THE
PRIVATE DIARY
of
LYLE
MENENDEZ

THE
PRIVATE DIARY
of
LYLE
MENENDEZ

IN HIS OWN WORDS!
AS TOLD TO
NORMA NOVELLI
WITH
MIKE WALKER

EDITED BY
JUDITH SPRECKELS
◆
CONCLUSION BY
PIERCE O'DONNELL

DOVE
BOOKS

Jacket photo courtesy of AP / World Wide Photos

ISBN 0-7871-0474-4

Printed in the United States of America

Dove Books
301 North Canon Drive
Beverly Hills, CA 90210

"Norma, buy me a yellow sweater. Ever see a violent man wearing a yellow sweater?"

—Lyle Menendez, January 8, 1993

Contents

Acknowledgments

◆

My grateful thanks are offered to the hardworking people who helped me with this book.

To Barbara White, for her painstaking job of listening to and transcribing the tapes.

To Wilbur Stark, who represented me with publishing contacts.

To Michael Viner, the publisher of Dove Books in Beverly Hills, who believed in this project.

To Judith Spreckels, for her patience in helping with the organization, preparation, and editing of this book.

To Lynette Padwa, for shaping the manuscript into its final form.

Thanks to my family and friends whom I have sometimes neglected during the Menendez years.

Special thanks to Lyle Menendez, whose daily telephone calls made this book possible.

—NORMA NOVELLI

Foreword
by
Mike Walker

◆

As a lifelong journalist, or voyeur for hire, I can tell you this truly: Nothing gets the heart pumping quicker than taking a brisk walk through the mind of a killer.

Murderers. The killer elite. Big Leaguers of crime. Famous outlaws who *did it* . . . went all the way down the taboo trail and snuffed out human life. We peer into the eyes of these beasts and we're horrified. Disgusted. And perhaps just a little bit . . . thrilled? Oh, we gasp, How could anyone *do* that? Next question: Could I?

There's no denying our morbid (dare I say fatal) fascination for the mind of the murderer. Killers are unique, not like other criminals. Crime reporters and whodunit fans enthusiastically study the quirks and aberrations of the lesser, or less lethal, outlaws; it's fun finding out what makes thieves, thugs, and perverts tick. But those pale minds won't suddenly pounce and make you shudder. What sets the mankiller's mentality apart is a cold, focused intensity, an hypnotic beacon that sucks us in as our imaginations thrash helplessly.

In publishing, only cookbooks sell better than murderers most foul. Which tell-all tome would you buy: Jim Bakker's unholy confessions of fleecing his faithful sheep, or a real-life Dr. Hannibal Lecter drolly describing his most unspeakable lamb sacrifices? For most of us, titillation ain't half the fun of feeling your heart thump wildly in the dead of night (while tucked safely in bed, of course).

The cold-blooded murderer rattles our cage. It's not the killing itself that rivets us. We easily accept that the most peace-loving human being can muster up the savage bloodlust required to blow away enemies in wartime; or that a mother will kill quite ruthlessly when defending a child. But what about the man or woman who doesn't look like a monster, yet suddenly commits murder in cold-blooded calculation?

Who *are* these killers? And how the hell do we recognize them? What if they're normal-looking people like, say, Lyle and Erik Menendez? These are two seemingly innocuous California tennis boys born into a prosperous family headed by a hard-working father and a mom who stays home. But suddenly one night, Lyle and Erik turn up at their Beverly Hills home carrying shotguns, and they methodically fire so many point-blank blasts into their parents that the family room literally becomes the smoking, bloody entrance to hell.

When my publisher first suggested this book about Lyle Menendez, I hesitated. I'd just chronicled an accused killer behind bars named O. J. Simpson. How was this different?

Going back over the Menendez case, I can remember when it first grabbed national headlines. Like a few million others, I immediately thought of the old joke about the kid who kills his parents—then throws himself on the mercy of the court because he's an orphan. Ha, ha. The joke's on Jose and Kitty Menendez. Lyle and Erik really did kill them. That fact is not in dispute. But the boys want mercy because they claim horrible sexual abuse by their parents. So unlike O. J. Simpson, this isn't a case of an *accused* killer behind bars. These guys did it. They just want the jury to set them free.

Shortly before I was asked to write this foreword, I had co-authored the *New York Times* No. 1 best-seller *Nicole Brown Simpson: Private Diary of a Life Interrupted*. My exposure to the megalomaniacal inner song of O. J. Simpson had exhausted me. And it frequently roused the ghost of another notorious inmate: convicted killer Gary Gilmore. I'd been the first writer, even before Norman Mailer, to sift through Gilmore's jailhouse manuscript. Nothing I have read in my life—nothing—has ever affected me so viscerally. Never have words on a page frightened me, made me shake and sweat and endure nightmares for months after I edited them. Why? Read Mailer's book *The Executioner's Song* and you'll feel the spooky threads of horror this manipulative killer uses to weave soft, paralyzing blankets around his doomed nymphet teen girlfriend Nicole, his family, his friends, and fans.

Mailer's book softens Gary Gilmore's tale somewhat, layering in sympathetic context. Before graduating to murder, Mailer learned, Gary was a charmy-smarmy smalltown thug whose life had been shaped by brutal childhood abuse. Unlike Mailer, I had no context when I first read the unexpurgated, unedited manuscript of this heretofore unknown white trash killer. That's why his writing hit me like a panicky scream from hell. This guy reached out through iron bars and grabbed your throat, shrieking, "Listen up, bastards!" Unlike Charlie Manson, a garden-variety geek who can barely keep his pseudo-sinister rap intelligible long enough even for quick TV sound bites, Gilmore could lay down words to make you tingle and buzz. Before his execution by firing squad, he wrote of goblins and ghosts visiting his cell, then of becoming a ghost himself. He described how, alone in darkness, he transmogrified in a burst of energy and propelled his spirit through the night sky. He'd materialize in Nicole's jail cell miles away and possess her sexually in the hours before dawn. And it's painfully clear in Nicole's letters to Gary that she believed it. Hell, I almost believed it. And therein lies the essence of the murderer's mind: the driving need to control other human beings, even if you have to kill them—and even when you're as good as dead yourself.

I'd been hired twice in my journalistic life to safari into the psyche of the beast and send back written reports for armchair voyeurs. Reflecting on those adventures with Gary Gilmore and O. J. Simpson, it slowly dawned on me that I was a pawn to my own premise: Who can resist the deluxe, all-expenses-paid tour inside the killer's mind! I was playing coy with my publisher, but who was I kidding? Here was my chance to stalk and observe a truly exotic mankiller—the parent slayer.

I called for the tapes and transcripts of Lyle Menendez. There were years of tape-recorded phone conversations between Norma Novelli and Joseph Lyle Menendez, popularly known as Lyle. I had followed the shocking case closely, all the way through the trial. I remember how people couldn't believe two such clean-cut guys could have killed their mom and dad and how easily people confused Lyle with his younger brother Erik—until you explained that Lyle is the one who wears a toupee.

When I listened to Lyle's conversations with Norma, I wondered if my premise that killers' minds have a commonality was about to blow up in my face. Would Lyle Menendez reveal himself as the cold, manipulative megalomaniac who settled for nothing less than the total preservation of his own ego at anyone's expense, or was he a decent guy caught up in a tough situation that had momentarily shoved him over the edge?

Another thing to consider: These were tape-recorded phone calls, not written journals. There's absolutely no doubt that Lyle knew Norma Novelli was taping him, so the possibility existed that he consciously hid his innermost self, knowing his remarks would someday become public, or even suspecting that his line might be tapped. This was different than the situation I had encountered with Gary Gilmore, in that I had read his actual writings; and it differed from my research into O. J. Simpson, whose mind I entered through the medium of his former friend and confidante, Faye Resnick, the book's co-author. Was Lyle playing hide-and-seek, and would I be able to find him?

The answer, though slow in hitting me between the eyes, was predictable. It's a time-honored concept among reporters and cops who don't rely on rubber hoses that if you let them talk, they will reveal themselves. A person who lets an interview go on for a long time can't help exposing himself to the experienced interrogator, even if he doesn't answer specific questions. In hundreds of hours of listening to Lyle Menendez coldly manipulate Norma Novelli, turning her into his literal handmaiden for more than four years, Lyle Menendez couldn't hide the ruthless, controlling mind of the murderer.

As Norma put it, "I knew all along I was being used and controlled by a master manipulator, but once you are drawn into a vortex, there is no way to extricate yourself, no way to come up for air. You are trapped."

And it's not as if Norma was some mindless do-gooder who believed Lyle was a sweet, innocent boy. In fact, she reveals, "He knew I thought he did it" long before he finally confessed to the murders. Even more astounding, Lyle knew that Norma never believed his sudden "revelation" of sexual abuse by his parents. "We had talked about every subject you can imagine for a couple of years," said Norma, "and there was no mention of molestation. It was obvious he was practicing on me . . . (but) he knew I wasn't buying it."

In March 1992, as Lyle carefully honed his parental abuse defense, he showed Norma a piece of paper on which he'd written down types of abuse children suffer. Then he mentioned a photo that had appeared on the cover of *L.A. Times* magazine of him with his father, Jose. Lyle told Norma, "He's got his hand on my crotch." It was an obscene manipulation. The photo was what any reasonable person would call a happy family portrait. Lyle, in his arrogance, didn't care if Norma believed in his innocence or not. She was just there to be used, to run errands, to operate his phone network, to visit him three and four times a week, year after year. And when she displeased Lyle, he berated her and treated her like a stupid child. Norma wasn't shocked. She'd learned that Lyle didn't care that someone's feelings could be hurt because "he doesn't experience those emotions himself."

Lyle's megalomania was boundless. "Everybody who meets me loves me," he'd tell Norma. Lyle believed he had the jury eating out of his hand. "I just come across as this really nice kid, and the DA hasn't produced a single witness to say otherwise. . . ." And in a world-class combination of self-aggrandizement and contempt for his dead mother and father Lyle told Norma: "I'm sure the jury are thinking to themselves, How the fuck did this guy get involved with these parents?"

Lest you think this mankiller is capable only of scaring kindly ladies and wimp journalists, consider this quote from an ex-inmate at the Los Angeles County Jail, who said of Lyle and Erik: "We were scared of them in jail, man. I mean, if they could kill their parents they could take me out no problem."

After five years in jail the cold malevolence of Lyle Menendez peers out through iron bars, unrepentant and arrogant. Norma Novelli and trial historian Judy Spreckels have spent hundreds of hours listening to scores of tapes to create this unique and utterly chilling "diary," Lyle's month-by-month account of his incarceration and trial.

Listen carefully to Lyle. He'll play hide-and-seek with you, just as he did with me. But he'll reveal himself, suddenly lashing out with claws unsheathed. Then he'll smile and soothe you, just like he does Norma. It's manipulation for aficionados; punctilious, cruel, and keenly focused. It's ringside, folks, and it's irresistible: The mind of a murderer. . . .

Mike Walker,
Palm Beach, April 1995

Preface
by
Judith Spreckels

◆

I met Norma Novelli at the Van Nuys Superior Court in the summer of 1993. An attractive, petite, vivacious mother of four grown children, she frequently hovered nervously near the hall pay phones.

Unusually dressed for a court watcher, she affected multilayered ensembles, usually topped off with a gauzy wide-sleeved jacket which floated as she darted about like an anxious hummingbird.

Norma exuded friendliness and enthusiasm, chatting animatedly with Menendez relatives and new acquaintances. The primary focus of her conversation, and apparently her life, was Lyle Menendez. It was clear that she truly knew him, that she had selected and purchased his courtroom attire, that she was in continual contact with him. I did not know at the time how this came about, nor how the communication system worked, but I was soon to find out.

In 1990, Ms. Novelli was publishing a small monthly paper called the *Mind's Eye,* devoted to allowing the free expression of interesting ideas by a variety of contributors, including some incarcerated individuals who welcomed the forum.

It was through her publication that Norma met Lyle and was drawn into his web of manipulation. What follows is Norma Novelli's four-year secret odyssey of telephone conversations, correspondence, and in-person jailhouse visits with Lyle Menendez.

Judith Spreckels,
Trial Historian

List of Individuals

◆

ABRAHAMSON, ALAN	*Los Angeles Times* reporter
ABRAMSON, LESLIE	Lead attorney for Erik
ANDERSEN, BRIAN	Lyle's uncle/Kitty Menendez's brother
ANDERSEN, PAT	Lyle's aunt/Brian's former wife
BAKER, TRACI	Lyle's former girlfriend/testified for him
BARALT, CARLOS	Lyle's uncle/Jose Menendez's brother-in-law/ executor
BARALT, TERRY	Lyle's aunt/Jose's sister
BERMAN, PERRY	Lyle's tennis coach/friend
BOZANICH, PAMELA	Deputy district attorney/prosecutor against Lyle
BURT, MICHAEL	Court-appointed attorney for Lyle
CANO, ANDY	Lyle's cousin/son of Marta Cano
CANO, MARTA	Lyle's aunt/sister of Jose
CIGNARELLI, CRAIG	Erik's best friend/prosecution witness
CONTE, JON	Professor of social work, University of Wisconsin/ defense witness
GOODREAU, DONOVAN	Lyle's former friend at Princeton (not a student)/ prosecution witness
HADERIS, HARRY	Lyle's friend since he wrote him in jail
JARRETT, GREGG	Court TV anchor
KURIYAMA, LESTER	Deputy district attorney/prosecutor against Erik
LANSING, JILL	Lead attorney for Lyle
LEANNE	Lyle's former girlfriend
LLANIO, HENRY	Jose's cousin/didn't know brothers before crime
McFADDEN, CYNTHIA	Court TV anchor/currently with ABC News
MENENDEZ, MARIA	Lyle's grandmother/Jose's mother/"Mama"
MONES, PAUL	Attorney/author/represents children who kill their parents
MORAN, TERRY	Court TV reporter at the courthouse

MORRISSEY, MARCIA	Attorney for Erik
OZIEL, DR. L. JEROME	Erik's therapist to whom he confessed
PISARCIK, JAMIE	Lyle's former girlfriend/prosecution witness
RAND, ROBERT	Miami journalist/writing a book about the Menendez family
RASCON, ART	Los Angeles TV reporter
SHELTON, MARTI	Woman friend in Virginia/taped Lyle's calls
SMYTH, JUDALON	Reported Oziel-Menendez conversation to Beverly Hills Police Department
STEVENS, GLENN	Lyle's friend/prosecution witness
VITERI, BEATRICE	Became friend of "Mama" after brothers went to jail/helped Lyle
WEISBERG, STANLEY	Judge of Van Nuys Superior Court, presided at the Menendez trial
WENSKOSKI, RICHARD	Lyle's bodyguard in New Jersey during spending spree after the funeral.
ZOELLER, LES	Beverly Hills Police Detective assigned to the Menendez case

List of Locations

◆

BEVERLY HILLS HOUSE 722 N. ELM DRIVE The Beverly Hills home the Menendez family bought when they moved from Calabasas. It was the scene of their deaths.

BIG 5 STORE The Santa Monica branch of the sports store. Lyle and Erik Menendez testified they tried to buy handguns there in August 1989. The store did not carry handguns at that time.

CALABASAS The area at the west end of the San Fernando Valley, where the Menendez family lived. The house burglaries perpetrated by the brothers necessitated the move to Beverly Hills.

CALABASAS HOUSE The fourteen-acre estate on Mulholland Drive in the mountains, that the Menendezes were remodelling at the time of their deaths. They never lived there.

CHEESECAKE FACTORY A Beverly Hills restaurant where Lyle wanted to meet Perry Berman after the killings. He wanted Perry to come to the house and discover the dead bodies of Kitty and Jose Menendez.

GUN STORE, VAN NUYS Where the brothers went the day before the murders, to purchase more lethal buckshot, after already obtaining birdshot, for shooting their parents.

LOS ANGELES COUNTY JAIL (Men's Central Jail) The huge downtown jail facility for men. Home since 1990 to the Menendez brothers who are housed in separate areas.

SHOOTING RANGE, VAN NUYS Where the brothers went to practice handling their new shotguns.

SPORTMART A chain of sporting goods stores Lyle called from jail, attempting to get handgun information to bolster his fabricated gun testimony.

TASTE OF L.A. An annual food festival held at the Santa Monica Civic Auditorium. The brothers were to meet Perry Berman there but were late due to the killings.

VAN NUYS SUPERIOR COURT (Van Nuys Courthouse) Scene of the July 1993 to January 1994 trial of the Menendez brothers in Department N of Superior Court, Hon. Stanley M. Weisberg, presiding.

THE
PRIVATE DIARY
of
LYLE
MENENDEZ

1

THE CRIME
AND THE CIRCUMSTANCES

On the night of August 20, 1989, just before 10:00 P.M., Kitty and Jose Menendez were unwinding after dinner, watching TV in the family room of their Beverly Hills home. They'd been eating a dessert of blueberries and cream while relaxing on the pale, plush sofa. Kitty snuggled in Jose's lap. It was the maid's night out and their sons Lyle, twenty-one, and Erik, eighteen, were at the movies, so Kitty and Jose were blissfully enjoying their solitude . . . and then they were dead.

At 11:47 P.M. Lyle Menendez, wailing and sobbing, called 911. He said he and his brother, Erik, had just arrived home to find their parents murdered. He yelled at Erik, "Erik, get away from them." Then 911 asked, "Who is the person that was shot?" "My mom and my dad," sobbed Lyle.

Before the police got there, Erik called his tennis coach, Mark Heffernan, who agreed to come over immediately from his home in Santa Monica.

The Beverly Hills Police Department is located only three blocks west and three blocks south of the Menendez home, located at 722 N. Elm Drive. The police were there in less than five minutes, but there was not a sound coming from the house. It was dark and quiet as they approached. The property is fenced by tall wrought iron, but the driveway gate was wide open.

Suddenly, ordered by the police, two young men burst

through the front double doors together, and ran out to the sidewalk. They were wailing and clearly distraught.

More police arrived and the street filled with official vehicles. While the brothers remained outside, watched over by a policeman, other officers entered the house cautiously in case the assailants were still there. Sgt. Kirk West, hearing the TV turned up loud and seeing the lights on, approached the TV room. He would not be likely to forget the carnage that met his disbelieving eyes and stopped him in his tracks.

Officers searched the rest of the house for intruders or other victims while they waited for Det. Les Zoeller to arrive. They found only Kitty's dog, Rudy, in her bedroom upstairs, and one other dog.

The crime scene was the goriest, more gruesome sight most of the officers had ever viewed. Both victims had been blasted beyond recognition. The male was seated on the couch, awash in blood.

The fatal shot had left a huge hole in the back of his head from a close-range shotgun blast. The female was on the floor, blasted from head to toe, lying in a pool of blood, with one eye, her nose, and her teeth blown away due to a shotgun having been placed right up against her cheek and fired. Her other eye was wide open, staring in stark terror. Blood and viscera were splattered all over the furniture, walls, and floor.

In a news clip, aired all too frequently since the killings, everyone saw the body bags on gurneys being wheeled from the house and placed in the coroner's vehicle. What home viewers fortunately did not see were Kitty's shattered limbs, her broken arms and legs, her shotgunned breast, and the pulverized remains of her once pretty face, with the mouth wide open in a final scream of horror.

The viewers didn't see Jose's collapsed facial structure, nor the gaping hole in the back of his head, so big that when his body was lifted into the body bag his brain fell out.

The people watching television in their homes that night didn't see the last sight Kitty and Jose saw, the murderous faces of their killers.

*　*　*

After 1:00 A.M. Lyle, now under control, and Erik, considerably calmer, were transported together in the back of the same police car to the nearby Beverly Hills police station. This was not normal police procedure, but it was deemed expedient. Unknown assassins were possibly still in the vicinity.

Given the chance to speak to each other privately, Lyle told Erik that if the police questioned Erik first, he should give Lyle a signal when he came out, indicating he had stuck to the alibi they had devised. That way Lyle would know whether or not to go along with their prearranged story. Amazingly, Erik stuck to his story, amidst great protestations of grief.

Erik cried such copious tears the interrogation was halted within twenty minutes. Lyle, on the other hand, was apparently not grief-stricken, speaking matter-of-factly, suggesting business rivals of his father might have been responsible.

In an excerpted portion of that August 21, 1:42 A.M. interview, Lyle rambled on as follows:

Mark [Heffernan] said it might be a robbery or something, but from the looks of it, it didn't look like that, it looked—it looked like they definitely wanted to make a mess and it was really sad. . . .

I would think that, unless they find things that are missing from the house or something strange like that, it would be my father that would be the reason that it would happen. He used to work for RCA Records which was a lot bigger than what he does now. He works in a smaller company and with a group of people that from the stories that he brings home and the people that I've met, these are a real seedy group and even though he was very aware of that . . . I don't know if anyone would ever try to kill my father.

When the interviews were over, Lyle and Erik left with Mark Heffernan for his home in Santa Monica. It was 2:18 A.M. The police had not performed the standard gunshot residue tests on their hands. After all, they were not suspects anymore than everyone was suspect, and Erik, at least, was considered to be emotionally devastated.

By 8:00 A.M. Lyle, the normally very late riser, was already back at the Beverly Hills house asking for permission to retrieve the brothers' tennis racquets. Det. Zoeller refused him admittance to the yellow-taped crime scene. Undettered, Lyle and Erik returned later. They received permission from an officer to get some tennis gear out of Erik's car, still parked in front of the house. Equipped with an empty sports bag, and unsupervised, Lyle removed several items of evidence including shotgun shells, then casually departed the scene in a friend's car.

As the numerous relatives of Kitty and Jose, the Andersens and the Menendez families, arrived in Beverly Hills for the funeral, Lyle and Erik got an early start on what was to become a monumental spending spree.

Although their house was heavily guarded by a private security firm, their dad's company felt they might be in danger and offered to pick up hotel expenses for them. The relatives stayed at the Bel Age Hotel, a popular celebrity spot, adjacent to Beverly Hills. The brothers favored tonier digs at the posh Bel Air Hotel, where in only a few days they ran up an $8,000 bill, which included $2,000 for room service.

During the trip to the Century City shopping mall a few days after the murders, Lyle and Erik purchased sports jackets at $1,500 each. Then they went to a jewelry store and bought three Rolex watches and some money clips. Their late father's credit card had treated them to $14,000 worth of ostentatious jewelry, of which he would not have approved, and neither did his brother-in-law, Carlos Baralt (married to Jose's sister, Terry). Carlos was the executor of the Menendez estate and Jose's lifelong friend.

The memorial service was held at the Director's Guild of America on Sunset Boulevard in West Hollywood. The first floor is dominated by a beautiful movie theater and a spacious foyer.

Lyle and Erik were over an hour late, while the guests grew increasingly irritated. The unrepentant brothers' rudeness was later said to have been due to Lyle's pit stop at the wig maker for an adjustment on his toupee.

At the service Jose's friends were sickened at the behaviour of Lyle, who despite his tardy arrival, conducted himself like the cool host of a cocktail party.

Erik, looking grief-stricken, spoke briefly and movingly, shedding a few tears, but keeping himself under control.

Lyle was very much in command of the situation, speaking appropriately before calling the other speakers to the podium. Erik and Lyle hugged each speaker in turn. Two months later in October, when Dr. Jerome L. Oziel suggested to the brothers that they hug each other after a therapy session, they refused, saying, "We hate that hugging shit."

Three days after the Hollywood service, the Princeton University chapel was the scene of a more traditional funeral service. The Menendez family had made their home in the Princeton area before moving to California, and Lyle was an on and off student at the university. He had been suspended for a year due to cheating, despite the best efforts of his father who flew to the university to plead for him. Lyle's Princeton education had meant everything to his father. Lyle, now off suspension, was expected to attend the forthcoming fall semester. Toward that end his parents had selected a condo for him, which Kitty had been planning to decorate at the time of her demise.

At the Princeton service Lyle spoke for half an hour. He read a letter from his father which said in part:

Dear Son,
    Thank you for your very thoughtful and moving letter. As you know, to me the family is the most important thing in my life and I hope it will be in yours. I can't tell you how much I miss not being able to speak to my father . . . I miss him a lot.
    Ecclesiastes 4:10 states: "For if they fall, the one will lift up his fellow, but woe to him that is also alone when he falleth; for he hath not another to pick him up."

As we have discussed in the past, we are the heirs to a very special heritage and with that good fortune comes duty and responsibility. I know that you sometimes worry about your future. I have total trust in both you and Erik, and have no concerns about your future and your future role in your country.

I urge you as you go through life and enjoy the fruits of your work and the good fortune of your heritage to think of your family, your country, and your fellow citizens. I believe that both you and Erik can make a difference. . . . I believe that you will!

I encourage you not to select the easy road. I urge you to walk with honor regardless of the consequences and to challenge yourself to excellence. The future does not belong just to the brightest but also to the more determined.

The letter speaks movingly of Jose's love for his sons, and perhaps his realization that they were not of the genius caliber he had envisioned, but that they still had a big future as heirs to the Menendez mantle, if they were willing to work.

One thing on which everyone agreed was that Jose's life was his family and work. When Lyle was born, he was, in Jose's opinion, the perfect child. He was the scion who would carry the Menendez name to greater glory. Jose would mold him, and teach and train him to achieve success (just as he had done) and then go on to a career in politics or business. Jose stuck to his plan. When Erik came along he was the crybaby, the sissy, his mama's boy. Neither child was to be criticized or disciplined. They were not to be stifled or punished. Growing up they were permitted to run wild in stores and restaurants, annoying other patrons. They were not forced to obey and did as they pleased. Their clothes fell where they dropped them. They did not concern themselves with chores. Nothing was to quash their free spirits or stymie their brilliance. They were to devote themselves to sports and education, urged on and doted upon by their parents. Swimming gave way to soccer, which was superceded by tennis. Practice, practice was Jose's command. Kitty became a chauffeur during the day, driving both boys to their various lessons and endless practice sessions, and a teacher at night, often doing their home-work for them.

Their father always pointed out to them that they were special, better than everyone else and not subject to the rules and regulations by which everyone else played. His personal motto had been, "Lie, cheat, steal, but win." The brothers paid attention to that credo more literally than Jose had anticipated. They lied about everything. The lies became more elaborate as they grew older. If they were not believed, no one let on. Thus Lyle became a master storyteller, with his worshipful brother never far behind.

In the last few years of their lives, Jose and Kitty lost hope in their dream of the perfect sons who would achieve greatness, the best of the best. To their relatives and friends they covered up the poor academics. They covered up the criminal behavior, and condoned the lies and cheating. The boys' uniformly lackluster performances were blamed on teachers, coaches, and outside influences. Their tennis rankings never approximated what Jose had hoped for. The brothers sassed their parents and swore at them. In their final year Lyle's unbridled spending and Princeton problems caused Jose concern and heartache. He was proud of Lyle's success with women, but he disapproved of his choice of older women, whom he perceived as gold diggers.

Erik's sexuality was a cause for further distress. His mother had set a deadline for him to get a girlfriend. Erik met the deadline. He got a girlfriend, briefly, but the "romance" was short-lived and physically unfulfilled. His mother listened in on his phone conversations and spied on his selection of magazines. Because his dad was rabidly homophobic, the suspicion of Erik's sexual preference was devastating.

Gradually Jose became convinced that Lyle might never gradu-ate from Princeton or any other college, that he was going to continue to date women Jose perceived as tramps interested primarily in his money, that both sons had criminal tendencies, and that Erik was a wimp. These failings on the part of his sons came as a crushing defeat to Jose, who told them both he was taking them out of the will.

Kitty was nervous and unhappy. After obtaining Erik's permission, the boys' therapist, Dr. Oziel, informed Kitty that he thought the brothers might commit more crimes. The word sociopath entered Kitty's vocabulary. She checked it out with her therapist, Dr. Lester Summerfield, who was later to testify at the trial. Kitty was aware of her sons' narcissism and lack of conscience, and she was frightened. She had remarked more than once, "I can't believe my kids. I can't believe this is happening to us."

Prior to the memorial services, the brothers sustained a monetary shock at a financial meeting with the top executive of their father's company. Escorted by their uncles Carlos Baralt and Brian Andersen, they went to the offices of LIVE on Sherman Way in Van Nuys. There they were informed that their father's $5 million life insurance policy, of which they were the beneficiaries, had not gone into effect. Jose had been required to undergo a separate physical for that policy, which he had put off while he attempted to quit smoking to improve the test results.

The news that the $5 million that they had expected would not be forthcoming stunned the brothers. Erik broke the silence with a businesslike inquiry regarding the status of the company's $15 million Key Man policy, which was in effect, but benefited only the company. The brothers would not be recipients.

As it turned out, the brothers' aunt, Marta M. Cano, had talked Jose into buying an insurance policy from her years before. She later had him upgrade it so that it was valued at $650,000 upon his demise. With lightning speed Ms. Cano had the policy paid off and each brother received $325,000.

During the trial Ms. Cano testified as to the poor financial condition of the brothers. "Didn't they each receive $325,000?" asked the district attorney. "Peanuts!" shouted Aunt Marta, startling the assembled, especially blue-collar, jurors.

The estate was rumored to be worth about $14 million. Like so much about the Menendez saga, this turned out to be a far cry from the truth. The Beverly Hills house was mortgaged to the max, as was the Calabasas house. Jose was over $1 million in arrears on his taxes. The properties had been illegally overinflated by Jose to secure larger loans. At the same time the economy took a nosedive, and real estate values were plummeting, the enormous monthly payment and upkeep expenses continued to accrue. Without Jose at the helm of LIVE Entertainment, the public company Jose had headed, his stock share prices plunged, further reducing the value of the estate.

Nonetheless, Lyle Menendez immediately commenced a spending spree worthy of Imelda Marcos. Like a young Midas, at ease in the back of a limo, and followed everywhere by bodyguards, he blazed a spending trail through the Princeton area.

He bought a Porsche convertible, originally ticketed at $68,000, for which he paid $64,273 in cash. He bought clothes by the carload. Apparently forgetting that he was supposed to be worried about mob-hired killers out to annihilate him, he strolled out of stores laden with purchases. His bodyguard, Richard Wenskoski, testified at the trial that Lyle didn't act like there was any danger, and that he never appeared to be upset or in mourning, though it was less than ten days after his parents' death. He was, in fact, "happy-go-lucky." If he ran low on money, he went to Uncle Carlos's house for a pecuniary transfusion. His coffers replenished, it was back to buying . . . laughing all the way from the bank.

In his first foray into business, Lyle, so hilariously inept it challenges credulity, lost a fortune. He bought a small Princeton restaurant specializing in chicken wings. This was not a Kentucky Fried Chicken franchise, it was a privately owned enterprise with a probable value of around $200,000. Lyle, anxious to become an instant executive now that he had the car, the clothes, and the jewelry, gladly handed over $300,000 for the *down payment.* The total price was $550,000 . . . and that was just for the business. On top of that he signed a fifteen-year lease at $2,100 a month, which included the apartment over the restaurant. He could have collected rent on the apartment to offset the expense, but didn't. For $550,000 he had not purchased the land or the building, and was shelling out an additional $25,200 per year for rent.

The entire ill-fated venture become a total loss for the wannabe entrepreneur, but a major windfall for the restaurant owner. Lyle couldn't pay the note for the balance when it came due. He was in jail and his relatives wouldn't take any more money from the estate. The restaurant had not paid its way. The original $300,000 was money which would have gone to Jose's mother, Maria, when the estate was settled, if Lyle had not lost it.

The restaurant owner took his restaurant back, plus the $300,000 and the lease money. He gave a small portion of the money back. Lyle, who did not profit from his mistakes, used it to fund yet another branch of his stillborn empire. The person Lyle placed in charge of his latest venture couldn't make a go of it, and so that money also disappeared, and Lyle's career as a restaurateur collapsed into a black hole.

Not long after the murders the brothers decided to buy a fancy Marina del Rey penthouse, for just under $1 million. This deal fell through but they did get adjoining apartments in the Marina. Lyle moved in with his girlfriend. Each apartment rented for more than $2,000 a month. As a bicoastal executive, Lyle needed a Princeton setting for his budding business empire. He leased a spacious office suite and filled it with expensive furniture. He signed on his friends as junior executives with healthy salaries, though their business experience was nil. Lyle and his version of the Billionaire Boys Club never occupied their offices, because Lyle got arrested.

The brothers had thought they were home free. They had committed the perfect crime, although they had some nagging worries when they learned that the store where they had purchased the guns had a video camera monitoring the customers. They did not know that the camera did not contain any film. After calling the store, they ascertained that the "film" was kept for three months. This was not the truth, but they didn't know it. By the end of November, they figured, the film would have been destroyed.

Their biggest concern was their knowledge that a new will had been started in the computer in their parents' bedroom. Lyle found out a relative was planning to have a computer expert go to the house and try to get the new will from the computer. It would not have been valid, but the fact that the will existed wouldn't have looked too good. In the midst of his shopping marathon, Lyle told Richard Wenskoski that he was flying to California on business but would be back the next day. Lyle beat his relative to the punch in hiring a computer expert. He called a local man selected at random from the phone book. The expert came over and Lyle told him what to look for on the computer: "Lyle, Erik, and will." The expert thought "will" was a third name, not a document. Lyle asked him if he could erase everything in the computer so it could never be regained, because he was going to sell it, and didn't want personal information going to the buyer. The computer man assured Lyle there was nothing readable left to be found. Lyle wrote him a check for $150 and returned to New Jersey where he was met by his bodyguard. Apparently he was not in danger on the trip to California. The computer man, however, came up empty, because Lyle's check bounced.

On Halloween, October 31, 1989, Erik went to see his therapist, L. Jerome Oziel. He suggested his therapist accompany him on a walk, as Joe Hunt had done in the Billionaire Boys Club (BBC) movie. Then Erik told Dr. Oziel that he and Lyle had killed their parents. Erik went back to the office with Dr. Oziel and told him about the crime. Dr. Oziel immediately called Lyle and suggested he get right over, because Erik had told him something. Lyle arrived in minutes and began berating Erik. If their crime had been perfect, that was no longer the case. Dr. Oziel tried to keep the brothers calm, but Erik was crying and ran out, so Lyle and the therapist went after him. At the elevator, Lyle said something to Dr. Oziel which he perceived to be a definite threat. There was later testimony that Erik told Lyle to do whatever he had to do, but that he (Erik) was not up to any more killing.

The brothers continued sporatic visits to Dr. Oziel and he informed them that he had notes and tapes of their meetings in a safe place. He suggested that for their own benefit they come to his office and record their version of what happened and why, which he felt could help them if they were ever caught and brought to trial. On December 11, 1989, they made the tape which was to haunt them forever.

Dr. Oziel never turned them in. For safety he asked his

girlfriend, Judalon Smyth, to sit in the outer office and listen, and if there was trouble, to call 911.

In a session with Dr. Oziel, Erik explained that the brothers had watched the BBC movie on TV three weeks before the murders. By coincidence, the younger brother of one of the convicted murderers from the BBC was a classmate and friend of Erik's at Beverly Hills High School.

At trial they denied having seen the program, but it appeared to be more than coincidence that in talking to the police and others, they verbalized exact terminology from the film. There were innumerable other copycat actions, including their purchases, that coincided with the BBC members' behavior.

During the trial, Leslie Abramson, who said she had not seen the film, argued strenuously and eloquently to keep it out, which was an indication of the importance of that evidence. The judge ruled the tape inadmissible, a victory for the defense.

Good fortune had been with the brothers since the night of the murders. The brief police questioning, the failure to test their hands for gunshot residue, the boys' ability to remove evidence, the lack of film in the gun store camera, the will being erased from the computer, and Dr. Oziel not turning them in . . . all that good luck was about to run out.

In March 1990, Dr. Oziel and Judalon Smyth were having romantic problems. While sitting in his waiting room she overheard the Menendez brothers confessing their crimes to Dr. Oziel. Dr. Oziel and his wife, also a psychotherapist, shared office space in Beverly Hills. Although both Dr. Oziel and Judalon knew of the confessions since 1989, it was not until the following March, when they had a parting of the ways, that she went to the Beverly Hills Police Department and told the story that made the case against the brothers. She provided the missing links.

Early on, the detectives were sure that the brothers did it, but proving it was something else. They couldn't link them to the shotguns, which were never found. Along came Judalon to tell the BHPD that the brothers said they purchased the guns in San Diego. Bingo!

Three days after Judalon Smyth went to the police, Lyle, accompanied by two of his associates, was en route to the

Cheesecake Factory in Beverly Hills for lunch. As they pulled out of the driveway in Erik's Jeep they spotted a car blocking the street to the south. It had a flashing light on top. Lyle, who was driving, threw the Jeep into reverse and banged into another police vehicle that had pulled up behind him. Police came from everywhere and ordered the young men to lie down in the street where they were handcuffed. His companions were released, but to this day, Lyle gets his suntan from a bottle.

Erik was in Israel playing in a tennis tournament when he heard the news. He flew home, via Florida, where his Aunt Marta and Cousin Andy joined him for the flight to California. At Los Angeles International Airport he was handcuffed and placed in custody by Det. Zoeller.

It was revealed in court that near the end of his life Jose Menendez had said to Lyle, "You can kill me, but you won't get the money."

How true that turned out to be. At long last, many months later, when they finally confessed to killing their parents, the money was gone.

Lawyers for each of the brothers cost $750,000, knocking a $1 million hole in the money bag and decimating what would have been the estate. The remainder went to taxes, repayment of loans, fees, and commissions. Their relatives, clinging to the erroneous belief that outsiders had committed the crime, had authorized the legal expenditures. The two relatives who might have known differently were not in control of the estate funds, and kept their mouths shut.

When the Menendez murders took place I, like everyone else, was shocked and horrified. I took particular notice because I had lived near the Beverly Hills location. For a true crime reader like me, a local whodunit is especially fascinating. I was sad for the murdered parents and my heart went out to the brothers who had come home to find their parents dead. But I had little intuition that the case, and the life of Lyle Menendez, would gradually come to eclipse my own life, my every waking hour.

2

---◆---

LYLE MENENDEZ UP CLOSE

E arly in 1990 I began publishing a paper called the *Mind's Eye*, as a forum for people who liked to read and write interesting original articles.

I was divorced and had recently moved from Beverly Hills to Toluca Lake with my four grown kids. Toluca Lake is a charming, primarily residential area between Burbank and Studio City, a quiet upscale community near major entertainment giants such as Disney, NBC, Universal, and Warner Bros.

Starting a new endeavor takes a lot of time, so most of mine was spent working and developing that project. My hobby of collecting and reading books about psychology and true crime had to take a backseat while I worked on the paper. Before starting the *Mind's Eye*, I had worked as a private duty nurse. I was eager to try my hand in the creative field of writing and publishing. I knew at any time I could resume as a caregiver, because nursing skills are always in demand.

That August the Menendez saga began to unfold, and I followed the case in the papers as various theories regarding the assailants were espoused. I didn't think it was a mob hit as was suggested by the papers. Beverly Hills is not a hotbed of organized crime assassinations and the Menendez killings didn't fit the pattern of other Mafia slayings I had read about.

As I was getting established in my new community and starting the paper, the press reports on the crime were infrequent, and the case went to the back of my mind. It was not until Lyle was arrested seven months later, in March 1990, that the story came back to the headlines. When Erik surrendered at the airport a few days later, causing further notoriety, my interest was renewed.

On June 12 I wrote a letter and sent two of my papers to the brothers who had been downtown in the Los Angeles County Jail since their arrests. I already had several subscribers in jail who enjoyed the paper and contributed pieces to it. I thought Lyle and Erik might be interested in it to help pass the long days and nights.

Lyle answered my letter, but Erik did not. Lyle also wrote a reply to something I had written, and offered to write additional pieces for the *Mind's Eye*. I replied to him, and so our sporadic correspondence began.

Mind's Eye

THE PAPER FOR CREATIVE PEOPLE
Studio City, California

June 12, 1990

Lyle & Erik Menendez #1887106
Terminal Annex, P.O. Box 86164
Los Angeles, CA 90086

Dear Lyle and Erik,
   I read about the trouble you are having and that you are now languishing in L.A. County Jail. How boring for you both. I hope your problem is resolved pretty soon. In the meantime, I'm enclosing a copy of a magazine I publish for creative people like artists, poets, writers, inventors, etc. I hope you enjoy reading it. I'll keep sending it every month if you like. I send it to many other jails and prisons because that's where many inmates discover their hidden talents. You might find a few of your own.
                    That's all for now.
                    Best wishes and good luck with your
                    case.

                         Norma Novelli
                         (Publisher)

Lyle Menendez Speaks to the Mind's Eye

Hello Norma,

Thanks so much for your letter and two copies of the Mind's Eye. *I have lost great faith in our media system and so have thus far refrained from any contact with it, however your papers were so enjoyable and refreshing I cannot help but reply and congratulate your herculean efforts. Good for you! I am presently reading the book* Solitude *by Anthony Storr and was very pleased by Mr. Cooks' article.*

I am going to ask my grandmother to reimburse you and send you the necessary funds for a subscription. Also, if you would like me to write for your courageous young paper I would be glad to. I enjoy writing and am a great believer in creative opinion. You have my permission to print whatever I write you. Please let me know how else I can contribute.

You will forgive me but I cannot help but respond to your article on the cover of Volume Number 6: "Did You See."

You are welcome to print this as a rebuttal or letter to the editor, if you feel it has merit and are so inclined.

I agree with you that birth control would help many of the impoverished nations of our world, however it seems to me that some of your criticisms lack perspective and are somewhat unfounded. The Catholic religion is based on the premise of love, forgiveness, brotherhood, and the celebration of life. It is therefore opposed to abortion and includes birth control within that circle of immorality. Birth control is a complicated issue and in my opinion does not violate this religion's premise, however I cannot agree with you that this religion and this controversial issue are the cause of Mexico's poverty and suffering. It is clear that the economic greed and antiquated political policies of that nation's leaders are the cause of its rampant poverty and widespread starvation. I would further suggest that for many of its citizens the Catholic Church and its spiritual teachings are the only refuge and source of relief.

I am also surprised you have attributed the representatives of this religion with mental incompetence, when they are in fact the most scholarly and well-educated fraternity on earth. I think you should also have mentioned that the Catholic Church, with all its "ancient ideas," is this world's chief advocate and contributor for public education, and the fight against hunger. This is particularly evident in Mexico.

Lastly, I am concerned about your criticism of Pope John Paul II. I think you would be hard pressed to find a man who cares more and loses sleep over the world's poverty and suffering. No other person or Pope for that matter has done more to battle the evils of hunger and poverty than John Paul and I commend his great efforts. We must remember that he is the appointed leader of a religion and is therefore not the servant of his own desires, not even of the people, but of his God. I am pleased that John Paul and his interpretation of religious laws are not swayed by the times and the emotionally volatile influences of popular opinion.

Norma, I hope you are not offended by that rebuttal. It is not a personal attack in any way. And I realize that your articles are published in an effort to arouse peoples emotions, whether for or against.

Actually, from your various articles and your paper's structural tone, I believe we would get along quite well.

> *Sincerely,*
> *J. Lyle Menendez*

---◆---

Thank you for writing, Lyle. Your opinion was very eloquently stated.

And, as I said in my letter to you, any publisher who gets offended has no business creating an opinion forum.

So, we look forward to reading more of your views in future editions of the *Mind's Eye*.

> Norma Novelli, Publisher

When we first began writing, Lyle did not have an answering machine. He employed a service where people could leave messages. When it was his time to use the phone, he would pick up his messages and call people back, collect. Obviously, people in jail can't receive phone calls, so unless they have an answering machine they are stranded. They must also have a large supply of dimes to initiate calls. Lyle was a world-class phoner before his arrest and being in jail barely slowed him down.

After I learned the phone system we began conversing now and then. Of course I had to agree to accept collect calls. Lyle said his grandmother would reimburse me. We spoke from time to time. He always was cheerful, upbeat, polite, and seemed intelligent.

One day Lyle suggested I meet his grandmother and accompany her to the jail to visit him. We had been corresponding for a few months, and I was receiving frequent phone calls from him, but I had put off an in-person visit because my magazine kept me so busy and I did it all alone. I'd heard warnings about·the rigors of jail visits, the crowds, and the time lost waiting. I knew Lyle already had a few visitors to get him out of his cell for breaks, so I wasn't eager to go.

Lyle called one day with his grandmother on another line, so I could speak to both of them at once on a conference call. Maria Menendez was warm and friendly. We chatted for a short time and then Lyle said, "Okay Norma, Mama will pick you up and bring you down with her. She'll show you the ropes about visiting."

We made arrangements for the following Saturday afternoon. I agreed to meet Mama, as she prefers to be called, at the Radisson Hotel on Ventura Boulevard in Sherman Oaks.

By Friday I was really looking forward to seeing Lyle in person. I'd seen him on TV but this was going to be different, so I was quite excited. I was to meet Mama at 1:30 for the 3:00 P.M. visit.

I arrived first, and waited inside the hotel doors, where it was air-conditioned. Soon I saw Mama driving slowly along Ventura Boulevard. She looked nice in a black outfit, her grey hair in a tidy bun. Mama is a tall imposing woman, with proud erect carriage, though she is in her seventies. She had been a world-class swimmer as a girl in Cuba.

Seeing her for the first time, I was overwhelmed with compassion for the enormity of her loss, and tears filled my eyes. Even to this day, even now as I write these words, I have to pause, because the memory of that meeting makes me cry again.

As we drove out of the hotel driveway, I felt my first feelings of hostility toward Lyle Menendez. I was suddenly confused and ambivalent about going to see him.

Mama speaks limited English and I speak no Spanish but somehow we managed to converse. I have no memory of what we talked about, but I certainly remember that all the way there my mind was in a turmoil. How could I have gone from being so excited about seeing Lyle to feeling cold and hostile toward him after meeting his grandmother?

Since the first day I met Mama Menendez, I loved this woman, and I do today. She has been the only person I've cared about throughout "the Lyle years." I'm not sure how she feels about me since the publication of this book, but I still care for her.

The Los Angeles County Jail is a terrible place to spend a summer afternoon. On my first visit in 1990, I found myself standing beside Mama Menendez in a long double line inching its way down the walk toward the visitor waiting room. It was crowded, noisy, and very dirty. The line, comprised mostly of women, many with children, usually takes an hour to snake slowly toward the glass entrance doors where two deputies wait to hand out the visitors' passes.

At the door the deputy searched through my purse. After I showed my driver's license, he handed me a blank pass and I was admitted to the building. Another very long line led to the counter where a deputy, seated in front of a computer, tapped in the visitor's name and the inmate's name and number. I was visiting Joseph Lyle Menendez, booking number 188 7106.

We filled out our passes and the deputy stamped them with a large date in purple ink.

Mama and I went to a separate area of the jail allocated to high-security inmates, where we sat on wooden benches for another thirty minutes, waiting for the inmates to be called.

I spent my time nervously wondering what I would talk about with Lyle. I was used to talking to him on the phone, but I'd never seen him face-to-face.

I wondered what I was doing, sitting in this unpleasant place, visiting a man accused of blasting his mother and father to death. Of course at that time, Lyle was still maintaining his innocence.

It was strange how my mind darted about. I was struck by the realization that I was now under an umbrella of rules and regulations just like the inmate I was visiting.

An unseen person commanded, "Ma'am, put that purse in a locker now. You can't take that into the visiting area."

Who me? Mama had gone upstairs to visit Erik, so I was alone. It was eerie. I walked to where the voice had emanated and a brass key with a number on it suddenly appeared through a slot at the window. A row of metal lockers lined one wall. I stuffed my purse into #53 after removing a few items. I'd brought along the latest edition of the *Mind's Eye*, my asthma inhaler, and a photo of the little truck just purchased for distributing my magazine. I added the locker key to my skirt pocket, which was now looking rather lumpy.

I hated not having my purse in hand. I'd planned to dig into it from time to time so I could divert my eyes. I didn't want to keep staring into Lyle's face for the entire visit. Later I learned that in that section a visit might last thirty or forty-five minutes, depending on the deputy in charge.

Crash! Clang! Slam! Now I knew why they call it "the slammer." The iron doors clang open and shut and the noise was jarring. My ears were ringing and I was shaking from the deafening banging of the metal doors. I wondered if jails were deliberately made noisy.

I pushed on the door but nothing happened. I pushed again, nothing. I looked toward the one-way mirror where I thought a deputy might be standing. "Deputy, it won't open."

"Ma'am, you have to push it."

I leaned my whole body against the iron bars, which barely moved, and quickly squeezed through into the visiting area.

There I stood puffing from exertion, looking at Lyle through the glass that separated visitors from inmates. I recognized Lyle immediately, but he was much paler than he appeared on television. The color control on my TV must have been set too high because Lyle appeared pinkish, though Erik looked alabaster white.

"Hey, Norma, finally, at last!" Lyle said into the telephone receiver on his side of the divider.

"Hi, how are you Lyle?" I said into my phone. It was so strange to be speaking on the phone face-to-face with someone a few inches away. Lyle said, "Oh, I'm doing great."

How could anyone be doing great sitting in the county jail, facing the death penalty?

We took a few seconds to look closely at each other's faces through the glass. I noticed his white skin and his little short nose. I leaned forward for a better look into his eyes because they were so dark. I couldn't see where the iris ended and the pupil began. His eyes were such a deep brownish black . . . the windows of his soul?

While we talked easily the visiting time went by rapidly. When the deputy came to take Lyle away, he stood up quickly of his own accord, not giving the officer the opportunity to order him to stand up. Lyle does what's expected so he doesn't have to take orders. He stood immediately and put his hands behind his back without being told.

This is the way most inmates seem to behave. They hate to take orders from deputies, especially when they perceive some deputies to have attitude problems.

The deputy clicked the handcuffs on Lyle, who bent down to the phone mouthpiece, "Did you bring me some dimes?"

I nodded yes, waved good-bye, and made my way to the exit. It clattered and clanged indicating it was unlocked. I pulled with all my strength and slipped out. I felt free, as though I'd been found not guilty.

After that I volunteered to further help Lyle with clothing for court (the Beverly Hills courthouse being the location at the time), or any other things he was allowed to have, but couldn't buy in jail. (The Mailroom Regulations on p. 22 give you an idea of the restrictions.) He told me that the jail "store" came around on Fridays and that he could get candy and personal needs, but his taste ran to finer things. I agreed to shop for what he needed and his grandmother would pay me back. I kept a careful

COUNTY OF LOS ANGELES
SHERIFF'S DEPARTMENT

DATE   NOVEMBER 10, 1993
FILE NO.

OFFICE CORRESPONDENCE

FROM: LEE C. MCCOWN, CAPTAIN   TO: CONCERNED
        INMATE RECEPTION CENTER   INDIVIDUALS

SUBJECT: MAILROOM REGULATIONS (RESCINDS PREVIOUS
          BRIEFINGS)

Food and cosmetic items which can be purchased through the Jail Store will *generally* not be accepted through the mail.

The list below is intended to assist you in determining what may and may not be sent to inmates housed at the Los Angeles County Jail Facilities. Any unacceptable items will be returned to the sender.

1. Stationery items: No more than ten envelopes or pieces of writing paper no larger than 8 × 10. No more than ten stamps.

2. No personal checks, second party checks, or out of state checks.

3. No gum, candy, cigarettes, or food items.

4. No musical, blank greeting/post cards, or plastic cards. No identification cards or facsimiles.

5. Photographs: Limit of six per letter. No nude, suggestive, gang, tattoo or logo signs, groups, or men's face photos larger than a quarter. Polaroid photos will be examined by cutting open the photo.

6. No paper clips, staples, glitter, stickers, glued items, or gummed labels. No pens or pencils.

7. No balloons, rosary beads, string bracelets, or other jewelry items.

8. No magazines, newspapers, books, packages, or booklets except those sent directly from the publisher or bookstore. Limit of five (5) books or magazines at one time. No magazines of an explicit sexual nature.

9. No lottery tickets.

10. No newspaper clippings or tape on letters.

accounting of every charge slip or register receipt as she required.

I also helped Lyle with a new, improved telephone network. It was basically a conference call system. He'd use the jail pay phone with dimes I provided. He needed to deposit only twenty cents—there is no time limit on any call to the same area.

Lyle would dial my number and tell me to call another number for him. I'd press the hold button, which would cut him off temporarily, and I'd call the number he wanted, anywhere in the world. When the person answered, I'd press the "conference" button and all three of us would be on the line. If I was not joining the conversation, I'd put my receiver on the table and leave Lyle talking to the person I dialed for him. The bills for these calls were sent to me.

Lyle had the same setup with a few other people, so his phone network was limited only by the time he was allowed out of his cell. Before and after this phone network was established, Lyle had an answering service. I later bought him his own answering machine, which was installed in another person's house.

Lyle was always charming, ingratiating himself with me. I felt badly for him, a young athletic type, caged in almost all the time, except during visits . . . even though I knew it was his own fault. I hated going down to the jail, but I wanted to make his situation better if I could by giving him some time out. For a very long time only his accountant visited once a week, and his attorneys came to see him sometimes in the attorney room. While his grandmother was back in New Jersey I was his only chance to get out for a visit.

All this time the brothers continued to maintain their innocence, but there came a time when I told Lyle I knew he did it. He didn't seem surprised and passed over my remark to talk about something he wanted me to get.

One day Lyle told his longtime girlfriend who had stuck by him that he had killed his parents. She was gone shortly thereafter, still wearing Lyle's diamond ring.

Throughout 1991 and 1992, when there was almost nothing in the papers about the brothers, as the case dragged on through the higher courts Lyle still had no one else to visit him. So I continued. He was very unpopular in jail, constantly in trouble with other inmates and the deputies, though he made light of those problems.

After the brothers lost their legal maneuvers to keep out the Oziel tapes (the issue which kept the case from going to trial until mid-1993), Lyle and Erik finally admitted they killed their parents.

Why didn't I stop helping Lyle? everyone asked me, even my mother in England. I know it is hard for people to understand, and maybe no one will, but for three years I knew I was Lyle's only link to life outside. His grandmother had obtained my promise that I would visit him and so I did, and the years went by. I bought him books, notepads, pens, and clothes . . . whatever he wanted. Silk thermals were important to both brothers. I brought clothing catalogs to the jail and held them up to the glass, turning the pages so Lyle could pick out what he wanted.

I have always rooted for the underdog, and though Lyle may be an atypical example of an underdog, I felt that I was helping him primarily for that reason.

I came to know Lyle well, and it was a fascinating experience. Through our writing, visits, and phone calls I was studying and learning about him, and at the same time I was his puppet. Lyle was always interesting. It was mesmerizing to hear him talk, to listen to his extended monologues. I realized that he was a spoiled brat and always had been, and there I was, continuing the spoiling.

After more than three years, as the trial neared, Lyle's visitors increased, and I didn't have to go downtown anymore. I was pleased about that. We spoke on the phone more often after the trial started. I operated the phone system for him, continued to run his errands, tape the TV to play back over the phone, and, in general, was there for him.

The only times I found Lyle to be in less than his normal good spirits was once when he caught a cold and again when his phone time was drastically curtailed. The phone is Lyle's most vital concern, almost as important as the court activities. It is his grasp on the puppet strings he pulls.

Before I met Lyle, I was well read regarding the psychopathic personality. If I displeased him in some way, I was not shocked by the patronizing and arrogant manner in which he berated me at length. I knew he wouldn't notice or care that anyone's feelings could be hurt, because he doesn't experience those emotions himself. Oh yes, he cries easily on demand, as he did on the witness stand, but he could and did recite the same information previously on the phone in a trial run, without a tear or even a sigh, in a matter-of-fact, cold and calculated manner. He mentions with pride how well he controlled his emotions testifying at an earlier hearing, saving the big emotions to his best advantage for the trial, which was indeed dramatic and believable on TV. Lyle is a very good actor. As I grew to know him better, I realized that Lyle was like a tightrope walker, revelling in the thrill of taking risks and chances, balancing precariously between disaster and a safe haven. Self-destructively, he does not profit from his mistakes, often engaging in the same course of behavior that was calamitous initially, with the repeat performance also doomed to fail.

Although Lyle caused so many heartbreaking problems for his parents, they continually tried to solve and gloss over these transgressions. He leaves chaos in his wake without a backward glance. No matter the gravity of his "mistakes," he maintains a positive, upbeat, confident attitude, while revising a solution for his latest mishap.

The conversations herein give insight into the mind of a man who finally admitted to shotgunning his parents, after denying his participation until it became expedient to confess. He tells his thoughts each day in jail, reveals his hopes, and dictates exactly how his case should be handled. Lyle tells me how the jurors perceive him (a really nice boy), which prosecution witnesses are lying (all of them), and who is telling the truth (himself). He tells how he comes across to people and voices opinions on a wide range of subjects. Even when he is misinformed or has no independent knowledge about some matter, Lyle can explain and rationalize everything.

Beginning in 1992, I began to keep a diary documenting my visits and phone conversations with Lyle. Then, in the fall of that year, the taping of our conversations began.

The longer he rants and raves, the more the real Lyle emerges. It is fascinating and chilling to hear as he expounds at length, making comments so outrageous and ludicrous that they bring gasps before laughter. Lyle carries on with his virtual monologues, secure in the belief that he has fooled the masses yet again.

3

LISTENING TO LYLE

1992

Killing Time

During 1992 media coverage of the Menendez case dwindled: The *Los Angeles Times* mentioned it only four times the entire year. At the end of August the state Supreme Court ruled that the tapes of Dr. Oziel's notes, taken from two therapy sessions, could be used. On December 8, Judge Lance Ito set the arraignment date for December 29 for both brothers. At their arraignment, the brothers, handcuffed to each other and sweater-clad, answered "not guilty" to the charges of murder and conspiracy before Judge Ito.

While Lyle had languished in jail since 1990, he came to count heavily on Santa Monica attorney Paul Mones, who had focused his practice on defending children who had killed one or both parents. Mones had written an interesting book, *When a Child Kills,* recounting some of his cases, citing numerous accounts of abuse against the young defendants. Mones was to appear in court (as a spectator) during the Menendez brothers' testimony. He told Judge Stanley Weisberg that he was not a Menendez lawyer, but the judge said his name was on the list.

I continued to visit Lyle faithfully throughout 1991 and 1992 several times a week, when he was, for the most part, out of the public eye and without other visitors.

March 1992

Lyle's attitude of bravado and arrogance never wanes; even his handcuffs haven't taken that away. He says his attorney, Jill Lansing, is "brilliant" and "she believes in me so much she would defend me for nothing." Except it is a matter of record that she has been paid over $770,000 up front.

Lyle takes strange pride in his case, saying, "Norma, this is going to be the biggest trial in the country, this is parricide!"

"It's gonna take at least six months, so I'm gonna be here for quite a while yet."

Saturday, March 28, 1992

Lyle talked to Paul Mones today. Lyle said, "It was okay, but sometimes I get tired of going over the same points, but I guess I have to get it exactly right." He brought out a piece of paper with conditions and types of abuses that children suffer at the hands of their parents. He was hinting to me that his father had sexually abused him, which he has never mentioned before.

He said, "Well, look at the photo on the front of the *Los Angeles Times Magazine*. He's got his hand on my crotch."

I have studied this picture since he said that, but it looks to me like exactly how an arm and hand would naturally rest, sitting in this position. It looks like any normal family photo.

Wednesday, April 15, 1992

Got to the jail at 5:30 P.M. Mama was there saving a place for me in the line. I waited an hour while Mama went to see Erik, then came back down to wait with me. We finally made it to the visiting room. Lyle was waiting for us, smiling because he had no cuffs tonight. During our visit he reminisced about the time he cleaned his Dad's car with a Brillo pad. He got all the spots off, but when the car was dry, the scratched paint showed; his dad was not very pleased with him.

He showed me his new Reebok high-tops, the only pair he has right now. He said he now dreams about being in jail. This means "you've been in jail too long" in jail thinking. Lyle has been there since 1990.

Thursday, May 7, 1992

Lyle said, "I felt bad today in court because the chief of police in Beverly Hills was telling the prosecutors that he believed our grief was real on the night of my parents' deaths, which it was anyway, but I felt that this guy might have thought we'd fooled him, but we didn't. It was a terribly emotional time for us regardless. I'd like to reach him somehow and tell him I'm sorry, and that I appreciated his feelings for us that night."

He made me think he genuinely felt sorry about this man.

Friday, May 8, 1992

Lyle's leg muscles were aching tonight. He said, "I've been standing on my feet all day since this morning, about five hours altogether. That's a long time for me, but the cell is looking nice and clean and the passageway is looking whiter. I still need to get a fuse for the radio. A guy came in today to do something to the ceiling but he looked like he was an inmate, too, so I can't get a fuse from him."

"Could Michael get one for you?" Michael Burt is Lyle's other attorney. Lyle looked at me as if I'd said "Could he get you a gun?" so I let the matter drop.

"Oh, and guess what? That mouse Buffy came back. I gave him some pigskin chips and he carried them off to the drain, but they're still there, just stuck. Maybe he's storing them."

May 1992

We got into a discussion about men being more interested in women's looks than their brains. Lyle argued, "Only at first, but then I'd like a woman to be a good cook, a prostitute in bed, not too independent, and waiting for me when I get home." So I told him to design one, and "good luck!" He announced he could intellectually out-converse me on any subject, and was still arguing into the phone as his guard came and handcuffed his hands behind his back, holding the phone in place with his shoulder and chin. Then he had to stand up, so the phone dropped. As usual he got the last word!

Monday, May 18, 1992

I saw Lyle from 7:00 to 8:00 P.M. tonight. He was distracted and couldn't concentrate.

I took him fifteen dollars in dimes, ten dollars of which was for other inmates.

All four defense attorneys are in New York. I forgot to ask him why they were there. Lyle had talked with Jill Lansing earlier. Tonight Lyle made a rare negative comment saying, "I'll be lucky if I get out of here, Norma."

I'm wondering what Jill said to him.

Tuesday, May 19, 1992

Tonight another inmate called for Lyle because Lyle was in lock-down—not allowed out of his cell—and no reason was given to me.

I could hear Lyle in the background saying,

"Tell her thanks for the dimes."

"Tell her I got the book catalog."

"Tell her I'll call tomorrow."

Wednesday, May 20, 1992

Today he didn't call because he was locked down again.

Friday, May 22, 1992

Lyle was over his depression, which was brought on by a number of things.

He mentioned he was glad I visited today because he has been in a bad mood and needed to get out for a break. I responded, "It will be better once your case begins. Maybe you will be able to talk more and get rid of some tension."

He said, "No, I still won't be able to talk until after I have testified."

I showed Lyle a clipping from the *Daily News* regarding Harvey Rader, an inmate accused of killing a Northridge family of four. Lyle said, "Things look good for him up to now. Anyway, they have no bodies, so they have no case." Lyle later proved to be correct.

Lyle has sent for a catalog of log cabins so he will have a place to go for solitude.

Thursday, May 28, 1992

Lyle was in a good mood again today.

He has a hearing coming up June 4, then he thinks there should be no more hearing dates, and that they'll set a trial date.

When Lyle is not depressed (a spell which usually lasts two days) he's in a good, positive mood.

Lyle was telling me that if I think his name is notorious now, I must wait until later this year and I will see a big increase.

"People from all over the world are interested in this case," he professed with pride.

Lyle has lost his treasured early morning trustee job and his 11:00 A.M. until 1:00 P.M. freedom, so "no more daytime phone calls for you," he said, "but my friend can call you and leave messages."

Lyle was once again making the best of a bad situation. He said, "I'll get to sleep in the mornings, so my days will be shorter. I will also get a chance to read more."

Friday, June 19, 1992

No visit today but Lyle was able to call me collect at 10:30 tonight. He sounded in good spirits. He said Erik talked to a chief of police, but he didn't know which police force, probably Beverly Hills.

I asked Lyle if Erik was nervous. He replied, "Oh no, he was fine." The answer I expected from Lyle. He said he received the book I sent him, *The Prodigal Daughter*.

I told him I'd bring him a book I found in my library called *The Anxiety Disease* by David V. Sheehan, M.D.

Wednesday, June 24, 1992

Today was another wasted journey down to the jail. I had parked my car in the underground lot, hiked up the steps, and was heading for the visitors' line. Suddenly I spotted a sea of people coming toward me, heading for their cars. "Oh no, another lock-down!" That is the most frustrating thing about these visits. All the planning, scheduling, driving, paying the four-dollar parking fee . . . then having to turn around immediately to drive back home. The parking fee is never refunded, even if you paid two minutes before the lock-down. There was no way to guess when a lock-down might be ordered.

After driving home, I was sad because Lyle didn't get out of his cell today. My main reason for going there wasn't to talk to Lyle; we could speak on the phone. The important thing was to get him out for at least a little while every day. The girlfriends are long gone now, and Lyle isn't having any visitors except me, his accountant, and his lawyers. I just hated to let him down, so I did an instant replay and repeated the entire procedure for the evening visit.

This double roundtrip makes for a terribly exhausting, frustrating day. I can't remember how many times this has happened over the years, but it averages once a week, and I hate it every time.

Saturday, June 27, 1992

Lyle phoned tonight. He told me that next month he has to do a lot of talking to different therapists. He's not looking forward to this at all. He said, "Norma, when you come down, or when I talk to you on the phone, tell me when I come over cold and how to correct this problem. Help me to see how I am, because you know me from the outside and I know me from the inside. Leslie

Abramson said I come over too cold and don't care enough about Erik or others, and that I'm too wrapped up in myself. I have to contact my relatives and ask how they're doing. But only those who are going to be witnesses."

Thursday, July 2, 1992

I received a phone call from another inmate. "Lyle wants to talk to you badly tonight. Will you please come down?"

I went down thinking there was a problem, but no. He just wanted company and a break from his cell.

He told me that I was "his right arm, both legs, his eyes and ears." That was a nice compliment. He also said that I was the only person he ever wants to see. "You're the only person who makes me forget where I am."

I was concerned when Lyle said he'd received a letter from a girl in jail who was arrested on a "DUI." He said he'll write and tell her he can't correspond with her.

I said, "Lyle, don't write back anything at all, because if she was sent to jail it's not her first offense, so you will be corresponding with a drunk—and drunks are trouble."

He looked at me as if he had never considered this. "You're right, Norma. Okay, I won't answer her."

Wednesday, July 8, 1992

Lyle called to say that he was in trouble, "not his fault," he said. A homemade knife was found in his cell. He felt "somebody had it in for him." Now he thinks the disciplinary action will be ten days in solitary confinement, probably in a week's time. He's going to call Jill to get her to complain to the captain of the jail.

He said if he gets solitary he will use my advice about mind control. Ten days is a long time in solitary. If he doesn't get out of his punishment, he'll be denied visitors, books, and phone calls for the ten days. Although he insisted the knife was planted, he didn't say who did it or how.

Mama was waiting for me today to give me twenty-five dollars for Lyle. A guy whose visitor left was sitting alone. Mama sat and talked with him for forty minutes, so he could stay out of his cell. She's a very unusual woman with tons of strength, patience, and love. She will leave in a few days for New Jersey again, but Lyle won't care.

Monday, July 13, 1992

Bad news today; Lyle did get sent to the hole for ten days. He couldn't prove the weapon found in his cell was planted, so now he gets no visitors except his accountant on Tuesday and his attorney next week. No books and no phone calls.

Tuesday, July 14, 1992

Erik called me tonight. He seems sensible, telling me that Lyle will have to learn to do without the sewing needle I sent to Jill and the watch I bought for him.

Erik said he [Erik] received mail when he was in the hole. The problem is if I write to Lyle now, he'll probably be out by the time he gets it in his hands. Sometimes it takes nine days to be delivered, sorted, and then handed out to the detainees.

Monday, July 27, 1992

Lyle looked fine and none the worse for his ten-day ordeal in the hole. He said he felt very tense without any outlet for his energy. He had paced his cell last night because he couldn't sleep. I think he needs a punching bag to release some of his pent-up energy.

Wednesday, July 29, 1992

Lyle was really talkative tonight. I had to shut him up at least twice so I could speak, then he interrupted me three or four more times.

I showed him the book *Home Planet*. He loved the photos but couldn't concentrate on the writings of the astronauts. He kept chattering as I was turning the pages. He was in an up mood. I showed him the newspaper I had underlined for him. It got sent back to me. He said, "You're unbelievable, Norma, the way you get things done for me." So I said, "Well, I'm a doer." Lyle asked me to send him the book *A Brilliant Madness* by Patty Duke. He asked me not to let Jill know that I was sending it to him.

Saturday, August 8, 1992

Lyle was peppy again today. He showed me his book about businesses. He wants to start a food delivery service, plus anything else deliverable besides food.

I told Lyle I hoped Jill would speak up louder in court, like Leslie Abramson does, and Lyle said, "I know, I was thinking the same thing." He went on to assure me that he had confidence in her, such as her preparation skills, plus the fact that she is a lady . . . very soft, very honest. "She couldn't tell a lie," he said. "My overall opinion of her is good and positive. I'm not going to divide her up into negatives and positives, just like I don't with you, Norma. I don't say Norma Novelli is great at this but not so great at something else. I just remember you in a good, positive way because I feel good when I see you and I like thinking about you when you've left. I view you overall."

Sometimes this guy leaves me mute. He's always surprising me, jumping from something outlandish, that no one would believe, to something perfectly plausible.

Saturday, August 22, 1992

I encountered another big mix-up tonight as the deputy on the computer told me Lyle was back in the hole. I came home, heard a message from Lyle to bring dimes, so I knew he couldn't be in the hole. I then called the captain who determined that Lyle wasn't in the hole. He told me if I wanted to come back he'd leave a message to let me through, so I received a pass.

It was a long way to go back, but Lyle was in a good mood, real gabby and joking a lot. He showed me a card he was sending Lianne. It had been painted by another inmate who did beautiful airbrush work. Lyle told me that the guy who did the airbrush work was doing two life terms. He said, "He's a really strong guy mentally. Weak people die by killing themselves because they can't stand the prospect of life in jail, but he's a strong guy. I like him."

We talked about friendship. He stated simply, "If you're my confidante, that means I'd have to tell you everything, and there's a lot I could tell you, but I can't." I said, "Well, I'll be your confidante to a point," so we agreed on that.

Sunday, August 30, 1992

Today we talked about Mama going to the trial. I suggested keeping her at home to shield her from some of the mud throwing about her son Jose, which she isn't going to like, but then again, she's not going to enjoy the prosecutors pulling Lyle and Erik to bits either. Poor lady, she's between a rock and a hard place.

Lyle says there's no way to stop her from coming to the trial unless he gets her barred.

I said, "You can't do that. It will look good for you to have her standing behind you in support." "That's true," he said, "well, she will have to put up with it then. Anyway, she has an idea what we are going to say."

He thinks he'll be taking the stand for about five days. He said quite a few of his relatives will be coming to court every day, especially if the Calabasas house isn't sold. They can stay there. Free.

He's glad his mother's brother won't be coming. He was going to testify against Lyle but begged off last week.

Today Lyle said he felt good because "I've really cleaned out my cell . . . killed a hundred roaches because I managed to get some Ajax . . . and now it feels really nice and clean in there."

"Have you noticed my voice has gotten deeper since I first talked to you two years ago?" he asked me.

"Not really, no."

"Oh well, that's because you talk to me so often. When you talk to somebody every day you don't notice these changes. Norma, I've got to get more letters written to get me moved upstairs to Erik's row. I mean, I like it here, it's nice and quiet and nobody bothers me, but it's kinda lonely and my phone privileges are less and it's a punishment row also, a discipline area. I wanna move upstairs where it's safer. Plus there is a TV up there and I could watch reports of my trial on the news."

Then we discussed the crying issue. Lyle said he needs to be able to cry at the appropriate times when he's on the stand. If Jill cries during his testimony he won't be able to. It will block him off. So I said, "She probably won't cry anyway, attorneys never do." Lyle said, "Oh yes, they do. She cried last week." I said, "Weren't you afraid that she was crying?" This threw him a little bit but he responded with, "Oh, she was just crying because she felt sorry for me being in this situation and because she loves me."

I'll see him in court in Beverly Hills on Tuesday. I told him not to smile at me or anything. He said, "I'll try not to look at you, but I probably will, just to make sure you're there."

Saturday, September 5, 1992

Lyle seems to have disassociated from his mind the possibility that he might be in jail for years to come, or forever, which is natural when you realize that he thinks killing his parents was justified.

His biggest problem so far is to endeavor to explain the inexplicable, excuse the inexcusable, and reconcile the irreconcilable.

Monday, September 7, 1992

Tonight when I visited Lyle he was very agitated and depressed. He explained he'd had a horrible weekend of anger and rage. Jill Lansing had left for Russia so he has been without her for two weeks now. He is worried about the phone being tapped. I doubt it, but I gave him the benefit of the doubt. I feel frustrated for him. He thinks he is being singled out for unfair treatment regarding his visitation rights.

He still wants to move upstairs with Erik but doesn't seem to be able to get anyone interested in moving him. He is particularly upset that his phone calls to Erik might have been tapped. He says if they have, he will be damned, meaning that the calls will be damaging to his defense.

September 1992

Tonight Lyle left a message on my answering machine: "Hey, Norma. It's Lyle and I just wanted to let you know I'm out. It's 7:00 P.M. and I came back from court. You don't need to call. Thanks, Sweetie, I'll probably talk to you a little while later. Okay, bye-bye.

"Actually I wanted to let you know . . . if you could look for me in a store or call around and see where they have a real good one—that lotion—a suntan kind of lotion that they use to make your skin tanner. It has nothing to do with the sun. It's a lotion to make you look like you have a tan. I don't want the kind that makes you turn orange or whatever. There are some decent ones, I think Bain de Soleil is the best one but I'm not sure. If you could research that a little bit—check into it and call around. I'd like to try some of that. Okay, thanks."

Friday, September 11, 1992

Lyle was pleased tonight because he had been able to cry about his father while talking with another lawyer who came to see him today. We were both pleased. I told him he needs to practice those same feelings and get rid of the block that prevents him from being emotional.

He repeated to me that this will be the biggest case the courts have dealt with in twenty years.

Thursday, September 17, 1992

Lyle was telling me that he was talking with Paul Mones today and Paul thinks he can stop them getting the death penalty. He said, "What I'd like to do is make a deal with the DA that will do away with the trial."

Lyle was a bit concerned that his mail had been opened today, as it hasn't been for quite some time now.

Saturday, September 19, 1992

It was quiet at the jail today. Only four of us. Lyle was chatty and upbeat. He talked about what a nice guy Paul Mones was, but that "he's a bit too optimistic."

He was also telling me how he insisted on paying Jill and Leslie because that way he would have more control over them. At first Leslie was adamant about not having Paul Mones join the defense team but "I insisted," said Lyle, "and now they're all happy together."

"Paul said a deal is most unlikely in this case—it will have to be tried by a jury."

Lyle thinks if he goes to prison it will be Lompoc in Santa Barbara County.

Lyle said he wanted no part of anything to do with insanity or mental imbalance. I was thinking, if Lyle and Erik get twenty years, who is going to know them when they come out of prison? Who will ever want to know them? They'll have no money, no status, only faded notoriety.

Lyle told me how nervous he is going to be when the trial starts. So I told him once the trial starts his anxiety will ease. It's only because he's waiting expectantly right now. He said there will be about one hundred witnesses for the defense.

Thursday, September 24, 1992

We had a long visit tonight and Lyle was quite chatty again. Lyle is the only inmate on a block of eight cells (he is in the discipline area). We discussed at length the roles of women versus men. He argued that women are becoming more independent and more likely to cheat on their husbands than men are on their wives. He said that was what he has read, and he believes it.

He feels excited about how his case is going. He said Jill enjoyed her trip to Russia, but there was no milk or veggies.

Lyle often mentions how everything is gray around him—he'd like some posters for color. He is also not as bored as Erik, and Erik has television. He said Erik wants him to come upstairs to his floor.

Saturday, October 24, 1992

Leslie Abramson called to give me a stern lecture on the seriousness of this whole situation. She also told me she had a good long talk with Beatrice about her interview on "Hard Copy."

Her last warning to me was, "Norma, I want to trust you. Do not tell anybody, especially Lyle, that I have called you—or he will have a nuclear!"

Tuesday, October 27, 1992

No word from Lyle. I feel nervous.

Beatrice called me to say Lyle is deprived of all phone calls and visitation rights for now. She doesn't know why.

Jill called me to say that Lyle has been deprived of his privileges for the time being, but I can write to him and send him books.

She said, "I can't discuss why he has this ban, but I will call you when you can visit him again—he will have a nuclear."

--------------------◆--------------------

[*Editor's note*: This transcript has no date, but the conversation occurred shortly after Norma began taping the phone calls.]

NORMA: It gives you step-by-step stuff . . .

LYLE: OK . . .

NORMA: Yeah, I'll have two of those books on that.

LYLE: No, I don't think you'd want to publish it yourself, I mean, like a self-publishing type thing.

NORMA: Oh, no.

LYLE: You want it to go to a major publishing house and . . .

NORMA: Oh, yeah, let's get a good publishing house, yeah . . .

LYLE: And I guess you would go to them right after the trials, and you would go, "We already have an outline and we want to do a book."

NORMA: Yeah . . .

LYLE: Ask them if they think they—do they need a ghost-writer involved in it, and, do something, and say, OK, we'll do an eight-month deadline or something . . .

NORMA: OK . . .

LYLE: You know, and deliver within eight months . . .

NORMA: Yeah . . .

LYLE: The book comes out, I mean, if it was something we wanted to do . . .

NORMA: Yeah, because, uh . . .

LYLE: The screenplay would be like a whole different thing.

NORMA: Well, I'd want to be involved, because I'd want it to be—

LYLE: Well, I wouldn't want to do it unless you were involved, because I don't trust these writers.

NORMA: You don't what?

LYLE: I don't trust the writers.

NORMA: Yeah, OK. Well, this is good.

LYLE: Because I mean writers can come down and they'll sell you a good story, and, "Oh, I promise it'll be just like you want it," and then it's not.

NORMA: Yeah, and the thing is, it wouldn't have our personality. You know what I mean, a book has to have, the writer has to have some personality, and I'd want to go in with some humor here and there. You know, I wouldn't want it to be like, just a serious book.

LYLE: Right . . . and the writers (overlapping) . . .

NORMA: And we don't even, we don't know the personality of the writers, do we? Of ghostwriters.

LYLE: Right.

NORMA: So, he's just a total stranger.

LYLE: Right.

NORMA: So, we don't know how he's . . . how he writes.

LYLE: Right.

NORMA: Well, at least—

LYLE: Well you could, you could—one possibility is for you to look at a lot of the people that have done these kind of books, and read their work, and then we can sort of narrow down a few people that maybe could work with you.

NORMA: Yeah.

LYLE: . . . doing . . . (overlapping) . . .

NORMA: Well . . .

LYLE: And I think we could get any—just about any writer would want to work on it.

NORMA: Yeah.

LYLE: Just to have it . . .

NORMA: As long as we like how his style is.

LYLE: Yeah.

NORMA: Right.

LYLE: You know, or you could, uh . . . I mean, it would take longer because you have never written a book, but see, this is like a unique situation, 'cause, like let's say that, and I'm not saying that this would work, but let's say that you did the book, right?

NORMA: Yeah.

LYLE: Did the book, in a year, or eight months, or however long it takes. And you're not a—a known writer, and whatever, and it's not a book that a publisher would normally jump on, but because it's this book, and it has me involved—

NORMA: Yeah . . .

LYLE: —and it's this trial, it—there's a power.

NORMA: Yeah.

LYLE: There's no doubt about it. They're not gonna go, "Oh, no, we've never heard of Norma." You know, as long as the book is even decent, they're gonna do it.

NORMA: Yeah.

LYLE: Because of—because what's gonna sell the book is the fact that my name is on it.

NORMA: Right.

LYLE: And that, you know, and I, and I can promote selling it.

NORMA: Yeah.

LYLE: Because regardless of what happens in the trial, whether I win or lose or any of that, is not going to have any effect on a book.

NORMA: No, that's—Well, I don't know, I think if you were acquitted, a lot less would be done regarding the book, don't you?

LYLE: Oh, no, I think it's the other way around.

NORMA: Do you?

LYLE: If I'm acquitted—first of all, if I'm acquitted, or if I get out?

NORMA: Yeah?

LYLE: I could tour the book.

NORMA: Oh, of course—well, yeah, there's that advantage, of course.

LYLE: The publishers would just definitely want to tour the

book. And two, if I'm acquitted, there's a much more, uh, desire, or—any kind of good result at the trial—

NORMA: Well, I read—

LYLE: —more desire for my side of the story, because people will accept my side of the story, because a jury would have accepted it, and they would be much more eager to publish that side. Because all the other sides to it, the kind of guilty sides?

NORMA: Mm-hmm?

LYLE: —have already been published.

NORMA: Oh, sure . . . yeah.

LYLE: There's no market for another book that's like Dominick's or like *Blood Brothers* or anything like that.

NORMA: Yeah . . .

LYLE: The market is gonna be for a book that has the other side of the story, you know?

NORMA: Mm-hmm, of course, yeah. Because, I'm—of course it's so different as well, isn't it?

LYLE: Yeah.

NORMA: To get it from the inside out, you know.

LYLE: Yeah. And obviously, if the—if—the other side of the story, the one that I would do, is, is the one that at least partially wins in the trial . . .

NORMA: Yeah . . .

LYLE: . . . then, that makes it easier to sell the book.

NORMA: Mm-hmm.

LYLE: Because, I mean—either way, the book's gonna sell, because it'll have all that stuff from me, and that kind of that view of it—that inside view.

NORMA: Right.

LYLE: Because, I mean, people might want to buy, you know, they'll buy a book with some writer's view of this whole thing, but it's not the same as the participant, you know.

NORMA: Yes.

LYLE: I mean, you can write a book about Amy Fisher, but it's not the same as a book that was written with Amy Fisher.

NORMA: Oh, no, absolutely not.

LYLE: And it, and it really doesn't matter whether—

NORMA: And there's not even many of them out. Because I

think I've bought almost all the books on every crime that have—all the crimes that have been committed in America. And there's—I very rarely see one from the inside out, you know.

LYLE: Right.

NORMA: It's always the reporters that write them, or the authors.

LYLE: Right.

NORMA: The usual authors, yeah.

LYLE: Right, exactly. And whether Amy won or lost the trial, it would not affect the book.

NORMA: Mm-hmm.

LYLE: I mean, if she were out, it would be much easier to tour the book, that's all I'm saying . . . you know.

NORMA: Right.

LYLE: You and I would have much less easier time getting the book sold, and—

NORMA: Yes.

LYLE: —getting the book out, obviously. Or, or, if I got a good result to the point where, people would—the book would be much more accepted. 'Cause I mean, if I go to trial, and I totally lose—and hopefully that's not gonna happen but—the book is still gonna sell. But my version of it is gonna be less accepted. Because the jury will not have accepted it.

NORMA: Right, it—yeah.

LYLE: Do you know what I mean?

NORMA: Yeah, that's true.

LYLE: So, if I'm gonna do my version, it's, it's gonna be—people are gonna be much more eager to read it if the jury's accepted it—

NORMA: Yeah.

LYLE: —than if they had rejected it. You know what I mean, I mean, like, well why do we, you know—I mean, they'll still want to buy the book, but—

NORMA: Yeah, I think it'll still be like, uh, fifty-fifty anyway, Lyle, even if you were acquitted, you're still gonna get the other that's gonna buy it, and vice versa, and if you're not acquitted, you're still gonna get the other half that's gonna buy it.

LYLE: Right.

NORMA: So it's gonna sell about the same.

LYLE: Right, with the exception that if I'm out, I can tour.

NORMA: And I'll finally go to that Italian restaurant. (laughing) Yeah.

LYLE: Yeah. And more importantly—I'll go. (laughing) Right. That's true. Yeah . . . one of those fireside things.

NORMA: Yeah, yeah . . .

LYLE: At the fireside . . .

NORMA: . . . with a cup of tea. (laughing)

LYLE: Yeah. Yeah, now that would be nice, huh?

NORMA: Yeah.

LYLE: Although I, you know, even from a—if I got a manslaughter, or if I'm in another prison somewhere, you could, you could, uh, promote the book from—

NORMA: Oh, sure, of course I could.

LYLE: Could you, could you? Well, you could promote the book, but I could do it from there, through satellite interviews and things like that.

NORMA: Yeah. And then, well, can we still, can you still, uh, have, a bank account, I mean, could I still open a bank account for you? And uh, well, you'd have to keep it quiet.

LYLE: Well, I think what I would—like I say, I, I'm "Trial Lyle"—it's not, uh—I would rather just, you go ahead, and, uh, when the right—whoever—if there's another writer involved, he'll want some. The publisher's gonna take a great deal of it.

NORMA: Yeah.

LYLE: . . . some of it. And then the large part that's left, it might as well just go to, uh—I mean, they can't take the money from you, so it might as well just go to you. I mean, I'd rather give it to you than the government.

NORMA: Hmm. well, that would be nice.

LYLE: Well, I mean, you gotta put a lot of work into it.

NORMA: Oh yes, I know that.

LYLE: And, and uh, you know, you might as well profit from it.

NORMA: Yeah. Sure.

LYLE: You know? I mean, my feeling is, I'm doing this book

because I want to do something good. You know, if it sells well, and it gets out there, and people see a, a different version of it—

NORMA: Yeah.

LYLE: —than what, the books that are out now.

NORMA: Right. Which is what I always said in the very beginning. It'd be different.

LYLE: Yeah, you said it in the beginning, and you know, I wish I would have started that, you know, thought about it more then, but, my feeling then was like, I don't want to do a book for money, so that's not the motivation. And I don't want to, uh, I don't have an interest in just doing it for the hell of it.

October 1992

LYLE: We were discussing movie rights. This guy feels that you get the best deal before the trial rather than when the whole trial is already out. And the information is already disseminated. The movie won't come out until after the trial though. But the rights should be negotiated before. And there is some merit in that argument. But I'm not so sure that, you know, I mean obviously if it were to be found out that you were selling your rights, that would be very damaging at your trial.

NORMA: Would it?

LYLE: Course. And so, you would have to do it through a third party like Beatrice or whatever who is selling "The story of the Menendez Brothers" type thing. And you sell the rights that way and try to keep it under the lid. But I would think that the whole appeal to tell the story is that it was coming from us. And the question is, do we really want that to be floating around? You know, it's hard to keep under the lid. There's obviously a whole side show that we don't really need to deal with before trial.

October 1992

LYLE: What were you doing tonight?

NORMA: I was making a typical English meal. You might like it. It would probably be delicious compared to what you're eating down there.

LYLE: I ate about twenty crackers tonight—well about ten crackers tonight and a piece of bread.

NORMA: Saltines? That's not much is it? Crackers?

LYLE: It's good. It fills me up a little bit.

NORMA: I feel awful now telling you what I ate.

LYLE: Like all my other friends. They tell me excruciating details—lamb chops, mashed potatoes, we had a big Breyer's ice cream with big—

NORMA: Really laid it on for you. Nice friends you've got.

LYLE: That's what I say. Who needs you. I'm fine, I don't need anybody. I talked to Jill, she's in Vancouver.

NORMA: When is she coming back?

LYLE: Tomorrow night.

NORMA: Was it like a little vacation for her?

LYLE: No. She's got a meeting all day tomorrow with one of my experts—my other expert. It'll be a grueling day.

NORMA: For her?

LYLE: I'd give anything to be out and at these sessions. If they'd let me out now. Then I could have input.

NORMA: That's an unusual thing. It would be great for you to do that. But you can't.

LYLE: I'd be helping my case left and right. I'd be in therapy—serious—trying to help myself. Overall it is better that I've been here but it would probably be nice if it happened.

NORMA: It's just unusual for you to think of it that way. Being on the outside. You're probably trying. I don't know whether you can really envision being out and looking in like that. Can you?

LYLE: Yeah. I think I would spend a great deal of time in the office. I wouldn't have picked Jill, though, as an attorney. It's probably better that I'm here.

NORMA: Who would you have picked?

LYLE: I would have ended up with somebody from New York or something.

NORMA: Some aggressive bastard who fights to the—well, anyway you are with her now so you'll have to make the best of it. I just hope that she's able to—she might surprise you. She might just surprise you, Lyle. You never know.

LYLE: Who?

NORMA: Jill.

LYLE: I'm not saying that Jill's bad. Jill is incredible. I would never have anybody else, I know.

NORMA: I thought you just said you wouldn't have picked her?

LYLE: No, no. Oh, if I was outside?

NORMA: So, if you were outside you wouldn't have picked Jill?

LYLE: If I was outside I would have made a mistake and not picked her. That's why I think it is overall better that I'm in here.

NORMA: Why? Why wouldn't you have picked her?

LYLE: Because I wouldn't have picked somebody that was in touch with feelings, because I would have a girlfriend, I would have other things for that. A lot of the reason that I picked Jill is because I was so isolated here, I wanted somebody who was motherly who could give me some love. And that turned out to be the best for the case. But I did it for selfish reasons pretty much. I wanted somebody that was a little bit more in touch. If I was on the outside, I would have girlfriends, I'd have advisors, I'd have this. I'd have that. It would be bullshit. So fuck that.

NORMA: I see what you mean now. You have good vision, good insight.

LYLE: I have pretty good—sometimes I make decisions and I look at them later and I go, oh.

NORMA: In retrospect it wasn't right. That's the way you learn, isn't it? How not to do things. There is no successful man that hasn't made mistakes. Otherwise he wouldn't be a success.

LYLE: I've learned that the strong men, the men that you think are strong are still so fragile.

NORMA: Of course, I think a lot of this is a mask.

LYLE: Full of doubt, full of fear. Some of the most courageous men, you think. Most people—

NORMA: It takes courage to do that anyway. To be fearful inside and to show—put on this slick show. It takes a lot of courage to do that.

LYLE: Well that's what courage—

NORMA: This is what you're doing anyway.

LYLE: I don't think so. But as far as acting, when you have fear. That's what courage is.

NORMA: Absolutely. Being free of—that's why I have a motto

on the phone that says "First be afraid, then do it." I like this because it is courageous. To do something that you are afraid of doing.

LYLE: I don't know what else courage is. Because if you are fearless, then it is not courage.

NORMA: No it's not. Absolutely not.

LYLE: I learned that.

NORMA: I think it would be more foolhardy or just not thinking to be fearless. You'd have no brain.

LYLE: Well, some people feel it is because they haven't had fear in their life. They walk around—they never had bad things happen to them. I know people like that. Well, something is easy for them, so they are fearless. They know what it is.

NORMA: Yeah, they feel it until they feel fear. Let's put it that way.

LYLE: They know little fears but not great tension in their life. But some people are just fearless because they are warriors or whatever but—I think it holds a lot of men back—most men are held back because they are so aware of their insecurities and their doubts and their fears and their mistakes and their lack of talent in certain things. They figure they can't be anything extraordinary. They can't achieve any greatness. They can't achieve any notoriety. They can't plunge ahead because they look at their whole package and they see themselves flawed.

And they think that guys that are like Sylvester Stallone or Ronald Reagan or this as flawless people. They think—I can never be Jack Kennedy. I could never be Ross Perot. I don't have what it takes to be Luke Perry or Elvis or whatever. And not even people like that—they go, I could never be Lee Iacocca or this. I don't have what it—and they don't—if the men could just see that they could still have all of their fragileness, they could still have all of their problems, but they could still do some great things with their life. They could go so far.

NORMA: That's good thinking.

LYLE: It took a long time for me to learn that. I've always thought—I always thought my dad was like invincible. And me as flawed. I could never be like my Dad because I just don't have it. I'm just too sensitive, I just make mistakes, I can't concentrate sometimes. I can't learn quickly enough sometimes. I can't be like Dad.

NORMA: Well, he probably had fears as well. But he never showed them to you. Right. So he was a good actor also.

LYLE: Sure. I mean I—[sound of call-waiting beep]

NORMA: Never mind, they'll call back later.

LYLE: It's probably just Ross Perot and he wants to give me some money. Now you are nervous, aren't you?

NORMA: Oh, sure, it might be Ross Perot. Maybe I should tell them to call back because it is interruptive to our mental thinking. Hold on—

NORMA: Hello—hello, Lyle. Nobody answered so I think they must have hung up.

LYLE: I made you nervous when I said it could have been Perot.

NORMA: Oh, yeah, I was shaking in my shoes. So that was good thinking—you should write some of these things down. Well, mind you, what would you do with them? Well, you can send them to me.

LYLE: I write them in the letters. I actually write these—this stuff to my girlfriends. It goes over their heads. But Leanne is pretty deep. She can figure this shit out. I get in those moods and I just write.

NORMA: Sometimes it takes mood to make you write. I can write out of habit now. Cause I'm always writing something for the paper or making corrections and stuff like that. So writing to me is nothing, it's just like having a cup of tea. It's just the normal part of my life, writing. But for other people it's a big effort, isn't it?

LYLE: Yeah. I was talking to this girl in Texas, Angel. About the fact that I can't seem to use—I use the same words over and over and over again.

NORMA: When? When you're talking to somebody?

LYLE: When I write.

NORMA: When you write?

LYLE: Or even when I talk to someone but when I write—I use the word "great" and "how" and "well" and "very" and "so" and "much" and "then" and "often" and—it's like the same twenty-five words over and over and over.

NORMA: That's sort of Lyle's vocabulary. You could always change them.

LYLE: Right. It's like I never use the next grade of words. Like tenacity or—those words that are just a little bit—

NORMA: Yeah, so instead of saying "Oh, that's great" from now on I want to hear you say "Oh, that's terrific." What about that?

LYLE: I use words like "terrific," "fabulous," "fantastic," "this and that" occasionally "here and there," but pretty much I'm still saying "very" and "so much" and "really, really, really," and "how."

NORMA: You've got to say "how" when you are asking a question. There are some words that you cannot avoid using.

LYLE: But I use it over and over and over. I say "goddamn it." I'm amazing, I can write sixty different letters with the same six lines.

NORMA: I don't think that is at all amazing. I think it is very unamazing. I'm a clone of myself.

LYLE: I don't want to get as bad as my brother. My brother writes me letters—he'll go—at the end of his last letter he goes "Well, I guess this letter is sort of a catharsis."

NORMA: I hope he knows what it means.

LYLE: I said, "What the fuck does that mean?" I still don't know what the fuck it is. I didn't look it up. I'm not wasting my time to look up that fucking word. As far as I'm concerned "it is what it is," I told him when I wrote him back. I was in a bad mood. I said, "Listen, I haven't had that much schooling, don't use these advanced words when you write to me because it kills the moment when I have to stop and look them up."

NORMA: Yeah, really. It stops the flow of the letter. The flow of the words.

LYLE: I have to stop and look up this word to figure out what the hell his letter is. Because he says his letter was a catharsis. As far as I'm concerned his letter was ununderstandable.

NORMA: Well, maybe he is trying to seem intellectual as well as wear those glasses.

LYLE: I'm going to try to use that thesaurus. I've got a great thesaurus, maybe I should start trying to use words.

NORMA: Oh, you've got one there?

LYLE: Yeah, a great one.

NORMA: Shame on you then. Especially when you happen to notice that you are doing those things. I haven't noticed that you're using the same words all the time because I'm more interested in hearing what you have to say.

LYLE: I express myself very well.

NORMA: Oh, even though you say so yourself.

LYLE: Some people don't—they use big words—you don't know what the fuck they're really trying to say. Or they can use small words and you don't know what the fuck they're trying to say. They just don't express themselves very well.

NORMA: Or some people say, "hey just try and get to the point."

LYLE: I can get across my meaning pretty well. The problem is, I say things—

NORMA: Well, if you didn't people would get bored listening to you. That's why you have to get it over because Americans do have a short attention span. So you'd better fucking say it real quick before their ears disappear.

LYLE: Plus, I think that you get your point across better when you use simple words. Because anybody can understand you real easily and as I listen to myself talk now, I probably almost never say a word that someone in third grade does not know.

NORMA: Yes. Just now, you mean? Of course.

LYLE: Like take this sentence. "I express myself very—

NORMA: "Clearly." Or, "very well."

LYLE: "Well." I won't use the word "clearly," I say "well" every time.

NORMA: Just because it is shorter and means the same thing.

LYLE: When you talk to people that are exciting people or they have a good personality, then it doesn't matter what kind of words you use. But still I would like to—because I write so many letters, sometimes.

NORMA: Listen to you.

LYLE: When have I gotten a letter from you?

NORMA: What me? What do you mean, the last time? Well, I have to think back to that. Yeah, right. Okay that is a few weeks, so big deal.

LYLE: You and I talk all the time, we don't need to write letters. But I write letters to friends around the country, to Jill—I have to write letters for the case all the time. I write letters to Leanne pretty often. So I wish I can use some fucking words. I get scared though, when I start to use a big word, I think to myself, no I just better put "good."

NORMA: You'd love that little thing I've got. That little thesaurus. That little mechanical thing I brought down for you that time? Type it in and then you get all of the meanings.

LYLE: I looked up the word "fear." Like I'll always say "fear." I never say things like the word "alarm," "anxious," those are words that I don't say. I should say those words. They mean more.

NORMA: It's habit, isn't it? People that you've grown up around tend to all copy each other's words.

LYLE: I grew up around parents that didn't talk to me. They only talked to my little brother. And he only started using big words in the last eight months.

NORMA: Since he's been in there reading.

LYLE: I swear. These big words—and I start to believe that you've taken this up in jail. The Mexican gang member next to you goes, "Oh, yo dude. While you're having a catharsis in here can you turn down the temperature?" I don't see that happening.

NORMA: Well, I think it's got to do with what he's reading.

LYLE: "The water jug is juxtaposed to the TV, will you please move it closer?" And I'm thinking, I think he's like trying a lot bigger words, which is fine.

NORMA: Yeah, he's amusing himself, I suppose. But he is learning anyway.

LYLE: Oh, I embarrassed the shit out of him when I wrote that letter back about how I haven't had that much schooling—he's had less than me.

NORMA: When do you write him a letter? How do you get it to him?

LYLE: I gave it to him in the attorney room.

NORMA: Oh, I see. Well, it saves you a stamp.

LYLE: Yeah, are you kidding. Everything I put on paper can be used against me.

LYLE: Songs always have easy words in them. I should have been a songwriter. That's what.

NORMA: Do you have any more songs?

LYLE: Do you want me to sing a song? What time is it? Do I have time to sing a song?

NORMA: It's about a quarter to ten.

LYLE: That's going to be cutting it close. I'll sing.

NORMA: I'm going to get my guitar. Plunking on it—

LYLE: I think there's one that goes—

> If I could give my life to you
> I could think of things that we could do
> If I could sing the songs of yesterday
> Maybe we could be okay
> In life there are no guarantees
> There's only what we both believe
> There are so many paths that we can take
> The choice is always yours to make
> 'Cause you don't have to leave me, girl
> Too many roads in your world
> If love ain't gonna change your mind
> Tell me, how do I say, good-bye
> 'Cause you came into my life and I can't let you go, girl
> You see the tears in my eyes
> Still you don't know, girl
> I'll never forget you
> But leaving my heart, you are the one for me.

Friday, December 4, 1992

Lyle is jittery as a bug on account of Jamie [his former girlfriend] turning on him. He found out that she is going to give evidence for the prosecution.

---❖---

December 1992

NORMA: Hi Lyle. How are you doing?

LYLE: I'm OK. How are you?

NORMA: Are you alright?

LYLE: Yeah, I'm doing great.

NORMA: Seriously?

LYLE: I'm having a great day.

NORMA: A great day? Why?

LYLE: Yeah. I was kind of sore actually from working out yesterday. But other than that everything is going real well on my case. I can't believe it.

NORMA: Oh, that's good.

LYLE: Yeah. It looks like the trial is going to be for sure in Santa Monica.

NORMA: In Santa Monica? How come?

LYLE: Yeah. That's where we wanted it.

NORMA: Oh really. Why?

LYLE: The DA wanted to have it in downtown L.A. But we don't want that because—too many blacks and you never know and all that stuff.

NORMA: Yeah.

LYLE: So we want white people and nice people in Santa Monica which you know are going to get along great with Jill.

NORMA: OK. That's good.

LYLE: So. The judge was firm and told the DA, "No, it will be in Santa Monica." She argued and argued and he said "No, Santa Monica." So.

NORMA: Oh. That's good.

LYLE: Then he told us a few judges that we might have. That getting the right judge is key and all three are great for us.

NORMA: Smashing.

LYLE: Yes, it's awesome. And the one we really want, right? His name is Judge Light. And we had two affidavits, I mean like two . . . you can remove for no reason at all, two judges.

NORMA: Really?

LYLE: And the DA can do also. So we have the choice of three. One of them the DA hates and they will automatically paper [reject] him. Even if he doesn't, Leslie can paper him. And we got Light. So we pretty much got a good shot at getting this guy Light.

NORMA: That's good. It does sound like everything is going your way.

LYLE: Oh, yeah. That was just a drag if we got that judge. Because we need the judge. Because the judge is the one who is gonna decide how much of our evidence we can put in.

NORMA: Yes, that's right.

LYLE: And what instructions to give the jury.

Saturday, December 26/Sunday, December 27, 1992

Lyle was saying that Tuesday will be chaos in court with all the media there and with their lawyers, too, all wanting the release of the taped transcripts of Erik and Lyle.

I was asking Lyle if he would have preferred Leslie over Jill. He said, "I don't want it to look like I'm so aggressive that I need an aggressive lawyer to defend me."

Then he was worried about what his grandmother would hear, once the defense starts talking about his father.

Lyle told me not to take any stuff into Jill regarding books, posters, or thermals on Tuesday, as it will be too chaotic.

Next court hearing is set for January 12, 1993.

JANUARY–JUNE 1993

Pretrial Hearings

The first half of 1993 found the brothers honing their defense and attending hearings. Lyle and Erik were deemed eligible for the death penalty for the double homicides because special circumstances were alleged. The special circumstances included (1) lying in wait, and (2) multiple murders. Special circumstances are found by a jury to be either "true" or "not true" rather than "guilty" or "not guilty."

When a defendant charged with special circumstances is found guilty of the murder, only then is consideration given to the special circumstances.

On Friday, May 14, Judge Weisberg ruled that there would be one trial but two juries. If testimony related only to Lyle, then the Erik jury would not be in the courtroom, and vice versa. If testimony related to both brothers, one jury would be seated in the regular jury box, and the other panel occupied the entire center section of the small courtroom, with overflow jurors sitting in extra chairs in the aisle. Two juries in one trial has happened many times before, but it is an unwieldy procedure that Judge Weisberg was reluctant to impose.

Jury selection began Friday, June 18. Many prospective jurors, when told that the case would take around five months, were anxious to be excused. Some were determined to serve in the high-profile case, which required they fill out a thirty-six-page questionnaire.

Lyle appeared to take a very active interest in the jury selection process, especially for his jury.

An unusual occurrence found a cousin of Jose Menendez, Henry Llanio, called for jury duty. California jurors are selected at random from the Department of Motor Vehicles' drivers' license holders and voters' registrations. Of course Mr. Llanio disclosed his relationship to Jose Menendez, as required by law, and was excused. He later returned briefly as a witness in the trial and was a frequent spectator. He became a self-appointed family spokesman, making numerous appearances before TV news cameras in front of the courthouse and on talk shows.

Friday, January 1, 1993

Lyle was saying that his case might be moved to Van Nuys according to a rumor that Jill heard. He said he would be pleased if it was moved to the Valley.

We talked about Tatum O'Neal's marriage breaking up. He said most divorces are the fault of women who are relishing their newfound independence. (What?) He said there are now more women in the workplace than ever before.

A discussion on what not to wear in court during his trial took up most of the visit today. We talked about how he seems to be the more dominant personality compared to Erik. I suggested lighter, softer colors regarding clothes for his trial. He also said Leslie is the more dominant of the two lawyers and loves arranging everything to her own satisfaction "which is good because it will focus more attention onto her and Erik and off me."

We discussed tennis and soccer. He said his father decided on tennis for them. "We didn't get to choose anything for ourselves."

He also said he would work on his marriage if he does get married, but "first I have to get out of here."

He missed out on his shower today at 3:00 P.M. because I was there for a visit, but he didn't complain. He seldom complains about anything.

I told Lyle about growing his hair longer on the sides, and he finally agreed.

Saturday, January 9, 1993

Lyle feels excited about Tuesday because that's when he finds out if they're going to lift the death penalty or not. He said the nervousness I perceived was due to the Redskins game he was watching just before I arrived.

He has now decided that there are too many women in his case, and if the death penalty is lifted he is afraid he will lose Michael Burt, whom he regards highly as a good speaker. Lyle will be entitled to a court-appointed lawyer, as second to Jill, if the prosecution seeks the death penalty. (Mr. Burt was court appointed.)

Lyle said he is far more sensitive now than when he first entered jail.

He said he does not want his grandmother there, if possible, for any of the trial. I said she should be there to give support to him and Erik. He disagreed with me on this.

Tuesday, January 12, 1993

The court approved the prosecution's motion to seek the death penalty—

Today's decision in court was certainly a blow for Lyle and Erik but it was to be expected on account of two special circumstances, and the questionable third one of financial gain, which is difficult to prove beyond a reasonable doubt.

I saw Leslie in court today. I was opening the courtroom door and she was behind it coming in. Our eyes met and I said nothing, and neither did she. She dislikes Lyle so much I guess she's cool to me for the reason that I see him three times a week. Anyway, I am not going out of my way to gain her friendship. She is probably suspicious or whatever, but that's her problem. I know she resents Lyle talking to me. She wants total control of Lyle, Erik, and Jill Lansing. She never stops talking in the courtroom, always looking as if she is giving Jill advice. She's often turned away from the bench, facing the spectators in the courtroom.

Thursday, January 14, 1993

I wonder if they ever say to themselves, We did wrong, killing our parents, and we deserve to be severely punished.

Whatever these parents were like, they didn't deserve to be blown away.

What do Lyle and Erik actually believe should happen to them? Serve a few years and be set free?

Sunday, January 31, 1993

Lyle was quite chatty tonight. This was also one of the longest visits, lasting over an hour, but Lyle chatted on and on. He asked me if I believe in the death penalty and I said "No," so he said, "Well, you're rejected from being on my jury."

I need to get a law book from the library and read up about jury selection.

He also said that when he and Erik were choosing and interviewing attorneys for their case, he realized that Leslie was brilliant and decided that Erik needed her more than he did "because I was worried about my brother."

"Anyway," he said, "we won't get the death penalty, it'll never come to that. Another thing about the case is that Jill has warned me what the prosecutors are going to ask me, so I've practiced my answers and I feel pretty good about that."

I told him he'll feel more confident a few weeks into the trial when he sees the style of the prosecuting attorneys and how they work. But he didn't agree.

We talked about how Leanne regarded Lyle as one of her best friends, and he said, "I'm not her friend at all. She's not somebody I can call, who is always there for me, to listen to me. As far as I'm concerned my best friends are you and Jill." This was nice coming from Lyle, as he is not the most generous with kudos.

———————◆———————

January 1993

LYLE: I was listening to this guy telling me that when he was up in Pelican Bay you can order a present of color TV sets, or stereos or whatever, but they have a list of things. You can only order certain sizes and nothing over $200—things like that. But what they do is, some of the guys have connections. There is no particular vendor that you have to go to get these things. So you can get the vendor. Let's say you know somebody that owns a TV store, whatever. Just put the price on there that it is only $200 even though it cost like $400 and you can get nicer stuff.

LYLE: So, did Jill talk to you afterward?

NORMA: Yes. She waggled that finger at me and she called me over and she said, "Norma, don't talk to [Miami journalist] Robert Rand."

LYLE: Don't talk to any of them.

NORMA: Oh, no. I said I'm not talking to him. He just showed me a photograph of Lyle and Erik from a foreign magazine. And she said, "Oh, but don't talk to him, okay?" I said, "No, I'm not talking to him, don't worry." He wouldn't dream of asking me anything anyway 'cause he introduced himself to me months and months ago and he has never ever tried to interview me. 'Cause, you know, I wouldn't talk to him anyway. I already told him that in the very beginning, once he said who he was. He was quite open about himself. He said he was from the *Miami Herald*. I said, "Oh, okay I know who to avoid then." You know, joking with him. But anyway that's the first time he has spoken to me since, so he is real laid back. He is not pushy or anything.

LYLE: I just would be cool—

NORMA: Don't worry. I never normally sit by him or anything. He's always in a different part of the courthouse. I don't walk down with him. He's alright. He's not a bit pushy. But today he wanted me to see the photograph that he had. That he said he was going to bring months and months ago and he forgot all about it. Anyway, today he remembered that he had it with him so that's all it was. Jill nearly had a nuclear fit—

LYLE: He says they got a publishing place where they can publish your books. If you want to write books in prison and stuff too.

NORMA: Oh, have they?

LYLE: So, when I write your life story, it'll be like one of those—

NORMA: It'll be kind of boring compared to yours.

LYLE: I don't know if they do comic books though.

NORMA: Very funny. I'm going to kick your ankle. My list is getting longer. The things I'm going to do when you come out. . . .

LYLE: That guy [Rand] is a big problem.

NORMA: Is he really?

LYLE: You think you got it all under control and—hey I have no problem.

NORMA: Well, this was my tongue. I'm not stupid. I've got more brains than I'm getting credit for. It's not fair.

LYLE: You don't really need brains. It's just what's to stop the guy from saying that he had coffee with you and you told him all of this stuff—and lie. What's to stop him from lying?

NORMA: Anyway, he just gives me the impression that he is not the normal journalist.

LYLE: Oh, no. He's worse.

NORMA: You think so?

LYLE: I do. That guy is fucking lunatic. He's crazy. He really is. He's way out there. He goes to the DA and tries to say that Leslie sent him and this and that—to get information and all kinds of stuff.

NORMA: Well, at any rate, he didn't ask me any questions. So I wasn't a bit worried. It wasn't like I was hiding something. I could have said, "Sure, he'll be downstairs," or I could have been undercover or said, "See me outside the courthouse." But I sat down there right in front of [Jill].

LYLE: He moved down here to do his book about us so I'm sure that he's just figuring that he's building your trust and slowly but surely you'll think, oh he's a great guy. And then he'll ask you this question and that question and oh yeah.

NORMA: Oh, yes. There could be a method to his madness.

LYLE: There usually is.

NORMA: Did you wear your [new] shoes today? 'Cause you can't see your feet even from the front row. You can only see like up to your thighs and that's it.

LYLE: Yeah, I wore them today. One of the shirts is just too starchy. They're business shirts.

NORMA: Are they all stripy?

LYLE: Some of them are just too starched. But I don't

know—I have some other shirts that are like that but more laid back. I just don't know where the stuff is. My grandmother has it or my aunt. So my aunt's looking.

NORMA: You have plenty of time to look, don't you?

LYLE: Yeah, otherwise she can just buy some more stuff. But I had—the blue sweater is not bad but I'd like to wear—

NORMA: It's a nice blue that sweater.

LYLE: I'd like to wear lighter colors. But that's not possible.

NORMA: The article was saying so too, wasn't it? It's true, you do think of more gentle people with pastel colors. 'Cause you know, men normally like dark maroon or black or a good grey or a solid blue. So pastel colors they think might be a bit too soft and feminine. But for you it is ideal in court, isn't it?

LYLE: I think so.

NORMA: I thought that was awful, that one Erik was wearing. It was kind of—he doesn't suit cream because he is so pale.

LYLE: That was my thermal.

NORMA: Was it really? I suspected it was because it was like really, really pale. I hadn't seen all of them before and I thought, Oh shit. What's he doing with this pale color on?

LYLE: We had this red shirt that nobody could wear and so—

NORMA: Oh, really, 'cause that was the only thing left for him. 'Cause he looks better in a color. He looks totally white when he's wearing a cream color like that.

LYLE: I agree.

NORMA: It looks like it reflects onto his face. Anyway, it doesn't do much for him.

February 1993

NORMA: So you want me to sew some buttons on—

LYLE: —some shirts and you just take about three-fourths of an inch and make them tighter. Just move the button. Take the same button out, there's buttons there. And just sew it in about three-fourths of an inch and make sure it matches with the hole.

NORMA: And this is on the cuff.

LYLE: On each cuff.

NORMA: And the body part is okay?

LYLE: Yeah.

NORMA: Alright. Both shirts? Alright. Even the pink and blue one? So, you're going to court again tomorrow? Well, I'll go at—let's see—lunchtime. I'll meet [Jill] there at lunchtime, then.

LYLE: Where?

NORMA: Jail. Well, what kind of arrangements did you make?

LYLE: With what?

NORMA: With Jill tomorrow.

LYLE: What do you mean?

NORMA: About giving me the shirt.

LYLE: We'll figure it out tomorrow. She'll give them to you. Don't worry about it. Grandma is probably going to be interviewed with the DA and Jill and Beatrice tomorrow. Just sort of stay out of their way until they're done.

NORMA: Yeah, I know. She said she wanted to talk to Jill.

LYLE: OK. Great. Listen, I'm going to call Jill and then if I have some time, I'm gonna call you back.

NORMA: Yeah, OK. So tell her then, that—OK—tell her that I'm going somewhere in the morning. I have an appointment to attend to in the morning—so did Mama come down this morning?

LYLE: No, she didn't. She's upset or something. But I called her at the house. I can't reach her.

NORMA: No, I called her this morning and I talked to her last night. She said she was going to get her car done today.

LYLE: Oh, maybe that's what she is out doing.

NORMA: I said, "Do you want me to come over?" She said, "No, because I'm going to stay there all of the time until it's fixed." She said she doesn't leave her car with anybody. You know, she says she doesn't go back home.

LYLE: OK.

NORMA: Is Beatrice there?

LYLE: Yes. She's here. You're not coming today, then huh?

NORMA: Pardon?

LYLE: You're not coming today.

NORMA: Yeah, I can pop over.

LYLE: OK. If you want to, why don't you pick up those shirts? We'll give you all the shirts because I probably won't be coming back until Monday.

NORMA: OK.

LYLE: So, if you can get the shirts done and back to Jill on Monday then I'll get them.

NORMA: Is it just the two or have you got a few you want altering?

LYLE: I think there's two. I'll put a little mark where I think the buttons should be—in pencil.

NORMA: That's a good idea. Because you said, what—about a half an inch?

LYLE: Yeah. I'll put a mark where I feel you should put the hole to sew—not the hole—

NORMA: Yeah. So they don't slip over your hand.

LYLE: And that will take care of that.

Friday, February 19, 1993

Well, tonight was a flop. I arrived at the jail for the 6:00 P.M. visit and the lock-down sign was posted across the parking lot entrance. (Another scuffle between inmates.) At least the sign was up before I paid the four dollars.

Driving back home at that time of the evening took me an hour. When I arrived home my answering machine was blinking. It was another inmate with a message from Lyle. "Norma, the lock-down has been lifted, could you come back down for the 7:00 P.M. visiting hour?" No chance of that. It's already 7:25 and I've just arrived home, but I do call the watch commander to get Lyle out of his cell, as they sometimes forget about him because he is on a row by himself. If I didn't call and remind them, he wouldn't get his phone time.

Saturday, February 20, 1993

Lyle was a bit depressed tonight and didn't concentrate too well. He's anxious about moving and is nervous about how removed he's going to be, more than any other factor. As of now, I'll be visiting him tomorrow for the last time in L.A. County Jail. Then he is being transferred to Wayside Rancho at Castaic, a long way to go.

I think he's bothered about how the other inmates will react to him. He keeps other worries to himself because that's the way Lyle is.

When Lyle called tonight he was saying that he thinks the move won't happen. Jill isn't keen on the idea and I don't blame her. It's much too far for her to travel, especially as the trial is getting closer, she'll need to see him more often. Now he thinks if he stays in L.A. County Jail he'll be moved to another row for more protection.

February 1993

NORMA: They didn't deliver some defense thing because the father didn't have a gun in his hand when the kid did. . . . After the father ran out after him. So they discounted the self-defense thing. Well, he did say that he felt that one of them was going to die. You know, so—

LYLE: You mean the jurors discounted it?

NORMA: They discounted the self-defense thing. Right.

LYLE: What do you mean they discounted it?

NORMA: OK. They said they didn't go for it. They didn't go for the self-defense.

LYLE: Why?

NORMA: Because the father didn't have a gun.

LYLE: You just said that some of the jurors didn't want to give him manslaughter.

NORMA: Right, they didn't. So I assume that they couldn't come to a conclusion quicker than they did.

LYLE: Right. So they compromised.

NORMA: Sort of.

LYLE: Some of the jurors did think it was self-defense.

NORMA: Right.

LYLE: Yeah, because it can be self-defense. He doesn't need

to have a gun. You know—a person doesn't need to have a gun to be possible to kill you. As far as I'm concerned.

NORMA: Oh, I figured with the lack of—they were saying—somebody came on at the end and said something about he was the only one with a gun. The kid. And so I figured—that it was because he didn't have a gun, that they didn't want to give him self-defense.

LYLE: Well, it's possible that some jurors thought that way, other ones didn't. They certainly could have given him self-defense. He could have come up and killed him with his bare hands.

NORMA: Oh, sure. Oh, yeah, yeah. That's true.

LYLE: Or he could beat him with a gun and he could kill him easily.

NORMA: Yeah, sure. Yeah, and it was so dark and you see the father lying there. And he's got a dark suit on, and it is nighttime. And [the kid] said, "All I could see was his shoes." Which was also true, because you could barely see the father's outline on the dark ground. But you could definitely see his two white shoes. And the kid just shocked and panicked but he didn't think he hit his dad. But anyway—so—he got twenty-two months. And then you see him coming out at the end of the program and it was good.

LYLE: Yeah, but he came off good. He was lucky. He had Paul [Mones] through the whole thing.

NORMA: Yeah. He did.

LYLE: My attorneys are much better than Paul, but Paul, he is a miracle worker when it comes to that stuff. He was intimately involved in my case. And I get so much help from the guy, it's a miracle.

NORMA: And he's going to do the same for you, isn't he? Isn't he going to go into the court and speak?

LYLE: No.

NORMA: Oh, he's not going to speak?

LYLE: No. We may call him.

NORMA: Oh, I thought we'd been seeing him so regularly that that was what he was going to do.

LYLE: I don't think so. I mean he may be called as an expert.

NORMA: Yeah. So if he—

LYLE: In this kid's case, he was the lawyer. He tried the case.

NORMA: Oh, I see.

LYLE: In my case, he is not the lawyer that is trying the case, he is just the—he might be an expert that talks about it. You know. Child abuse in general.

NORMA: Right.

LYLE: So we don't—you know he is not the lawyer. He is not a great lawyer. He—I don't know. He might be. But he is not supposed to be. And I mean—Jilly I think can move a jury more than Paul Mones. And I think that Michael is a more brilliant guy than Paul Mones when it comes to lawyering for sure. And Leslie is a more dramatic person also.

NORMA: It would have been interesting for you to see Paul in action, wouldn't it?

LYLE: Oh, I see him in action all the time.

NORMA: Do you? Where?

LYLE: He comes down to the attorney room. And I—

NORMA: Oh, yes. But he has to be in a real courtroom for you to see how he—

LYLE: He does the same stuff.

NORMA: Do you think so?

LYLE: Oh, yeah. He's got one way about him and that's it. And he's great. I mean the guy is so much help 'cause, you know, my testimony is very much, you know, he has helped me get some of this stuff out expression-wise.

NORMA: Yeah, because that's what you have to do, express yourself. You get nowhere if you keep it all bottled up. The prosecutors are going to drag it out anyway.

LYLE: Helping me express is what he's good at. Exactly. So I mean, it's unbelievable, this guy. The way he can do this stuff. You wish he could testify for you in some ways.

NORMA: Yeah. So that he knows to say it exactly the way he wants you to say it.

LYLE: Well, he doesn't want me to say it a certain way because I have my own way of talking. But he helps a lot.

NORMA: Right.

LYLE: In having me express myself. It makes a big difference. You know. I mean, I'm more, I can move a jury, I think, more than most of these kids and him because, you know, because I'm the—I don't know. I get very emotional. . . . I just affect people more. I can affect people in a very negative way, sometimes. Affect them in a very positive way. People like that—it depends. And I'm obviously going to just be myself and affect them in a real positive way. And I hope it comes across real good. I think that it will.

NORMA: I'm sure it will once the time comes for you to get there and you'll be nervous and stuff a little bit.

LYLE: I want to show them how much I believe in what—my past. You know, how much I feel for it. All the pain involved and there is no way the DA is going to get me. You know, that's stupid. I mean I'm thoroughly, you know, I'm a product of what happened and I just feel like I want to make sure that they—the jurors—understand that.

NORMA: Yeah.

LYLE: And every time I feel real sad. Like today, I cried a lot today.

NORMA: Did you?

LYLE: And I feel like there is no way that I would be on the stand and a jury not believe what I say.

NORMA: Right.

LYLE: You know they are going to absorb what I say.

NORMA: Absolutely. They are going to be hanging on your every word.

LYLE: Yeah, absolutely. And I don't give a fuck how many people lie, which you don't have that many people, but you have a few people, or how many people come forward on my behalf, or all the arguments and opening statements and stuff like that. You got the person sitting a couple feet away from you and they are telling you things that are very hard for them to say—are very embarrassing, very difficult—you know. And they are telling you that. Because they need to. They have to. They are being forced to in a way. But they also—they need you to know. And you know—I can easily—I always envision the jury that they are hearing me. And then he sends a note to the judge saying we don't need to hear anymore. We don't want to hear anymore. We don't want to spend another four months here. And that's what I want. And that's what I believe will happen. I could be wrong. But I don't think so.

Friday, March 5, 1993

Lyle said he was sobbing yesterday during his meeting with Paul Mones and Jill, as it was about his parents.

He also told me that Paul played prosecutor with him, flinging negatives and insults just as it will be in the courtroom, and that he felt well prepared for this.

Then Lyle said, "Norma, I don't know if I want to stay in Los Angeles, maybe I'll go to Seattle." I was startled as he's never mentioned Seattle before, so I said, "Why Seattle?"

"Oh, it's a beautiful place," he said, "quite a bit of rain falls there so everything is nice and green."

As far as I know Lyle doesn't know anyone there, so who knows what brought this about. Lyle confuses me quite a bit because he doesn't seem to have any well-thought-out reasons for his statements. I've never heard him say "I don't know," except as an expression at the end of a statement. He has an answer for everything. It's a habit with him, even if he doesn't know the answer he will say, "Well, probably because . . ." and then take a guess, assuming his answer could be right. His mind never slows when I am with him.

"Norma, Paul Mones thinks I'm the best defense witness he's ever dealt with . . . and even though he won all these kid's cases, they didn't know how to defend themselves properly."

Lyle likes Paul and I get the impression he boosts Lyle's spirits quite a lot.

Lyle was saying he had to take a test to weigh his moral values. Later he said he scored the topmost marks for his moral values test. Mercy!

Although Lyle has committed the terrible sin of parricide, he probably believes he was justified in doing so. He tells me, "Wait until you hear the evidence of my abuse," as though I am going to say, "Oh, my God, Lyle. I don't blame you."

I personally think some of his problems stemmed from too much attention and smothering by his parents, and not enough freedom for himself.

March 1993

Tonight there was a big upset. A girl called to tell me what Lyle had done. She said, "Grandma got there at 4:30 P.M. for a 6:00 P.M. visit, and everyone's so upset 'cause she had to drive so far. She showed us her face where she fell at the airport and was hurt. She decided to see Lyle first. The deputy told her Erik already had a visit today, so she couldn't see him. The deputy was upset when she told me she didn't know how to tell Mama that Lyle had refused her visit. I told Mama that Lyle had refused her visit, and she said, 'Why?' The guard lied and said, 'He's sick.' Mama said, 'Tell him it's *me*.' I told the deputy, 'She's really upset.' The deputy called up there again, and I guess Lyle told the deputy to fuck off."

The girl asked me, "Were you on the phone with him? They said he was on the phone with someone."

I said, "Yeah, I was." I felt bad about that because I didn't know what he was doing at the time. Then she tells me what else happened: The deputy came back and said again, "No, he refuses the visit." Then the girl asked, "What if I put in the pass for her at 7:00 P.M.?" The deputy responded, "No, he pissed that deputy off so bad, Lyle won't get a visit tonight, no matter what."

Then she asked me, "How did Lyle explain that to you?" I told her he said it was a mix-up over Beatrice. She said, "That's a lie. Beatrice and I had talked, and she wasn't planning on coming." I told her I knew that because I had called Beatrice, too, and anyway, Beatrice never comes at night. Lyle hadn't seen his grandma for *eight months*, and when she comes over, he refuses her visit. It made me sick.

The girl said, "I don't know how he can face himself. Everybody was so mad at him. All the B Row inmates were mad. I'm sure he got his head full when he got back, because everybody was on a visit. They were all pissed! All the girls, everybody! She's an old lady. I'm so worried about her. It was so sad. She said to me, 'I might as well go back to Princeton. He doesn't want me here.' He broke all our hearts tonight. He couldn't get off the phone *one time* for his grandma? Mama said to all the women waiting, 'You know my house is so far away, and I come here and wait, and I sit here.' She was all by herself. We all felt so bad for her. The deputy felt bad for her, too. No one knew what to do. Lyle didn't give a shit. He's got to learn how to talk to his grandma. You have to respect your elders. I was so worried and upset, I called her house but there was no answer. Everyone on B Row ragged on him because he ruined their visits. They yelled at him, 'Your grandma was all upset. She fell down and hurt herself, and then she came here and stood in line to see you!' They all yelled at him for an hour and a half. They were really mad. He disrespected her."

The next day Lyle called me. "I'm kinda in the doghouse with Mama for refusing her visit, so it's not a good idea to call her or have too many discussions with her about things, unless you're getting along with her good."

That was it. No mention of them yelling at him for an hour and a half. No mention that he was sorry. He wasn't sorry, he never is.

------------------------◆------------------------

March 1993

NORMA: You know another interesting thing that I thought of the other day that I haven't mentioned to you yet was when something traumatic happens like on that morning—it happens in slow motion. This is what I've read—two books now said this. Now that's a real interesting point. I thought, I'm going to tell that to Lyle. And it said when something really traumatic happens and you are in shock, it happens in slow motion. That's only if you are in shock, right? Now, if you are not in shock, it doesn't slow down and it is cold and ruthless. It happens just as if it is a normal thing that you are doing. Do you see what I mean? But if the thing that's happening turns into slow motion, it means that you've gone into shock. And I thought, that's an interesting point.

LYLE: Well, I'm not so sure it's true.

NORMA: Well, it sounds logical if you think about it.

LYLE: I don't know. I haven't had an experience with other shock victims. I know with me, I experience shock. I often see things in flashes. And they go on at lightning speed and then I'll remember exactly what happened sometimes. Other times, it is slow motion. It's both.

NORMA: Well, it's like when—you know when someone is in a car crash? When they crash and it is actually happening to them, they go into such shock that it happened. Now this is a normal reaction to a body. A body immediately goes into shock because something extraordinary is happening. And then it happens in a real slow-motion kind of way because of the sensitivities all being aroused. You're extra sensitive to everything. And then, afterward, you don't have a lot of memory of it. But at the time it happens, it is in slow motion if you're going into shock. But if you're just totally doing something—

LYLE: I don't think so. I disagree. It's a nice little pat theory that people put in books and sell. I don't think so. I mean, people experience shock in different ways and I don't think you can say it's slow motion or not slow motion. It's called—

NORMA: Well, I think it might be something—I don't know it might be worth mentioning to Paul. Just someone you can confide in anyway.

LYLE: I don't feel it. I've been in shock many times. There have been times where minutes have gone by and I can only recall it as if it happened in seconds. Certainly not—

NORMA: Well, I think it sort of depends on which sort of shock you're talking about, doesn't it? You know, it depends on how severe the shock is.

LYLE: I'm talking about trauma. I don't know what you mean by shock. But I'm talking about trauma. Traumatizing stuff. I think people experience trauma in different ways. Some people are—it may happen in slow motion and detail. Some people blank it out completely. They have no memory of it.

NORMA: Right. That's what happens. Yes.

LYLE: That's certainly not slow motion. That's like it never happened. And then some people experience it—it just happened so fast. It was like everything was pushed together and it happened in like five seconds. You know, I don't think you can say that people experience trauma in a certain way. Blanking out is certainly a common thing.

NORMA: Yes. It did say that too.

LYLE: Slow motion is one of them. You know I would think that slow motion would be less of the answer.

NORMA: Less of a shock?

LYLE: If someone is very traumatized by them, his mind is constantly rejecting the pictures as they come forward. Let's say that you see something that is very brutal or whatever. Traumatizingly so. His mind is saying, no I can't experience that—too painful. And it's constantly cutting it off, right? So what is a long two-minute episode, every time something comes in visually it is cut off and so it happens like it happened in two seconds. He doesn't have a very good memory of it. Happened real fast. Because the mind couldn't—his mind couldn't handle it being in slow motion. He couldn't handle seeing a two-minute thing as it was happening for five minutes. There is no way a person can register that if they are really traumatized. It would be too painful. The mind would reject it. It wouldn't be able to recall it that way.

NORMA: The memory would, yes.

LYLE: That would be my thinking.

NORMA: You're talking about the afterward though. I'm talking about the time that it was happening. Whatever you remember about it. You know—did it happen in slow motion?

LYLE: Well, you're talking about your memory. I mean you can't go back. Your memory of the event. Your memory of the event would be all chopped up depending upon how traumatizing it was—

NORMA: Yeah, depending upon how much of a shock you go into. Yeah.

LYLE: You know. I don't think it's slow motion. I don't know. I only remember the—

NORMA: This is like—these books were written years and years apart. So—it would be interesting to find them again. Whichever psychology book it was in. So you could read that particular passage.

LYLE: I know that—fear, fear can seem that way. Five seconds of fear can seem like ten minutes.

NORMA: That would be different. But it's hard to say. It's hard for me to say unless—well I've been in severe shock. Yeah. When my daughter was killed but—it's hard for me to remember that far back now to the exact feelings, you know. 'Cause it is like you're blanking out. Because you don't want to remember the horrible words that this person said to you about it. And, you know—but that's too difficult for me to remember and compare it.

LYLE: That is very painful.

NORMA: Yeah. Well, I hope you're not feeling too sad now. You don't—you sound okay anyway.

LYLE: I'm okay.

NORMA: You were just sad about memories this afternoon, I suppose, were you?

LYLE: Yeah. Sometimes, you know. I just can't get it out of my mind. But—

NORMA: I would imagine more than sometimes.

LYLE: Sometimes—I don't let myself think about anything too long—too often. But you know, I'm forced to do it.

NORMA: Yeah, I know.

LYLE: You know these experts want more and more and more from me.

NORMA: Constantly taking you back.

LYLE: And I can only go so far for them. Some things I can't talk about. Some things I won't. So for me I don't see the difference in the case. And so—I wanna—I can't—I won't.

NORMA: I think it is difficult to get at you every week anyway, you know. You need a break. You know, sometimes so you don't have to keep on saying it over and over again. I mean do they expect you to be emotional when you're telling this? They don't expect that too, do they?

LYLE: Sure.

NORMA: When you're just explaining something.

LYLE: No, no. I am quite often.

NORMA: Because you're going to—

LYLE: It's emotional. I don't talk about this stuff too often in a scientific way. I can't. But, you know, sometimes obviously I do that. Just talk about it monotone. But I don't like to do it that way. I get very upset when I'm forced to do it that way. That's why I don't like these emotions where they talk about it in such casual way, you know. I feel like, What the fuck is this? You know, let's get the jury in here and let's do it in real life. Because it bothers me. So I get emotional in the stupid motion—'cause it upsets me. This guy talking about this letter—this is an exhibit. You know, it's unbelievable.

NORMA: Do you ever sometimes just forget what the hell you are there for? Sometimes do you get all wrapped up in your conversation and you even forget what you're discussing sometimes? I think I would.

LYLE: A conversation with who?

NORMA: You know, when you're talking to these guys. I mean, they are not always saying—about your father and your mother to you. Talking about your friends and all the rest of it and your friend's friends. You know how they go off in two different—all the way down the avenue and talk about different people. Do you sometimes lose track of what you are there for? I think I would.

LYLE: All the time.

NORMA: Do you?

LYLE: I have to.

NORMA: And then you get jolted back to certain—to reality about what it is they're asking you all these things for. Yeah. That was one of the hardest things I think for me to put up with—the constant going away of it and then the jolting back of it.

LYLE: I prefer to be jolted back on the stand.

NORMA: I'm sure you're used to that now.

LYLE: I'd rather be—you know the escapes are important. Absolutely.

NORMA: The escapes are important. For the relief you mean?

LYLE: Lately as I get closer, I've been allowing myself to escape less and less.

NORMA: Have you? Do you feel better this way?

LYLE: Yeah. I think it's a way of escape. That's why I moved to this row. I moved to this row because they don't give me a TV set, forget it, I'm not asking for it. Fuck it. I don't want the escape. You know what I mean. I don't want to play chess with guys. I don't want to have people to talk to, to cheer me up. I don't want to watch "Gilligan's Island" or lose myself in a movie. I'd rather sit here with my pain more.

NORMA: Would you? Do you feel better doing that?

LYLE: Work on it. Save myself so that when I get to where I got to be, I'm there. I'm there emotionally. It's important for me. And I'm not going to screw up.

NORMA: Right. This is a great way to be. This is the way to go, Lyle. Especially now, as you say, you are getting nearer. This is the best way to go about it. You're grasping the thistle by the thorn so to speak.

LYLE: That's why we take the vans instead of the buses. A lot of it is helpful, yeah whatever. No harassment. A lot of it is just, I want as little stimuli as possible, you know. As little stimuli as possible. I just want to concentrate on what I have to do. And it's painful and whatever, but I have plenty of courage to get through it, so I'd just rather do it and then when it's over it's over. So I don't think about consequences, results, future. I'd like to have a girlfriend so I [could] talk to her and I hope to talk to her. But she's a pretty serious person and so it's not like having some silly dumb blonde. So I can talk to her regular and so on. But other than that, I don't really want too much and, like I said, I work on my case every day.

NORMA: So you're staying there. You're not losing sight of it. Right.

LYLE: And I'm willing to go back over it. I'm just kind of—I mean obviously I know it all so there is no real reason to work on it but—other than just to keep writing it out. Just to see if I can get in touch with more feelings. And it clearly shows. I mean I think it showed between Erik and I when we testified. I was clearly the person who was emotionally there. I was the only person in the room who was emotionally there.

NORMA: Were you?

LYLE: And it was obvious. Man, I got on the stand and everybody stopped talking. And it was like riveting. Because you know, I care. And it shows that I care. Everybody was like quiet and like a little bit embarrassed 'cause you know you can ask all of these nifty questions and try to trick people and do this and that. But you know, when there is somebody there—this is like important to them—their feelings—they care. You're going to make no progress with a person like that. That's a witness on and off as far as they're concerned because you're not going to make any progress. It's like having some old lady who is crying on the stand or something. You're not going to ask her any questions if she's not there for you.

NORMA: Right.

LYLE: You just want her off. That's the way they are going to feel about me. I don't think they are going to want to ask me a lot of questions. They are going to get through part of their cross-examination and I think they are just going to go—no more questions.

NORMA: Which was the part that embarrassed you? Because the embarrassment you'll definitely get rid of.

LYLE: I don't think—

NORMA: You were embarrassed. You testified for the first time.

LYLE: I'm not going to be embarrassed. I'm not going to get rid of the embarrassment and I don't want to.

NORMA: Yeah. That's what I'm saying. What made you embarrassed last week?

LYLE: Well, lots of things. But basically the fact that this is a personal letter that is now public exhibit.

NORMA: Oh, okay. The letter to Erik.

LYLE: It's embarrassing. Everything about my life being in the public domain is embarrassing to me.

NORMA: Yeah.

LYLE: You know, everything is embarrassing to me. The first thing I told the guy before I got interviewed that night was, "Is this going to go on to the public? Is this going to remain quiet? 'Cause if it's going out tomorrow on the news, I'm not talking to you."

NORMA: When did you say that?

LYLE: On arresting. That's what the cops said the night when my parents died. When they interviewed me.

NORMA: Okay.

LYLE: That was my main concern.

NORMA: Really.

LYLE: That was my main concern. I'm not any voyeuristic person like all these people who lie. They lie because they want to be stars. You know, they want to be on camera. They want to be part of a big trial. So they say something to get them there. I wish I wasn't there. I wish it was somebody else who saw it. I'd go watch.

NORMA: Huh? I know.

LYLE: But, you know, Jilly understands. So it is nice to have her there.

NORMA: Anyway there's all sorts of shit in the paper already. So you won't be—you're embarrassment will soon go away. You'll get tougher.

LYLE: My aunt told me today. She said, "Don't worry Honey. You're not going to scandalize the world. There is too much stuff out there already. You gotta say your stuff and when it's oh, wow it's going to sell a lot of programs for about a year and then it's going to go away."

NORMA: Yeah. Sure it is.

LYLE: "And in fifteen years they're going to forget about it. There will be another case. And so, don't worry. You say what you gotta say. Don't hold back because you are afraid."

NORMA: That's what I told Erik. Stop worrying about "Hard Copy." Because as soon as that's finished they are going to click with their little gizmos, click to the next channel, and you are forgotten. That's the way it is in America. Everyone's got a short attention span, you know. And people do watch shitty programs like that anyway. So don't even worry about them. They're just looking for instant excitement. Yeah, and then it is not even the Menendez brothers. It's just two guys in trouble—entertain them for half an hour and then click. Onto the next channel. And that's the way it is. They don't even give a shit what your name is or anything, you know. Just two guys to watch for awhile and then turn over.

LYLE: Thank you, Sweetie. I need to know that someone's got it.

NORMA: But this is real life. That's the way it is.

LYLE: Believe me. I know it's real life. I hope it works out like that kid in Olympia. You know, I remember when he [Paul Mones] went up there for that case and then he came back down with that result. And he keeps coming back with results like that all over the country. And I keep getting pissed off. I don't want to see you anymore. Give me—He keeps telling me that mine is the worst case that you've ever seen.

NORMA: Who said this, Paul?

LYLE: He feels the best about it. As far as the worst—the stuff that happened to us. And you keep going out and winning all of these cases in five weeks and I'm still in jail. And I've got no guarantee. On the one hand, I feel confident. I go, "Great, all these other kids are winning, I should win too." On the other hand, I feel like jealous, you know, like all of these other kids are winning and they don't even—they haven't been through anything—that kid spent what, like two days in jail or something? A couple of months in jail or something? You know he got time served by the time he got his sentence.

March 1993

LYLE: This room sucks, the other one was much better. I'm all packed, ready to go. I feel good, but tired. It's lack of sleep, I have so much on my mind. It's enough to wear me down. I don't know why I let myself get into these stupid situations. You women are so emotional.

NORMA: Don't include me.

LYLE: I'm serious. All these women are in love with me, right? It's true. It's real obvious, too. They'd be happy as hell to be in a relationship with me. I'm not interested. So I get interested in one girl; then they change completely. They turn into a monster or something. All emotional. It's awful. _____'s a wonderful girl, but too sensitive. She mentioned something about fantasizing about me in a bathtub. I told her to put the fantasy on tape and I'll listen to it. She freaked out. She's embarrassed about what she said. Too sensitive. It's a form of trying to control someone and makes me nervous. I don't need the pressure.

NORMA: Tell her to send Polaroid shots instead.

LYLE: I got in trouble for that already. I can always call _____ to get that.

NORMA: I'll call *Dirt and Track* this morning and order it.

LYLE: Have them send everything to the jail, obviously. And next time you're at a book store, buy *Unique Homes* and *Architectural Digest*. Just this month's. Do you have an Audi dealership nearby? Get a brochure on Audi, their new S4 and the lower line model. I'm tired, I've been out two and a half hours now, since 6:30.

NORMA: It's 9:00 now. Shall I come over with a helicopter?

LYLE: Yeah, I'll probably still be out. I keep worrying they're taping my phone calls. They haven't done it before.

NORMA: Just be careful what you say. Try not to worry about it.

LYLE: I'm not real concerned.

NORMA: I won't be able to see you tomorrow.

LYLE: OK, so I'll just see Grandma. I'll call her to come at 3:00. _____ isn't picking up her messages. She's at her sister's house. Last time I spoke to her was Wednesday. I'm gonna give her some space. It's better than arguing about the issues. . . . Next time you're in a book store, can you get *The Trial Lawyers* by Emily Couric? I'm already reading someone else's copy. It's very interesting—all their different tactics.

NORMA: I got your *Playboy* magazine today. It's labeled and will go out in tomorrow's mail. Plus two catalogs—lingerie and another one.

LYLE: Wait a day, just in case I get moved.

NORMA: Did you get the card I sent?

LYLE: No. Christie's birthday is the same as yours.

NORMA: April 1st?

LYLE: Maybe you two could just exchange your gifts.

NORMA: Cheapskate.

LYLE: Call a repair shop and explain the problem I'm having with my answering machine. The thirty-minute tape that came with it works fine. Longer tapes get tangled up when they rewind. Find out why. I don't want to be without the machine, so find out over the phone if possible.

NORMA: I have a friend who duplicates tapes, I'll ask her.

March 1993

LYLE: I need you to get me a pair of shoes, actually sandals with three Velcro straps. You can get them at Foot Locker. They're Nikes—"All Conditions Gear." Fifty-four dollars. I'd like all black with some purple, with "Air Des Chutz" in orange on the bottom. They have "ACG," that means All Conditions Gear, on the heel, size 11. Grandma came at 6:00—I denied her visit.

NORMA: Why?

LYLE: Because I thought Beatrice was coming at 7:00. Then she didn't come because she knew Grandma was coming. And you can't come tomorrow either because my cousin Anna Maria is in town 'til Sunday with her boyfriend. She'll come in tomorrow with Grandma. If you talk to Grandma, tell her to come during the day because I won't take a visit at 6:00. Call my Calabasas house right now and I'll talk to them.

NORMA: What did Beatrice say about the card?

LYLE: I got a new credit card from her and she doesn't want anyone to know what it is. I never expected them to call her at home, and they told her your name and everything. I told her you weren't charging things, you're doing things for me.

NORMA: When you get your monthly list, it has the exact items ordered.

LYLE: You can understand her concern, not letting anybody have the credit cards. She knows you're trustworthy, but nevertheless it's a bad habit to start. I used to trust _____, and you just never know. So, I got a new number and in the future I'll just have you do it yourself and she'll reimburse you.

I'll mail a letter to Leanne, letting her know that I bought her some gifts but I didn't send them because I don't want to overload her with gifts. I want to see what her reaction is to that. If her reaction is, "Don't send me any gifts," then I won't even get them. If her reaction is, "Well, if you've already got them, why don't you send them?" then I'll order them. It only takes a week anyway. She hasn't called me all week, so I may never hear from her again. Maybe it's PMS this week.

NORMA: I'm still not happy with Jill's explanation yesterday, when she said, "I don't think it's feasible for us to be traveling all the way out there [to Wayside]."

LYLE: It's not a question of that. They won't take me there. They refuse to set up a visiting situation there like I need with my attorneys, face-to-face. I'm not going to talk through a glass, and they won't provide that. They refuse to do that. They won't build an extra room. We wanted them to say no. They're willing to clear out G Row. It's hard to believe that a jail's willing to clear a whole row for one person, but they're going to do it. Jill's gonna call them tomorrow and demand a TV or let me be out all day. If they let me out all day I won't need a TV—I'll talk to people on the phone, I'll exercise, you know. I'm fine. I was fine with that before.

NORMA: But wasn't that just temporary?

LYLE: Three months. I'm not going over there if they're gonna leave me in my cell all day. I'm supposed to go to court tomorrow, probably with my brother. Do me a favor—definitely reach Grandma tonight and call Beatrice and let them know I'm going to court tomorrow. It's just a scheduling thing. The judge wants me there anyway, although I won't actually be in the courtroom. If I do, I'll be there for a minute. I'll catch the noon bus coming back. So you can visit me tomorrow night.

NORMA: I got *The Trial Lawyers* book you wanted. I've marked off some paragraphs that you might have missed.

LYLE: Good. You can mail all that other stuff—

NORMA: Shut your face a minute while I think of—oh, yeah, I'll bring the book tomorrow. I also have another one on order in case they don't let you have the one with the paragraphs marked. Maybe you can bring your copy and I can show you the paragraphs.

LYLE: OK. And maybe you could bring the shoes.

April 1993

NORMA: Erik said you did very well.

LYLE: Yeah. Oh, it went very very good.

NORMA: Even though you say so yourself.

LYLE: Very well. Erik did extremely well and my testimony was just as well, a bit more emotional. Which was good because that's what I want, getting myself to be able to do that.

NORMA: Right, yes.

LYLE: I mean, I didn't feel like I had any problem at all. I held back.

NORMA: Did you? And did you feel—?

LYLE: You don't know how bad I wanted to do that because I didn't know how good I wanted to do because I kind of wanted to wait for trial for some of this stuff.

NORMA: Yeah, right. And did it build up your confidence?

LYLE: Yeah.

NORMA: That's good.

LYLE: We're in motions right now. We're taking a recess so I gotta go right now. I'll call you tonight.

Thursday, April 1, 1993

If Lyle gets convicted, what sort of life will he have left? He will have no tomorrows worth talking about; no plans to make, just appeals.

He will have self-destructed himself and Erik. It is a totally devastating situation and even more so for his poor grandmother. I can only imagine the pain she has gone through, with more pain yet to face.

I dread her learning about the evidence the prosecutor says she has. I think the worst part for her is the waiting, which must put a terrible strain on her nerves. If Lyle and Erik are found guilty, she will have to live with the knowledge that her grandsons killed her beloved only son and daughter-in-law—their own mother.

Kids normally leave home if they can't stand their parents! Lyle could have moved out, but he was dependent on his dad's money, so he stayed. Why they killed their mother is incomprehensible to me—maybe this will come out in court during the trial.

Monday, April 5, 1993

When I first saw a photograph of the house in Calabasas, I thought, How beautiful it is. After I drove out there into the boondocks, I thought, Did Lyle's father actually expect Kitty to want to live way out here, so far from civilization?

No wonder no one is rushing to purchase that place. It is too far from any social contact.

——————————◆——————————

April 1993

LYLE: We have the captain of the Beverly Hills Police Department on the stand just now. Lying in there too. But not as bad as the other guys 'cause he's the captain. He doesn't lie as much. And so, you know, he says to this *Times* reporter that we were suspects from Day 1, right? For once, you know the DA is so stupid too. She's like, average. But she uses an average ploy which is—well, Isn't it true that you are also in charge of public relations and so obviously you are trying to make the department look good? They're trying to imply that maybe he was just saying that 'cause it made the police look good. Because this was right after they arrested me. "Yeah, we knew it from the first day" kind of thing. But that is an average thing. Doesn't he realize that my attorney is going to then go—like he did—"Well, you're not saying that because you have a role in the public relations department also, that you intentionally lied to that reporter?" And the guy, of course, says no. "Well, you don't ever fabricate reports or you aren't gonna intentionally perjure yourself like that, even to a layperson to make your department look good, would you?" This guy is a captain in the Beverly Hills Police Department and, of course, he says, "I would never fabricate anything—there is nothing in that report that is fabricated." What else is he gonna say?

NORMA: Was he in uniform?

LYLE: He was so stupid.

NORMA: Was the captain in his uniform?

LYLE: No. He was wearing some stupid suit.

NORMA: It's just that sometimes when he's standing there with his uniform on, we're supposed to think he wouldn't tell a lie.

LYLE: No. Not in Beverly Hills. You could tell he was the captain right off the bat though. He kind of looks like Ira Reiner. And he just looks like—he looks like he's a motherfucker.

Friday, April 23, 1993

No lines tonight at 7:00 P.M., I walked straight in. Lyle looked well, he had some color in his cheeks. "Hey, Lyle, your cheeks are pink tonight." "I know," he said, "I was up on the roof this morning. I called to tell you and left you a message." "Yes, I heard you when I got back. Anyway, while I remember, do you want a *TV Guide* because I can bring it tomorrow? I forgot it today." He raised his eyebrows, "I don't have a television, remember?" "Oh, that's right, I forgot about you being on G Row now, with no TV there."

(G Row is a high-security area where Lyle is held for his own protection, all by himself. No other inmates reside on this row.)

"Anyway," he said, "on Monday the court is having a closed hearing to discuss whether Erik's attorney, Leslie, will get to let Erik say he was frightened of me."

I said, "He's in a sticky position regarding his loyalties, isn't he? . . . Not wanting to turn against you, but also trying to keep Leslie happy."

He agreed. "Right, and more than anything I want him outta here."

Then I said, "The problem is, Leslie Abramson doesn't give a shit about you as long as she wins her case for Erik, or gets a lot lighter sentence for Erik and makes him the lightweight and you the heavy."

He agreed. "Right, exactly, and I don't want him to screw up and make out I threatened him, because he'll just make a fool of himself and Leslie, and he'll end up doing life without parole, and I'll end up walking out of here on my own."

I didn't know how he came to that conclusion, so I said, "Do you think so?"

He said, "Absolutely, so I don't think the judge will agree to this pitting one brother against the other as it could entail two trials."

I said, "Well, we knew Leslie would try this angle but I can't believe that this has suddenly come up now, so close to jury selection."

He said, "Well, it seems that the DA just recently spotted it in the paperwork and questioned Leslie about it. So now we have to straighten that out on Monday."

"Okay, Lyle, if it's going to be a closed discussion, I'll just stay at home and not go to Van Nuys. [The trial was eventually moved to the Van Nuys Superior Court.] You can call me at recess."

He said, "Okay, great. Anyway, I'm gonna pass you this envelope through the deputy, so will you put a fifteen-dollar check in it for me? It's for the Childreach operation, a charity that helps kids to survive diseases in impoverished countries." (Lyle's a softy when it comes to small kids.)

I said, "Okay, sure."

He suddenly brightened up. "Hey, y'know what I was thinking the other day?"

I said, "Oh God, Lyle, have you been thinking again?"

"Very funny! Listen, I was thinking when I get out of here, I could study and help Paul Mones with his defense of children; because who better to understand these kids than me? I've been there, I'd know exactly how to help them."

I said, "Lyle, I don't think when you get out, you'd want to get back into this sort of thing again. I think it would stunt your mental growth."

"No, not at all," he said, "I'd be helping to expand the minds of these kids."

"Well," I said, "you'll have to talk to Paul about that a little later."

Lyle doesn't seem to think that he himself needs therapy. Sometimes I'm stunned, and at a loss for words, at his ideas and suggestions, but he is always creative, if not always logical.

Saturday, April 24, 1993

Last night we were discussing his phone time. I'm always pulling his leg about him being a "phonaholic." I said, "Lyle, we have to be careful that the phone doesn't take root in your ear canal, or they'll have to disconnect it from the wall and leave it attached to your face."

He wasn't amused, saying, "Hey, you try sitting in a cell this small for twenty-three hours a day and you'd be concerned about *your* phone time."

Of course I agree with him, but I'm not going to stop making jokes out of some of his situations. It cheers me up. I need cheering up sometimes after the drag of driving down to that hellhole three days a week, month after month. I feel it is important to get Lyle out of his cell for a break and a laugh. Well, a break anyway. He doesn't always feel like laughing, that's for sure.

I'll go again to visit him tomorrow. He wants me to buy him some Post-Its to stick on his court legal pads. I'll take them to the Van Nuys court on Monday and give them to Jill before the hearing starts.

Sunday, April 25, 1993

I began showing Lyle the Post-It notes I'd bought, plus the stick-on labels. He said, "Norma, just hang onto them for awhile as Jill said she will bring me some. So you don't need to come to court tomorrow morning."

I immediately felt suspicious, so I said, "Lyle, did Jill tell you to tell me not to come to court on Monday?"

He said, "Yes, because 'Hard Copy' might be there and start giving you a label such as 'Mystery Woman' or my 'girlfriend' and she's worried about that."

This was news to me, not good news. Why does it matter to her what sort of description I am given? The media will always find something to say. I'm his best friend. Why is Jill Lansing so worried or concerned what a tabloid TV program says about me? They can't say very much, I've never spoken to any of them.

April 30, 1993

LYLE: They get all these cops on the stand and they just lie their fucking asses off—it's amazing.

NORMA: Did they?

LYLE: It's unfucking real. And it was obvious that they were lying because we had those other reports and he was trying to change what he had in the report.

NORMA: Really?

LYLE: It's so stupid. It's shameless, shameless lies:
"No, I didn't interview him."
"Oh, doesn't it say here in your handwriting that 'I interviewed him extensively?' "
"Yes, it does."
"Well then, doesn't that mean that what you said just now is not true?"
"Well, not really. What I mean is that I said hello to him and we talked for a few minutes."
NORMA: Yeah.
LYLE: You know what I mean? What sane person sitting there would not make this guy [out to be] not only a liar but a little scumbag trying to be sneaky? Man, these guys can lie.
NORMA: I was laughing this morning, though, when I read this morning's *Times* article. It said every page in your letter to Erik has the word *escape* on it.
LYLE: What did it say in the paper? That we tried to escape?
NORMA: Yeah, it just said that the motion was denied, that the cell was legally searched 'cause your letter seemed to be an escape plan.
LYLE: It didn't say "escape" on every page. . . . It's twice, and once it says "prison break."
NORMA: That's all—out of seventeen pages?
LYLE: Yeah, it wasn't seventeen pages.
NORMA: Well it says seventeen pages in the paper.
LYLE: You know the press.
NORMA: Yeah, I know. Confusion. I'll cut it out and you can read it tonight. . . .
LYLE: No, I don't want to read it. I mean the guy—guys think they're so sneaky, you know, and it's a big chance to interview me on the scene or something. You know, what can they do? They must think that I'm like one of these sneaky creative like assholes with no feelings. Like sitting and discussing things that are very important to me. And, you know, something I wrote to my brother which I'm pissed that he didn't destroy in the first place. I got all kinds of conflictive feelings about this. And it's just like some exhibit—the guy's like, "Well, isn't it true that this and this isn't?" I mean, I made it real. I took the whole thing and I

said, you know what, fuck this guy and I just, I got emotional and I said, "No. This letter is respectful and means a lot to me. I feel violated and I'm so surprised that it was taken. I was shocked." And you know, he started to go over what some of these things mean. And I started to get emotional and he about fell out of his chair so he stopped the questioning. What does he expect? You know what I mean? I mean, you know, if he pushes me I'll get as emotional as I can be.

NORMA: Yeah, you'll have to—

LYLE: I held back something because I felt like, I don't want to show this guy too much of what I am—he already got a big glimpse right there. 'Cause if they're going to go in and say that I don't have feelings and stuff like that, which they want to do. They've seen just in that little thing that—

NORMA: Who was saying you didn't have feelings, anyway?

LYLE: Well, that's what they're going to say.

NORMA: Oh, the psychotherapist guy?

LYLE: Yeah, the doctor. He says I said that. And—

NORMA: Well, anyway. This is kind of good training for you for what's coming, you know.

LYLE: Oh, yeah.

NORMA: You know how you used to just go once a week, once every two weeks to a court appearance? Well, now it's moving up to every day, so this is kind of good training for you, isn't it?

LYLE: I think so.

NORMA: Yeah, it's better than just going once every two weeks and then all of a sudden, every day, the trial.

LYLE: Right. You're right.

NORMA: Yeah. And so this will take some of your anxiety away 'cause you're getting a taste now of what you'll go through.

LYLE: I don't have any anxiety now.

NORMA: You don't? Oh, that's good. See? You're overcoming that even.

LYLE: Not after being up there. It was vitally important that I did it just for a little while.

NORMA: Exactly.

LYLE: And not only be up there but be up there and do what

I want to do, which is to make the situation become very personal and real. There are many different ways to testify, you know. And we just come across quite differently. One of the things that I'm seeing in these [pretrial] motions is that I get to see all of these different people testify. And I get to see which ones look good, which look bad, why, whatever.

NORMA: Right. Yeah, you can sit back and watch all this.

LYLE: My brother got up there and I was quite surprised. He was extremely sound, very firm. Very serious. Seems to be very sincere. You know, just open but no emotion at all. Void of emotion. Right? Which is fine, this is just a stupid hearing about a jail sentence. But I think they figured that I was going to be worse, even worse than Erik. More serious, more sneaky, more obnoxious. And I was quite the opposite. My feeling was I don't give a fuck if the jails are searching me. What are we talking about that was taken? I'm pissed off.

NORMA: And you know what else is good practice about this, Lyle? Right now you don't have a jury with you. So this is a good way to see and look back and reflect on how you did and what you think. What a pity though that people couldn't be there to look in. Like someone could say, do just a little more of this or a little less of that, you know. So you're going to have to do that yourself. Or Jill or Leslie of course. 'Cause they'll sit and watch you and base how you are doing. And you know, like I said the main thing is there is no jury there right now so this is good practice for you.

LYLE: Right. And yeah, I walked away feeling satisfied but on the other hand we all saw what happened.

NORMA: Well, you're going to have these ups and downs, aren't you? So don't concentrate too much about them.

LYLE: There's a guy that's back east interviewing that friend of mine that's an idiot, trying to find out things about him. We got his resume for the job that he has and on it he says—

NORMA: Which friend is this? If you can't say his name, it doesn't matter.

LYLE: Yeah. And he got a job saying that he was a valedictorian of his high school and he won the Yale Award. All of this is not true.

NORMA: Isn't it?

LYLE: No. That's why I need the graduating year book, so I can remember the names [of people] that would know him that would come forward and say that this is not an honest guy. To the guy who makes the story. Right. If we had his school records and so on, we could really go far. But they won't release the school records. We don't have access to anything. It's fucked up. But just that I think is good. You know, the guy wants to make himself be important obviously. He's a clever guy so you never know how he's gonna do on the stand, but I'm gonna get him.

NORMA: He doesn't play a lot of it by ear, so they say.

LYLE: You know, I'll really think and remember and think of everything that I can get him on. Because we're talking about a scumbag. Anyway, it's kind of like you've known a scumbag for all your life and all of a sudden you've got to prove he's a scumbag.

NORMA: Right.

Friday, April 30, 1993

When I finally got to visit Lyle today, he was telling me that Erik came over strong, cool, and unemotional at the hearing . . . how he, Lyle, wears his heart on his sleeve . . . how the color of the sweater will help to make him appear gentle. . . .

Lyle then said, "This is what I get for helping Erik out. I just wish things were like they used to be and my dad was alive, and I was out driving around free, but I can't do anything to change things. Y'know, Erik feels freer now than he did before. I have some real bad days about it, thinking of the way things were. I know Erik's not the gentle kid everybody thinks he is, he has his temper tantrums, he's bossy at times, and he's in control of things. Everybody thinks Erik's the sweet, easygoing kid and I'm the bad guy."

Friday, May 28, 1993

I waited quite a long time for Lyle tonight. He didn't get brought down to the visiting area until 7:25 P.M., instead of 7:00 P.M. He never knows what time it is because his cell is in the hole section (for his own protection) and there's no clock, TV, or radio. It's so quiet Lyle jumps when he hears what should be a normal sound. I think this is rather cruel and unusual punishment, especially in view of the fact that his trial will probably go on longer than usual and this is where he will come back to every day after court.

Even his phone calls are back to one or two hours in the evening, whereas before he used to get an hour or two in the morning also.

Saturday, May 29, 1993

Lyle's grandmother came to the jail today. She saw Erik first, then came to the visiting room with me to see Lyle. While we were waiting I showed her Lyle's receipts and phone bills, which amount to $296. Mama was telling me that the money she pays these bills with is from her own pension and not from the Menendez estate. That's why she has to check on the money being spent by Lyle, and why I have to make copies of the phone bills to take with me when I visit her in Calabasas next week.

She talked with Lyle for awhile and explained about the money to him. Then she handed the phone to me and Lyle said, "Take no notice of Mama, she has thousands of dollars."

I said, "But Lyle, she just told me that she is selling the house in New Jersey to pay for everything."

"No, she's not. She's selling it because she's thinking of moving here to California to be near Erik and myself." He always says "myself" instead of "me."

"Anyway, did you bring the answering machine booklet?" (Lyle's been having a problem with his answering machine so I brought the booklet down for him to see through the glass.)

The machine he has now "cuts off the message and is crackly," he said. Sometimes I think he invents these problems to give himself something different to think about (and me more errands to run).

"You and your bloody phones and machines, Lyle. I hope they have plenty of phones in prison, otherwise you'll go nuts." "Oh, they will. We'll probably go to California Men's Colony or another luxury prison. You can play golf or tennis, too." "That'll be nice," I said, "I didn't know they had golf courses with walls around them." "Well, they're very small golf courses, but I'll probably just play tennis." "Of course," I said.

As we were talking the lock-down signal went off but nobody came to get him so we carried on chatting. Mama continued talking to two other visitors which whiled away the time for her. I always feel bad for Mama because Lyle ignores her, especially since the visit ended up being two hours long due to the lock-down.

Amazingly we completely filled those two hours talking non-stop. That's a record for me—a two-hour conversation, with the intermittent burst from Mama, including her showing Lyle an article from a Pomona paper about the guy in the next visitor booth to us, telling how he was convicted for murder in a drive-by shooting. Lyle didn't want to read it.

One of the nicer points of today's visit was Lyle saying, "I can't imagine how I survived the first few months of my arrest with just Beatrice, now that I've got you." I said, "Well, it's nice that you appreciate that, Lyle. What I am trying to do is make your jail time as comfortable as possible and give you outside contact."

Sometimes when I come home from jail I feel exhausted, as though I've already done the errands he wants me to. Then when I get home he's left another message with yet another request. I'm burning out.

Sunday, May 30, 1993

Today I took Lyle a couple of fuses to look at through the glass. We're hoping the deputy will put them into the radio in the wall, so that Lyle can hear some music during the day. He said today that the quiet and the boredom are really getting to him. He is also suffering from a toothache, which the silence emphasizes because there is no distraction.

I suggested dental treatment but he said he doesn't trust jail dentists.

Then he got onto the "Fear" article I sent in from the book by J. Krishnamurti, *Freedom from the Unknown*. He actually enjoyed reading it. He should, because Krishnamurti talks rationally and with common sense.

Lyle said, "You should buy the book, *Mere Christian*. It's about a man who didn't believe in God, so he set out to prove his theory that God is nonexistent, and his searches and inquiries proved him wrong."

Wednesday, June 2, 1993

Today I went to see Mama in Calabasas. It was a sad day, but the surroundings were so beautiful. Maria is constantly reminded of her son, Jose, whenever she is there. No doubt she thinks of him all the time. This house was the culmination of his dreams and his success.

The place where Lyle and Erik live now is an extreme contrast to this place. Maria lives in both places, because her mind is always with her grandsons.

Friday, June 4, 1993

"One of the things that makes this case difficult is that we included my mom."

"I know, Lyle, and including Erik, too, doesn't help, it really does complicate everything."

"Well, on Monday in Van Nuys they're going to finally decide whether we get two juries or one."

"I thought that had already been decided," I said.

"No, it's still up in the air, but it'll be better for me if we just have one and my case gets heard first. Come to court on Monday, it should be interesting," he said.

"Yes, I probably will this time."

Sunday, June 6, 1993

I went down to the jail at 3:00 P.M. today instead of 7:00 P.M. because Mama wanted me to go with her to share the visit. Lyle was doing fine with his Spanish while talking to her. I was quite surprised he'd learned so much. The visit today was short because Lyle came down fifteen minutes after everyone else.

He wants me to take photos of the rooms in the house in Calabasas.

Monday, June 7, 1993

I was up early this morning. Erik called at 8:00 A.M. to tell me that court wouldn't start until about 10:30 this morning. "Lyle was up on the roof exercising and they forgot he was due in court this morning."

It made no difference to me as I had to meet Mama outside the Radisson Hotel at 8:30 because this was her first time at the Van Nuys courthouse. I was going to show her how to get there. We found a cheaper parking place (for four dollars all day) which is better than I'd been paying earlier this year.

Once the trial starts it could become very expensive, day in, day out, for months.

When we finally arrived upstairs outside the courtroom, we sat around for awhile, talking and killing time. The deputy district attorney, Pamela Bozanich, who is prosecuting Lyle and Erik walked by and Mama waved to her. Pamela smiled and came over. "Hi, I'm Pamela Bozanich," she said as she held out her hand. Mama said, "I'm Maria Menendez, Jose Menendez' mother."

"Mrs. Menendez, I'd like to talk to you about your son, if this would be alright with you. I could call you and come out to see you."

Alarm bells started ringing in my head. I looked at Mama as she said, "I have only good things to say about my son. He was a wonderful man. I loved him very much." I interjected with, "Mama, I don't think you should give any interviews to anybody just yet."

I had no choice but to tell Leslie what had happened. She was shocked. She told Jill, who took Mama aside and told her why it wasn't appropriate. Mama complained to me later that nobody can tell her who to talk to or what to do. She was quite annoyed at being chastised.

Later on in court there was still no decision as to two juries or one. Judge Weisberg will make a decision "very soon," he said. During this session, Lyle passed me a note about telling Mama not to be interviewed by anybody.

After court was over, I went home and there were three messages from Lyle. He called at 3:30 P.M. "Mama's not very happy with you, Norma, because you told Leslie that Pamela Bozanich interviewed her, so try not to tell her what to do." "Okay," I said, "I wasn't telling her what to do, or what not to do. I told her the deputy district attorney can't interview her, because that would be like Mama being on the side of the prosecution."

"I know that," he said, "but you know how she is."

After we hung up, I remembered that he had sent me a note in the courtroom saying, "Tell Mama not to speak to the deputy district attorney." Now he's telling me not to tell her what to do. Wait until he calls tomorrow.

Tuesday, June 8, 1993

I drove into the parking lot at 1:30 P.M. and there in front of me was Mama. The timing was perfect.

We walked to the courthouse together. She told me she is still upset over the treatment of Lyle . . . no television, no radio and hardly any human contact. It has been bothering me, too. Who can I complain to? I need to call the lieutenant and ask him.

There weren't many people in court this afternoon, which was fine, especially as there were no photographers waiting as we came out of the elevator. The only uncomfortable moment was going into the bathroom and finding ourselves surrounded by Jill Lansing, Leslie Abramson, and the prosecutor, Pamela Bozanich. We were literally bumping into each other around the washbasin and paper towels. I would have thought they'd have separate bathrooms for the defense and the prosecution.

During the afternoon debate about whether to have one jury or two, I scribbled a note for Erik and held it up for him to read. It said, "Leslie has a book for you." And a very observant deputy spotted it and mouthed to me, "You can't do that." Erik thought it was amusing as the deputy strode over to me to explain the rules of the court: "No communicating with the defendants."

"Sorry, I didn't know that. This is my first trial."

"Oh well, no harm done," he said, to which I felt relieved.

The decision to go with two juries was finally settled. Tomorrow they discuss whether to allow cameras into the courtroom.

Lyle looked good in his blue shirt and tie, but Erik's shirt was an awful red plaid.

Friday, June 11, 1993

Lyle had a lot of things on his mind today:

"A lot will depend on whether my parents were standing or sitting."

"Grief is shown in different ways."

"Trying for involuntary manslaughter instead of manslaughter."

"We didn't want to kill them."

"We also have to decide the difference between immediate or imminent danger."

"I'd like to do a deal with them but there's no chance of that."

"The prosecutors don't want to lift the death penalty."

"They'll take one look at us and there's no way any jury will give us the death penalty. Anybody who talks to us for an hour always comes away with a wonderful feeling about us."

"If we get involuntary manslaughter the most we'll get is five years, but for regular manslaughter we'll get eleven years."

"Self-defense will be decided upon depending on whether the fear was imminent or immediate."

Sunday, June 13, 1993

Today I went to visit Lyle with Henry Llanio, who is Jose Menendez' cousin. He did most of the talking to Lyle throughout the visit. He said, "Lyle, most of us in the family hope that the defense will be a united front. We hope that Erik isn't going to lay all the blame on you and you fry, and Erik comes out and kills himself over you, so I hope that the attorneys understand this."

"Don't worry," said Lyle, "that won't happen. Are you going to court tomorrow for jury selection?"

"Of course," said Henry, "I'm on the panel, remember?"

What a coincidence for Lyle's cousin, Henry, to have been chosen for jury duty in Van Nuys at that time. Naturally, the minute he revealed he was a Menendez cousin he was out the door.

Monday, June 14, 1993

Jury selection started today for Lyle but I didn't go on the first day, except to nip over at the close of the day to hand Jill Lansing a pair of earplugs for Lyle, but she backed off from taking them, even though there was nobody around. Really!

There's no court tomorrow, but more jury selection for Erik on Wednesday. I am going with Mama in the morning at 9:00 A.M. for his jury selection, so I expect it to be a long day.

I gave the earplugs to Mama to give to Jill. Jill doesn't mind being seen talking to her.

Wednesday, June 16, 1993

I went to court this morning at 10:00 A.M. It looked like there were about two hundred people lined up outside. They were perspective jurors.

Jury selection is a long but well-organized process, and I found it very interesting once it was moving along. Erik was wearing a yellow sweater which didn't improve his pallor. The sweater just reflected more yellow onto his already sallow face. He didn't look or act nervous; in fact he kept turning to stare at the jurors as their names were called out.

Friday, June 18, 1993

Lyle and Erik have confessed to killing their parents. Now that they are going to use abuse as an excuse (according to the papers), many people who were abused are getting interested in the case.

I wasn't surprised when they came up with that defense, since Lyle had mentioned Paul Mones and his "specialty" to me so long ago. I didn't believe it as it was taking shape, and I certainly don't condone it now. I was sad for Mama having to hear this vilification of her adored son. She does not accept that Lyle and Erik have confessed. Everyone feels sorry for her pain and grief.

Lyle and Erik are having one trial with two juries. It is hard to imagine how this is going to take place, but it is not the first time this has been done.

Tuesday, June 22, 1993

The courtroom was almost empty today, except for three or four court-watchers, one of whom spent the whole time sleeping.

Jury selection continues with what looks like mostly retired older men, and an occasional older lady. Many of these people seem confused, and some lacked understanding when the judge asked them fairly simple questions.

Those who appear to be getting chosen said they don't read the newspapers and don't watch the news. This must be an advantage for the defense, because these people may be more easily persuaded. On the other hand, most seem to be of modest means. This might not be a defense advantage with two rich defendants.

Thursday, June 24, 1993

Erik called from the court at the end of today's jury selection and said, "It was different in court this afternoon. Mama was seen talking to one of the jurors, and the prosecution brought it up. The judge lost his temper with Mama."

I said, "I bet she was nervous about that, huh?" and he replied, "Yes, she was, but she was pissed, too." I said, "She probably didn't realize what she had done wrong. Anyway, Erik, how did it go today regarding jury selection?"

"Oh, terrible, just terrible. Too many old guys. Where's all the women?" I said, "I know what you mean, Erik. It's been the same with Lyle. I've noticed the same thing, hardly any young people at all. The problem is that people are begging off because of the five months they've been told that the trial will take. Nobody can afford to sit that long. Anyway, Erik, there's two weeks to go yet so there's plenty of time. I feel that Leslie will make sure that you have a well-balanced jury."

Saturday, June 26, 1993

Lyle wasn't too happy tonight when he called. He now thinks the judge is an asshole as opposed to his first impression of him being a fair man.

I asked Lyle why he was pissed off with the judge and he said, "Because he's biased against us, saying that it was a heinous crime that was done for the money."

Lyle's impression of the judge is that the case is almost proven against them.

June 1993

We were discussing his move to D Row, or the isolation area as it is known, and I asked Lyle if he wouldn't be lonely back there. He replied, "No, I'll get used to it and, anyway, I don't want to be here on this row with this lot, they're just a bunch of killers."

———————◆———————

June 1993

LYLE: It's called *The Art of War*. I'd like you to get that for me too.

NORMA: OK.

LYLE: And I want you to send it to me and I'm going to send it to this guy Steve Homick [a fellow prisoner and hired gun, now on death row in Nevada for multiple murders]. I'm going to give you the number later.

Friday, July 2, 1993

Today was quiet at the jail. There were no lines. Lyle was in good spirits. He's been studying his jury list again, sorting out the answers different people have given in their questionnaires. It lets him see who he would or would not like on the jury panel. He has ninety-four people to choose from at this point, but there will be more by next week. On Wednesday, nine out of ten of the jurors declined to sit for one reason or another.

I showed Lyle the book *Ulterior Motive* again, so he could look through the photos. We'd talked about this book last week because Lyle's judge, Stanley Weisberg, had been prosecutor in the Kyle case, which is chronicled in *Ulterior Motive*. This didn't sound like good news to me. Maybe this is why Lyle suspects the judge seems to lean toward the prosecution, because he's dealt with a case very similar to this one before.

Lyle was telling me about a "girlfriend" who used to visit him every night. He made a hand motion to me, to indicate it was just too much. Apparently she felt the same way, because she hasn't visited for eight months now.

I laughed all the way home because Lyle told me he feels safer inside, where the Mafia can't get him. This was hilarious because there is a documented mafioso in the next cell. The man even wrote a book about being in the Mafia.

JULY 20–AUGUST 13 1993

The Prosecution

The trial commenced July 20, to a full house, with a large crowd of disappointed hopefuls turned away. The prosecution hoped to show that the defendants were consumed with greed and hate for their father. The brothers were tired of being under the parental thumbs, so they planned the crime, premeditated the killings, attempted to cover up with lies and alibis, and promptly commenced squandering their late father's hard-earned money. That money would have gone to their mother, if they hadn't killed her too, the prosecution pointed out.

The investigating officers testified about the crime scene. Former friends of the brothers testified against them. A bevy of witnesses detailed the bicoastal spending splurge, the computer erasures, the purchase of the shotguns in San Diego and more. Deputy Coroner Dr. Irwin Golden discussed the autopsies with an array of photos, and two small crime scene photos were also posted, depicting the appalling savagery of the killings.

The most prominently featured witness was Dr. L. Jerome Oziel, to whom the brothers had confessed. Although his character was assassinated by the defense on cross-examination, he remained cool, clearheaded, and steadfast in his testimony. There were two lots of the so-called Oziel tapes. Both had been subject to opinions of higher courts as the defense tried to keep them out. The first Oziel tapes were made by him from notes he took after the brothers' Halloween 1989 confession and one other session. The second tape in contention was the one recorded in his office on December 11, 1989, on which the brothers explain the killings. They knew they were being recorded and had practiced what they were going to say.

All the tapes were admitted into evidence. The sound was

generally of poor quality. During the trial jurors followed along on transcripts handed out just prior to the tapes being played.

Whenever the prosecutors were questioning someone or objecting to something, the brothers alternately glared at them or smirked with a condescending attitude. Throughout the trial Lyle tended to pay rapt attention. He would sometimes stare at someone or something for long periods without ever blinking. Erik frequently turned in his chair to glance at the clock on the wall directly behind him at the back of the spectator section, as though he had an important appointment. He yawned incessantly and chewed on his fingernails, which were already bitten to the quick.

July 1993

The trial has finally begun. Seating is at a premium, but if you arrive at the courthouse early enough to be one of the first eight or nine people there, you have a good chance of getting in. There are a total of nine seats allocated to the public if both juries are present. If only one jury is there, perhaps as many as twenty-nine "civilians" can go in. Some days there are as few as six seats if the judge has guests.

A hardy few arrive every day at 4:30 A.M.—the courthouse doesn't open until 7:30. Each person upon arriving asks, "What number am I?" Everyone on line knows to remember his own number, and to recognize the person directly in front and right behind him. There is no saving places. You have to be there in person. One day, in a comical scene, a young man running wide open from one direction was challenged by a middle-aged lady charging full-speed from the opposite direction. The young man won, but both got in. There is a lot of joking, laughing, and camaraderie amongst the regulars. Most newcomers are eager to learn the ropes.

After you have your spot in line and everyone has seen you, you can utilize the long wait by napping on a park bench, reading, studying, or chatting with others. People who've parked right by the building, in the dark of night, go to move their cars when daylight comes. There is limited one-hour street parking nearby,

Top: Kitty and Jose Menendez
© *Gamma Liaison*
Center: The Beverly Hills home of
Kitty, Jose, Lyle and Erik Menendez
© *John Barr/Gamma Liaison*
Bottom: The grave site of Kitty and
Jose Menendez
© *Yvonne Hemsey/Gamma Liaison*

Jail by LYLE

far I've been lucky. My brother seems
to be holding up well. And I have
just enough influence over him to
Bury him in the right directions.
To concentrate and open up. He's
very forceful and his own man.
The public perception of him is
way off. I know that

Top: Lyle Menendez
Bottom: Erik Menendez
© *Evan Agostini/Gamma Liaison*

Correspondence:
Excerpts of Letters from Lyle to Norma

OK, where shall I start? Let me first say that although I have come a long way in the last two years I still by no means understand the complicated phenomina of jailhouse love relationship, however I do have a pretty good feel for whats involved, at least in so far as my personal situation.

Looks like I'll be closing on a new restaurant in New Jersey next month. This is probably not the best time to spend cash and it leaves me very tight but the prices are so cheap because of the recession I find it hard to resist expanding.

Norma

I've always been glad
to share my joys with you,
Knowing you'd be happy for me.

And in times of sorrow,
I could count on you for support
and understanding.
Our friendship is something special,
something I treasure.

Love
Lyle

You're such a good friend...

What did I do before I met You?

... you, and Beatrice and you.
Right now I live day by day.
I believe that better days are ahead.
I believe that good things will happen
for me and my brother. The love and
...

From your letters I think
your a wonderful person!
I have the same proble... with

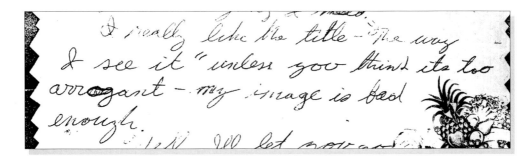

I really like the title "The way
I see it" unless you think its too
arrogant — my image is bad
enough.
I'll let you...

Norma,
hello. It's been a long time
since I've written. I'm all alone here
on the row. I don't mind. So far I
just read and think and write. The
music is nice. The plumber came
today and so now my cell is perfect.
I even have two mattresses, which
helps alot. I prefer the coolness of

Aug 25
1992

Attorneys Jill Lansing (left) and Leslie Abramson © *Gamma Liaison*

This a strange,
un natural experience and your
presence has added some sanity to it
Thanks sweetie.

It is really true that I treasure our
friendships. You are always there with
a laugh and a smile and those beautifu
eyes. I look forward to our contacts more
than you know. I do wonder how I got
by in here before I met you. You keep
my spirits up. You allow me access to
the outside world. You take care of all

May all your wishes
come true throughout
the Christmas Season

Life
XX

All the guys on the row love your newspaper. I show them your picture along with it so they can ~~related~~ the two. The jail's on lock down now. So I haven't been able to use the phone. I'll definitely let Grandma know about you wanting to visit. She'll give you a call. Between her accent and yours it should be an interesting conversation!!

This new job Ive got here in the mornings. 6-8 AM and 11-1 PM is stressing me out. Although I do get to use the phone alot. I'm also out 8-10 PM. I know, its alot of hours. I havent seen my brother is several days. Tommorrow we should be meeting in the attorney room.

I noticed [...] in your paper than when you [...] to me. What a surprise to see my Jail drawings! I almost died. Please don't scare me like that again! No publicity is good publicity. I'm in the hole right now. It sucks. No TV, No phone, No visits!

[...] was one of them. All that you do for me is way beyond what I deserve. I cannot possibly reciprocate except to let you know how much I appreciate it. I would love ya the same whether you did those things for me or not. But those extra gifts of love have made life here alot easier. I think you know that.

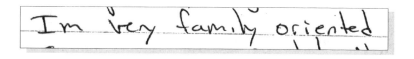
I'm very family oriented

A few words from Lyle

Alright lets begin.... First off you are right that when one of these relationships ends I should not take it personally. No doubt the jail situacion and my pending case add a tension and limitation that is beyond my control and largely the reason for the break ups. However ___ does not seem to

Monday Nov 2

Norma!
    hello. Boy you must be going crazy over this temporary silence. I can't do anything about it now. Things will change. Its certainly not your fault. Don't think that Has absolutely nothing to do with you.   Im doin fine. Ive been moved

gone down.
        Again, Norma, thanks for writing me and let me know if I can do anything to help.

                    Sincerely

                    J. Lyle Menendez

which is useless for court-watchers. One block away, the first lucky few get the coveted eight-hours-for-one-dollar spaces. The adjacent lots charge four dollars a day. This adds up to a tidy sum for the regulars not fortunate enough to nab a one-dollar spot.

———————◆———————

July 1993

NORMA: You know what bothered me the other day. I was reading—'cause don't forget I'm on the outside and if anything sticks in my mind I want to tell you about it. 'Cause I'm like a jury, you know. When you went to the theater on that same night [of the murders], you went to the theater for ticket stubs and then you talked to Perry [Berman, Lyle's coach and friend], so he said on the stand, at about 11:30. So, and then you went back and made that 911 call. Right? And so, is it going to stick in their minds, or do you already know what you are saying about that? Because aren't they going to think, Well how come he was talking OK to the theater people and he was talking on the phone OK but a little anxious to Perry, right? And then you go back to your house and start screaming over the phone, do you know what I mean?

LYLE: Don't worry about it. That's not an issue.

NORMA: Don't worry about it?

LYLE: No. I could explain it to you but it would take a half-hour and I don't feel like it. But there are no theater people coming in to testify so that's—

NORMA: Oh, that's good. So that's out of the way. But that just stuck in my mind when he was saying that on the stand the other day. That you were talking anxious to him—you weren't screaming and crying but you were screaming and crying later, you see.

LYLE: Right. I got emotional on the way to meet him.

NORMA: On the way to meet him?

LYLE: Nothing else makes sense, I mean, to me there is no way it can be seen any other way. Because here I am on the phone, I'm telling him to meet me at the restaurant, right? And instead for some reason I go to the house instead to make a 911 call myself and leave Perry at the restaurant and don't even go and see him. Now, why would that be? What would be the point of calling Perry, telling him to meet me at a restaurant and then not show up?

NORMA: But I thought you wanted to call him so that you could all go home together pretending to pick up this fake ID and then have Perry go in and see the scene with you.

LYLE: Right. I wanted him to make the call.

NORMA: Yeah, right.

LYLE: But the point is, Why would I go home myself and then decide to just disregard my plan?

NORMA: I don't know that. That is what the prosecution will probably want to know from you.

LYLE: And wouldn't the only thing that made sense is that we got so emotional that we couldn't possibly meet Perry and pull it off? So we just had to go home without meeting him? What else makes sense? Nothing else makes sense. If I was cool, calm, and collected there is no reason not to just go to the restaurant, have a few drinks, and then get Perry to come to the house. Right? There was no other reason then to call him and not show up so that he could tell the police, I had plans and he didn't show up. Nothing else makes sense. Trust me, trust me that we haven't left anything uncovered.

NORMA: Alright. Well, it was just—it just broke me when I figured, oh shit it was after that when he goes back to the house and starts screaming and then I felt I was worried a little bit about what you were going to say about that.

LYLE: And that phone call, by the time we got to the house, what caused me to go to the house was the fact that I obviously can't go to Perry's and while I am sitting here crying, my brother is hysterical. How was I going to go to Perry's? He was going to know that something happened. Right?

NORMA: OK.

LYLE: I don't have time to discuss it right now.

July 23, 1993

NORMA: I just read the article. You don't want the whole *Los Angeles Times*, do you? You just want the article. It's from the

Valley section, you're always in the Valley section. So that's the only section that you want when you want me to bring the *Times*.

LYLE: In that article, does it say what Perry said on the stand about what my demeanor was when I made that phone call? Was I anxious?

NORMA: It says that, yeah, you were anxious.

LYLE: Did it say that I was anxious or excited?

NORMA: Anxious.

LYLE: Who wrote the article?

NORMA: Alan Abrahamson.

LYLE: Good.

NORMA: Well, you would be anxious wouldn't you?

LYLE: Were you there when he was on the stand? I'm concerned about how that came across. I'm concerned that he used the word excited originally, remember? I don't want people to think that he meant that I was happy excited.

NORMA: No, people wouldn't think that. Excited—happy excited does not fall into the whole scene that you are in. It means the other excited like sort of shaky and nervy excited. Adrenaline type.

LYLE: The question is what came from Perry. 'Cause you are looking at the scene as far as what my defense is. The DA would like to think that I am excited happy.

NORMA: No. No definitely not. It didn't appear that way to me at all.

LYLE: Jill told him, "Hey, you said 'anxious' before." And he said, "Right, right. That's what I mean, anxious."

NORMA: That's right—because he just used the wrong word, which people do sometimes. And even if the wrong word is used, if you look at the whole theme, you really know what they mean.

LYLE: OK, you think that was clear?

NORMA: Absolutely, yeah.

LYLE: Alright, thanks. 'Cause otherwise, we could recall him and make it clear.

NORMA: Even so, even if you thought he looked the other excited, it wouldn't—oh, I see what you're thinking, like happy would be terrible. Yeah, of course it would. No he didn't come over at all meaning that word—or that way. No.

LYLE: Alright, that was the only thing. Otherwise the guy was just terrific.

NORMA: Yeah, he was.

LYLE: He was terrific. He was great.

NORMA: He was pretty good. But you know what, Lyle, I prefer to sit on the left-hand side. Because—

LYLE: It's up to you.

NORMA: Yeah, I know. It was just easier to get in because all of the spectator seats had been—tickets had been given out. That's why I was with Marta at the time because there were only four of us. But on the left, you could see the face of the witness like we could only see up to his forehead and his eyebrows. We couldn't see any more of him. I prefer to see their whole faces.

LYLE: I agree.

NORMA: Could you see all of him? You couldn't, could you?

LYLE: Yeah, I could see all of him from where I was sitting, yeah.

NORMA: Could you? Because I was directly behind you. But yeah, I must have been a little lower then because all I could see was his eyebrows. And plus, I can see the prosecutor's face from there and I can see you better because all I can see of you now is the back of your head. So at least I can see—you can turn around slightly there, if I'm sitting at the side. So I'm going to plunk myself there next week.

NORMA: So are you frazzled today, or what?

LYLE: I'm OK today. I'm a little tired. I couldn't sleep too well this morning because the store came and I had to get up and—

NORMA: I thought you would have got a good long sleep this morning.

LYLE: I would have if these fuckers didn't keep waking me up for stupid shit.

NORMA: Couldn't you go back to sleep again?

LYLE: No, I couldn't. Not really.

NORMA: Well, you could've if you wanted to, I mean. You could go there and just lie down.

LYLE: I'll try to take a nap—after your visit maybe. I won't have much of a chance though, because maybe, from 1:00 to 3:00

before I visit with you, I can sleep. Because otherwise, I won't really be able to sleep because I'll have to get ready for the visit with you and then I'll visit with you.

NORMA: Oh, what do you mean you have to get ready? You got to put your best suit and your tie on?

LYLE: Yeah. And then you'll come at 4:00—I mean you'll finish at 4:00 and then I'll have time to take a shower, and then I come out at 6:00. The food will come at 4:30. My social schedule is packed. Jam-packed.

NORMA: Oh, my God. Well, aren't I lucky I can see you today?

LYLE: You figure, my day is just busy and all I have is that going on. How does Bill Clinton squeeze in world affairs? I have no idea.

NORMA: I don't know. Well, so it's what time now? Twenty minutes before 1:00.

LYLE: I wanted to talk to Jill but she is on the phone.

NORMA: You're in—what day are you in next? Monday?

LYLE: Yeah, Monday comes next. The first thing on Monday is the Rolex watches. Hopefully that will be no impact. I don't know. But it was really good to end the weekend with Perry. That's what we wanted to do, leave them on that note because the next person was the Rolex watch lady. I told Michael, you know, you tell the judge I have a stomach virus and I need a break. He tried to put her on, squeeze her in.

NORMA: Seriously though, are you allowed to take breaks like that and have something else instead? Could they switch to Erik sometime if you weren't—if you didn't feel like going on?

LYLE: No, but if I told them I had a stomach virus and I needed to leave, what are they going to do? They'd have to break.

NORMA: Would they really? Oh, OK. I just wondered if those things could be possible.

LYLE: You can't use it often, but you can use it once. And so, we decided we were going to save it because he decided not to put her on anyway. They really—they got fucked over with Perry, that's for sure. So they are not happy.

NORMA: Yeah, like you said yesterday, it was funny though

they have two people on for themselves and it turned out better for you.

LYLE: Oh my God. Perry and this guy set up our case. This guy talked about the weekend itself. And Perry talked about my father and the secrecy and all this stuff. I mean the fucking—the judge was steaming. I was sitting there looking at Lester [Kuriyama] and going boy did you fuck it up. My feeling is that we have had three good days in a row.

NORMA: That's true. The only thing the policeman said he found odd was that you both commented on smoke. You know when you both smelled smoke.

LYLE: Yeah, but we were lying. That doesn't matter.

NORMA: Oh, no it doesn't. But he was just saying that as an afterthought, that he found it odd that you should both say it because smoke dissipates quickly. I didn't know that, did you?

LYLE: Did you watch that guy testify?

NORMA: Yeah.

LYLE: Oh you did, you were there in the early morning?

NORMA: No, but I saw him the day before. He was on twice. No I didn't see him in the morning time.

LYLE: Oh, OK, that was a big thing. The key that we get out of him was that we were traumatized. And that's what he felt. That's what he testified to. But then the only thing that they had is that Lester got up there and said, "Well, did you know that Erik was an aspiring actor, would that change your opinion?"

NORMA: Did he say, Erik or Lyle?

LYLE: Erik. But still, even if it was Erik, it goes over on to me and so—it was stupid, it was a low blow. Because an eighteen-year-old kid took one drama class and they are trying to make him out to be Marlon Brando? And everybody felt it was a low blow because the guy—

NORMA: It never has been mentioned that you were trying to be an actor anyway. In any of the papers, nor any of the magazine stories or any of those things.

LYLE: Well, the bottom line is that the cop said straight out, "They were traumatized. He was, I could tell by the way he looked, the way he acted and what he said." And so I think the jurors are sitting there going, well, you know. This guy is trying to weasel out of it. But the bottom line is that if that is what he wrote in the report, then that is what he felt. Which is really important to the case, a police officer on their side says that we were that way. My opinion is that it backfired twice. Because they should have brought it out that we were traumatized themselves, and then they didn't. They just did their direct and then it came out in the cross-examination. So like he looked like he was a bad witness for us and then suddenly he started saying, "Yeah, they were traumatized." So that's the third person now that they have brought in to try to make it look one way and it has left the jury with the opposite idea.

NORMA: You'll have to get yourself a part-time job as analyzer for the people on the outside that didn't quite get it all.

LYLE: You would not believe. I could not sleep for about two hours worrying about Perry saying that I was excited.

NORMA: Oh, no. Are you serious? Oh, you felt bad. No anybody with a half a brain could see that he doesn't mean excited like happy. No. Oh, no. Don't forget you are listening to a theme here and you are visualizing the whole theme.

LYLE: One of the things that I couldn't tell so well was because the guy said "excited" to Jill in the interview and Jill told him, "Listen, you don't mean excited. Don't use that word, use the word anxious."

NORMA: Right, this is what it is.

LYLE: Well, when he went in front of the grand jury, he used the word anxious. Jill was very happy. But here, right in the trial when it is most important, Jill asked him and he used the word fucking excited again. And I was like, oh.

NORMA: I know, but Lyle if you are not a writer or a professional person, you don't know the exact words to use. . . .

LYLE: Listen, I got to go. I'll see you today.

NORMA: Alright love, see you this afternoon.

July 24, 1993, morning

NORMA: How's court? You guys are getting a lot of publicity.

LYLE: Yeah, it's a joke out here. It's just unbelievable. The reporters are fighting with each other, beating each other up—it's ridiculous. It's going well in court, we've only had the first week of trial but it's been going unusually well for us but I can't imagine it will continue. So we'll just sort of go day by day.

NORMA: Are you scared?

LYLE: Yeah. Definitely scared. But I've been scared for three and a half years so it's no different now.

NORMA: It's finally coming to a head, right?

LYLE: I've had three good days in a row. We've only had three days of trial and we did the opening statements and my attorneys kicked butt and we were doing great after the opening statements. There was no doubt about it which I figured would be the case because I've got better attorneys and they just speak better. But obviously you've got to wait for the evidence to come.

So then the next day, the prosecution starts putting on their case, and they fucked up the first day because they put on this boat captain who was the guy who took my mom and dad and I and Erik on this fishing trip the day before they died, the Saturday night. And they wanted to put him on to show that it was a happy family and there weren't problems. And they just figured that that was what the guy would say and the fucking guy came in—the guy comes in—looks exactly like some boat captain too. And he goes, "No, it was unbelievable,—most people are enthusiastic about fishing trips. This family was very strange. They got on the boat and as soon as they got on the boat, the two kids went to the very front, like this little bow section that is hard to get to and they stayed there almost the entire seven hours." He said it was amazing because it was a windy, cold day—real choppy. He said, "And I remember I was standing on the bow and this huge wave that was under a crest came over the boat and soaked the two brothers and they were shivering and whatever and they still wouldn't leave."

And they said, "Really? They never came back?"

"No, they came back once or twice to use the restroom or whatever, but they almost never spoke and it was just very strange." And that was it.

Jill asked, "Well, what was their personality like—their demeanor?"

He said, "It seemed very gloomy and stoic." Obviously the DA was just dying. So that was the end of his testimony and that was a big blow for them. Because it's especially worse when they put the guy on and he fucks up.

NORMA: Oh, he was there to paint a picture of a happy family.

LYLE: Right. So then they say, oh fuck. So then they go a second day and they put on—actually that was the second day because the first day was opening statements. So then the third day was yesterday and they put on this cop who was the guy who interviewed Erik and I that night that my parents died. And they played the tapes of the interviews, which were hard to listen to—you couldn't hear very well, whatever.

But then they put the cop on the stand and they did the direct examination and they didn't bring anything out really. He said that he didn't give us that gun test to see if you fired a gun because we weren't suspects, right. That's what he said. And so then we got up there and cross-examined him—and it all came out on cross-examination. Because this guy had already written his reports at the time it happened so he couldn't change what he wrote. So we started cross-examining him and it all came out.

He said, "Well, isn't it true in the report that you wrote that the reason that you didn't give them the gun test is that the boys were so traumatized you didn't want to put them through anything more?"

He goes, "Well, yeah, they were traumatized."

And he said, "Even though you know now that they lied to you, do you still feel that they were traumatized? And that what you were seeing—the grief you were seeing was real?"

He said, "Yes." And he couldn't say no. He was trying to say no but he couldn't because he had written it in the report. So he said, "Well, yeah, I do."

NORMA: Yeah, that's what he wrote.

LYLE: So Jill asked him—the DA got up—she was dying because they need to show that we were faking—that we weren't grief-stricken in any way. That it was like a cold, calculated thing. And so they got up and they said—she did a low blow and she said, "Well, did you know that Erik Menendez is an aspiring actor?" I mean that is a low blow. "Would that change your opinion?"

And all he said was, "Well, I guess if I knew that I would have looked a little closer but that's all." And that didn't have too much effect really. It was just kind of a low blow—kind of ladylike, give me a break.

And so then they—Jill—asked him, "In what ways do you feel that Lyle was traumatized? How did you know that?" And he said by the pallor, the color that he had, by the way that he was so stiff, by his breathing, and by the way that his words were connected. So when somebody says that, I mean clearly, it's not something you can act out.

NORMA: Right, it's not guessing.

LYLE: Yeah, exactly. So then they blow up the fact that you are a thirty-one-year [veteran]—the DA tried to make it seem that he wouldn't know the difference. And he said, "Now, you are a thirty-one-year veteran—homicide detective. You've seen suspects lie to you, not lie to you, you've seen traumatized victims, you've seen people that you've called later and you felt that these boys were traumatized?"

He said, "I did."

"To the point where you didn't give them a gun test, is that correct?" You know, that was the end of him so they fucked up from the beginning. And then after that, they had about a good hour because we were really worried because the judge allowed them to bring in the shotguns. Not the actual guns. Can you believe it, they don't have the guns and he allowed them to bring in a shotgun that looks like it?

And we said, "You can't do that. That's just going to be prejudicial in front of the jury."

And he said, "Well, no I think it is relevant, the way you load it. I'm just going to bring them in to explain how you load it."

[We] said, "You can't do that without bringing in an actual shotgun into the courtroom." And the judge said—the judge is biased totally.

NORMA: I agree.

LYLE: For the DA. Well, how can you not be? He was a prosecutor five years ago in the only other case in Beverly Hills where a kid killed his father. And he lost. And the kid went home on self-defense. He actually lost the case because the father was wealthy and he argued that it was for the money and he lost. And he's out to get us. Plus he fucked up the McMartin case and he fucked up the officer case—the King case. He was the judge that let them go. So he doesn't want to be seen as a pussy judge. So—but he's pretty fair though.

NORMA: Has he run for political office?

LYLE: Oh no, he's going places. That's why he wants a politically correct decision here which he is starting to wonder what is a politically correct decision because we've been getting a lot of really good press. Since we're kicking butt so far. But anyway they were able to bring in the gun and we were dreading it, right because usually it's a real bad deal when they bring a gun in. And for some reason though, this is a real light-hearted jury and the judge is just a real humorous guy and he decided to make some jokes. And the guy that they brought in to show the gun was a funny guy.

So the whole thing was really light-hearted—one of the jurors laughed, and asked if it was loaded, everybody laughed and it was like not a big deal. And so that went over pretty good. We were actually amazed that it had very little impact at all. They were just kind of interested in how the weapons were loaded and this and that and asking questions. It was strange, and I was like, Man, this isn't having any effect at all. So that went by and then the last person that they wanted to put on was the lady to say that I bought these Rolex watches, which is really damaging evidence.

It's just—as stupid as it is, but it's what they—it's really their only evidence that is really crucial to their case. It's bad character evidence and so on. But in any case, they wanted to put her on last but they had wanted to get in Perry the day before. Perry Berman.

NORMA: Oh right, right.

LYLE: And they wanted to put him on because he was part of the alibi concoction. Because you know how he was involved in that right?

NORMA: Oh, he said you went to the movies or a wine-tasting thing or something.

LYLE: Yeah, he went to this wine-tasting thing and asked to—it wasn't for an alibi because this was me wanting to get together with him way after the time that my parents died. But it was just that I didn't want to go back home alone and call 911 myself. So I wanted Perry to go with me. So I called Perry and asked him to meet me at the restaurant and then I just got so broken up emotionally with my brother that I ended up saying, well, fuck it. We'll never be able to meet with Perry and pull it off so let's just go home and call ourselves and I just left Perry at the restaurant. In any case, they brought him in as a witness.

I don't fucking believe that they were going to kill me at that moment and I'm not going to go in there and say that I believe that now because I just don't.

NORMA: Well, you believed something was going on.

LYLE: Yeah, and they have a letter—this is a scandalous thing. Their two theories are that it was for money and that it was a perfect murder, and also that I hated my parents. But the main theory is money. They took a letter from me that I wrote to my brother and they confiscated out of the cell—that they felt we were trying to escape once so they just bagged up everything in my brother's cell while he was at court. And in there was a seventeen-page letter that I had written him all about what happened.

And basically—it was not all about just what happened; it was mostly about the fact that he wanted to move to another area of the jail and I wanted to go with him and how important it is that we stay close brothers. This one letter—and in it I say, only he and I know our family secrets—only he and I know what happened. I don't know what I can do about what happened. As far as I can see, I made a mistake. Right? And that I don't know what to do about it, I guess that I can't do anything about it now. Alright? That's what I say in the letter. And before that, I say, Don't worry about the press because you and I know that we didn't do anything for the money.

This is all written in the letter and they use this letter at the Grand Jury to get me indicted for murder. Because it was at that time the only piece of evidence that they had connecting me to proving that I was involved. You know the Grand Jury, right? And because they used it at the Grand Jury, the Grand Jury told them we reject your claim that they did it for money and they reject the financial gain because the fucking letter says it wasn't for money. You can't have your cake and eat it too. And they argue that when I said I made a mistake, that what I was saying was that I planned the perfect murder and because I got caught that was the mistake. And I was like, yeah, right. So anyway—they realized.

I got on the stand during the motion to the letter and they started cross-examining me on it and I got emotional. I cried. And they said, Oh fuck, we'd better not use this letter. 'Cause we don't want the kid to cry. So they told the judge one week before the trial, "We've decided we are not using the letter in our case." And the main reason they weren't going to use it—one is because they realize I'll get emotional; two, they realize it says there right in the letter that it's not for the money and now that I'm indicted and they've got Oziel and they realize that I'm going to admit to the killing, they don't need to prove that I was involved and this letter is just going to hurt their case. It's scandalous.

I told my attorney, I said, "How can they go ahead and say it's for the money when they got a letter that proves it's not? And they used it in the Grand Jury to get me indicted."

"Well, that's the law. They don't have to use what they used in one Grand Jury in the trial."

And I said, "Well, why don't we use it?"

"Well, you can't use a letter that you wrote. That's the law."

I said, "Well, there's got to be a way to get this fucking letter in, right?"

"Yeah, we'll get it in through the experts. When the psychologists come in and testify that they believe you and we ask them what is the basis of that belief, they can mention one of the things is this letter that the jail authorities confiscated. We'll get it in that way and don't worry about it. The jury will see that."

NORMA: You've got yourself into a fine mess.

LYLE: Thank God I wrote the fucking—and this is the best thing. At the end of the letter, I write to my brother, "Please destroy this." Like he hasn't got me into enough trouble already, going to Oziel. I write, "Please destroy this," this is before we had even gotten the decision about whether the psychologist could testify, so you can imagine my state of mind when I heard that they had this letter. There was no other evidence against me. My attorney said to me, "You're going home, they are not going to let—"

NORMA: Are you happy about the way Erik has acted so far?

LYLE: "Please destroy this." And I go, "Erik, why didn't you destroy this?"

"Well, you know, it was such a nice letter, I wanted to show it to my attorney so I held onto it and I forgot about it."

I'm like, Oh, my God. That sucker. And of course, I can't use it against my brother, they would just use it against me. So, it's just sad.

In any case, so they bring Perry in yesterday. And Perry gets on the stand and they only have a couple of questions about the alibi and then my attorney got on the stand and oh, my God, Perry has been on the front page of the paper all day.

NORMA: He looked great.

LYLE: First he argued to the judge that the judge shouldn't allow him to be on TV. And the judge told him to fuck off, he's got to be on TV. And he gets up there, man he reamed the DA. My attorney said—first the DA asked him, "You know the Menendez family, right?" He tells him about a story when he was at the racquet club where he was coaching my brother and my dad ran onto the court and started yelling at him for the way he was doing [it] and gave him dirty looks, yelled at him, and my brother started crying. And the DA was like—oh, my gosh. And the jurors are looking at Perry, man. And Perry said that was the most traumatic experience that he has had at the college in the whole fifteen years. And then my parents started talking about—the DA brought out the sign—they invited you over for family dinners and stuff—trying to make it look like they were real nice and it was just a nice, happy family.

And he said, "Yeah, I came over for dinner a couple of times," and they left it at that.

And Jill asked, "Well, what was it like in these family dinners?"

He said, "It was so tense, I hated being there."

Oh my God! And then the DA made a mistake and allowed him to talk about my girlfriend Christy, the model. Allowed him,

Perry, to say something Christy had told him, which was that my dad had ordered me to terminate my relationship with Christy because he thought Christy was a gold digger and I complied—which really was good form. And it will help the theory because one of the reasons I was taken out of the will was my dad was concerned that I had all of these golddigger girlfriends and he thought it would stop if he took me out and I knew about it. And so they ended up building up our case on the golddigger thing.

So Perry made this statement—that's been on the front page of every paper—that my dad, Mr. Menendez, ran his family like a company and he was chairman of the board. And so that's been on the front page everywhere. And then, the other thing Perry said was that when I called him that evening I was real anxious and jumpy—when I called him to meet me after my parents had died.

NORMA: I can't imagine why.

LYLE: Yeah, Jill brought out—Jill said, "Was there anything different about his voice when he left you the message in the morning?"

"No."

"Was there anything different about his voice when he called you at 4:00 to make the plans?"

"No."

"And what about when he called you at 11:30?"

"Yeah, he was anxious and jumpy."

And she is going to try and show that obviously this thing must have erupted sometime between the 4:00 call and when that happened or I wouldn't have had such a change in my demeanor. And so, so then Perry got off the stand and the DA is like—oh, my God. So the papers have it.

And the next lady who was supposed to be a witness is the Rolex lady and they ran out of time so Perry was the last witness and there was no court today. So they got three days of just dwelling on Perry. And so that was great. Perry was good for me. So it was good. So we've had three good days, between the opening statements, the boat guy, and Perry. I feel like they are building our case and not theirs. It's going well at the moment and oh check—guess what happened today?

Unbelievable. You know that the worst witness in my case is Oziel, right? Because—he is a lying shit and he's going to tell all these lies about me. And we've got a lot of girlfriends lined up to ream his ass and so on. That he has raped and abused. And the guy has been a practicing psychologist for this whole time, three years, and the DA is trying to make him out to be just this nice psychologist and we could—we tried and tried to get the Board of Psychology, the state authorities, to revoke his license.

◆

July 24, 1993, afternoon

LYLE: I don't know if you've ever fired a shotgun, but its a joke. I was like really depressed after I went to· the Range because I figured these things are pretty useless. If somebody is going to come in and get me or something, I'm not going to have time to whip out a shotgun. So because of that, I still wanted to get the handgun. So maybe I thought I could get one illegally or borrow one from a friend. I went the next day to one of my brother's friends, whom I didn't know and tried to get a handgun, and he didn't have one. He'll be testifying to that effect too. So I said, fuck it, then we'll just go with what we have.

That was Saturday anyway and the boat trip was that night. I still—I felt like I couldn't be positive about what was going to happen and I didn't want to like refuse to go on the boat trip because then my dad would know what was up. And it would bring it to a head and I would be in more trouble. I felt it was better to play it out and nothing would happen and maybe I could jump off the boat and swim away, I don't know. So I went on the boat trip and that's what the guy testified to. We just stayed in front of the boat and avoided my dad at all costs.

And we got back home and I had a—I went out with my brother to just kind of relax and stay out of the house in case there was something planned for me when we got home. Then when I came back, the door was locked. I rang the doorbell and my mother came down, and we got into an argument. And she told my brother, when he tried to interrupt in the argument, for him to shut up, and if he hadn't opened his mouth, things might have worked out in this family—[that] is essentially what she said. That's what I remember her saying. Erik remembers it slightly differently. And to me that meant that there was something planned. . . . I just felt like something was up.

And my mother is obsessive—has resented me from Day 1 from everything from the tennis on. Just—she felt like she had no life—the whole thing with the affairs, everything. I just felt like she was just a crazed, a dangerous individual at that point and I was glad that she had made that statement. So I became real ready for the next day. So we went to bed and whatever—making a long story short.

But the next day, we got up and my brother was gone, which was the way he was the whole weekend because he was too scared to be around the house even though he didn't want to run away. So I just hung around the house all day and I asked my—I went into the house and I asked my dad for the number to the . . . tennis camp that he had been bugging me all summer to go there. And my dad told me, I don't know where it is and what does it matter anymore? And just kind of like—without looking at me. I couldn't tell what that meant. But I knew it wasn't good, but then again of course our conversation Thursday wasn't good either so—I'm not expecting him to be joyous this evening. I don't know.

In any case, they kind of treated me like I was a ghost. That made me super nervous but my brother wasn't around and I figured I was safe as long as my brother wasn't around. So I waited for my brother to get back. But I called Perry and I asked him if he could go to the movies with me that night so that I would have somebody with me all the time at night—because I was mostly scared at night. And I had already made plans with this black guy out here who is a therapist—to go to the movies Sunday night because I wanted somebody with me.

And so he was meeting me at the movies and I wanted Perry to be there too to do something after the movies because I figured this black guy would go to bed early because he's got work Monday.

So Perry told me—I called Perry and left a message on his machine. He called back and apparently my dad answered the phone. My dad told him I wasn't there, I had been gone all day and was at the Beverly Center shopping and sorry and—Perry said, "Well, he wanted to do something tonight."

He said, "Well, I'm sorry. I guess he can't because he's not around. I'll tell him that you called."

NORMA: But you were there?

LYLE: Yeah, I was there. Obviously because I had just called him and left a message. He said, "I'll tell Lyle you called." He never told me. I called him back at 4:00.

He said, "Oh, you got my message."

I said, "No."

He said, "Yeah, I talked to your Dad."

"You're kidding, what did he say?"

"He said you went to the Beverly Center."

"Oh, really, that's interesting."

I said, "Well, can you go out tonight?"

He said, "No, I'm going to the Taste of L.A. and having dinner, why don't you come with me?"

I said, "I can't because I'm going to be with my brother and going to this movie—it's already prearranged."

He said, "Alright, meet me afterward."

I said, "Okay, I'll meet you afterward." And I figured, fuck—my dad lied. For some reason he wants me home tonight. That's all I could think of and I was just dying for my brother to come home so I could explain what had happened today.

And my brother comes home unbelievably late, like 9:30. Well, I've already missed my plans to meet this guy at the movies. He's waiting there and my parents are in the den and they're waiting. They look like they're just kind of watching TV but at that time I didn't know what they were doing. I didn't know that they were waiting. I just felt that they were watching TV or whatever and I was just kind of real nervous.

My brother gets home and my dad had tried to get into my brother's room Saturday night. And my brother, because the Beverly Hills mansion has special locks on each door, locked the door. He couldn't get in. He decided not to break the door down, my dad. He said, "I'll deal with it tomorrow night." My brother came home frazzled telling me this story and I told him what had happened with Perry and we got to get out of this house, let's talk about it somewhere else. And you're already fucking late, we're supposed to meet this guy at the movies. I go tell my mother, we're going to leave, we're going to the movies, I got plans.

She says no—she gets real nervous and tells me, "You can't go."

And I said, "Why?"

She couldn't answer me. "You just can't go out tonight—it's too late."

My dad comes storming into the kitchen and pulled her aside. And just told me—pulled my brother actually because for some reason he ended up standing next to me. Told him go upstairs and wait for me and I looked at my brother and said, "No, you're not touching my brother."

We got into this big fight. My brother left and went upstairs.

And I said, "Oh, man."

My mother came out and started saying something to me, and my dad pulled her away and said, "Come on, Kitty, let's go in the room." And just looked at me and then he closed the door to the den and—you don't know my house too well—but you're not supposed to close the doors to that room. He closed the doors to that room.

And I mean, I can't describe it too well but essentially I just panicked and I just said, you know, something is going on in the room. They have been waiting for my brother to get home, that's all this is and they can wait. I've been sitting here like a sitting duck and they've been waiting for him to come home and he came home late and it's fucking up their plans a little.

And so I ran upstairs to Erik, I said, "It's going down now." I didn't even think about running. I just said, "I'm getting my gun and I'm going in."

And I figured my chance was to just surprise them and I guess the DA is going to ask me, "Well, you could have just gone in your room and hid by the bed and just waited." But that's not the way that I'm trained from tennis on. I just rushed in there. My feeling was just get there as fast as possible and so I think—so that's what I did.

My brother I guess was of the same mind because he was willing to meet me out front. So we went running in and as—we went running in and the room was dark obviously so they could— 'cause the TV was on and there were like shadows and some shadow moved toward me and I started blasting and my brother started firing and we just fired and we fired. I had grabbed a bunch of shells and so we just kept on firing. And we continued to fire and it was still—there was still movement. Somebody was scrambling around the coffee table was all I could barely see because the room was so smoky and all I could feel was lots of shots going around the room and the pellets bouncing off the shotgun. I didn't know what was going on.

So I just ran out of the room and went and got another shell, ran back into the room. It was dark and smoky and I fired again at the person that I'd seen by the coffee table and I was in a crazed state. So I wasn't thinking. I probably should have gotten into the car and took off but we never even thought about that. So I came back in the room and I shot a final time. It turned out to be my mother, which is a great unfortunate thing to me but I didn't even think about it at the time. I just dropped my gun, I went into the foyer and waited. And I just slumped against the wall, I was exhausted from the event and my brother was there I guess in the room too.

The DA has been trying to say for the longest time that they were asleep on the couch. That they had fallen asleep watching TV and they tried to get one of my tennis player friends to say that they used to fall asleep in front of the TV often. And they said listen, "If they were on the couch sitting there, you can tell us the truth."

I said, "Listen I'm telling you what happened."

Only one and a half weeks ago, the DA's coroner come forward and said, "Listen, I'm sorry, it's really clear from the results that I have and I know that that's not what you want to hear—but it is real clear that they were not only awake, that they were in the standing position and Mr. Menendez was at one point kind of—at one point in one position and moving forward because his left leg was raised off the ground and shot to the side."

That confirms what I said. They figured that was a victory for us, and it is obviously. And so that's not going to be in dispute. There is not going to be any bullshit about sleeping on the couch. So anyway, I waited in the foyer for the police to come. And I figured, I'm going to jail but at least I'm giving it my best shot at this point. They never showed up. Nobody ever called. Whatever it is—twelve shots in the middle of Beverly Hills. Nobody called and everybody admits they heard it too. Because they got about ten people coming in saying they heard the shots. Nobody called. They just figured Beverly Hills, it just can't be.

We waited there ten minutes. And finally my brother and I just kind of snapped to it and we said, "Let's get the fuck out of here, we can just maybe come up with an alibi or something." I'm sure as hell not just going to call the police and turn myself in. So that's what I did. I left. I picked up the shells, I figured they might have some fingerprints on them. I left. And I tried to like make—so I went to the movie theater to try to buy tickets for the show that was started at 8:00 P.M. to show that I had been there. And I went, I wanted to buy tickets for *License to Kill*, because *Batman*, I figured my friend was already in there and I certainly—I was already fucked if the police ever got to him because he would say that I never showed up.

So I went to *License to Kill* and the lady told me it was sold out all evening. I said well, the only other movie that was playing that I knew the plot to—they would obviously ask me—was *Batman*. I said, "Fuck, just give me an 8:00 ticket for *Batman*. And she told me she couldn't sell it to me 'cause the movie was almost over. She couldn't sell me the 8:00 showing, she could sell me the 10:30.

I said, "No, I want the 8:00."

"Then I can't sell it to you."

I said, "Great. So, no thanks, I don't want . . ."—and we left.

I went to Taste of L.A. and Perry had already left. I called Perry and said, "Listen I got to meet you," 'cause I didn't want to go back home alone. I knew the police weren't there so someone was going to have to call 911 and I didn't want to do it.

And Perry said, "Alright, I'll meet you at this restaurant."

Like I said, when we were driving back, my brother started crying, I just started to unravel and I figured there is just no way that I'm going to sit down with Perry and him. . . . So I figured let's just go to the house and we'll call.

So we went and I called. I was crying. It was fucking—it was a fucking—a big scene. I figured my little plan is unraveling. It was a weak attempt anyway. After we went to the movies, 'cause we had just dropped the guns off in this ravine. And then we had gone to the Taste of L.A. That's why we were too late to see Perry. In any case, then Erik changed his clothes into a tennis outfit that he kept in the back and that's why he was in his tennis outfit.

But in any case, so the police show up and they find my brother crying. I called 911 and they showed the 911 tape recording and it's obvious that I'm crying and the whole thing. But they're trying to say that I acted it out and practiced and all this bullshit but I don't think that it came across that way.

NORMA: Plus no matter what—you're upset about what happened.

LYLE: Yeah, but you know what, the DA—they're not smart in that way. You would think that they would just say that. But they don't—they're not willing to concede a single thing. They say that no, they were faking it, they're an actor. Erik took a drama class, they're faking it. Stupid to have a theory that we're faking it when your own policeman with thirty-one years on the force says we are traumatized. Stupid.

In any case, they come and they bring us to the interview. On the way to the interview—what do you want to do? Obviously you're fucking broken up and I'm shaking here and I'm a little bit concerned that we are not going to be able to tell the story that we had just—we decided we'd just say that we were at the movies even though we don't have tickets.

And he [Erik] said, "No, no, I can do it. I can do it."

I said, "Well, I don't know. You go in first and you talk to them and you tell me when you come out if it's OK. Because I'm not going to go in there and lie if you're going to tell the truth."

He said, "Alright."

He goes in there and he's crying so bad that they turn the machine off after ten minutes. Boom, no more questions. The guy that was interviewing him said he was about to cry.

So my brother comes out and tells me, "Yeah, it's OK, you can go in." Because he had stuck basically to the story that he went to the movies and that was it.

So I go in and I do—the officer testified in court—it was very strange that the brother came out of the interview and said to the older brother, "Lyle, it's OK, it's OK, you can tell them everything." Right. And that was good for us, obviously. They don't know why it was good for us but it is obviously 'cause it fits.

So, like, I went in there and I wasn't crying or anything but I was obviously having trouble connecting words and stuff but I got through a long interview with them and basically just talked about my dad—yeah, maybe it's business related—I don't know. We went to the movies and we called Perry and—real simple story but it took a long time to tell because they asked me a million questions. And then the guy just—he—Erik and I were too upset about the whole thing to put us through a gun test, which he figured no way did these boys do it. So he didn't give it to us, so we left. And that was that.

Then my brother, breaking down to the psych—and he's a big part of the case, that's how it came out.

NORMA: If that hadn't have happened then there was no way—

LYLE: Not a chance—and then the DA started arguing it was a perfect murder. I mean, that's like a fantasy thing that people do crimes just for—they're trying to argue that one of the reasons is because we just are obsessed with perfect crimes. Only because Oziel said that that was mentioned. He's just a liar—they shouldn't just accept anything that he says because of his stupid theory. But their feeling is, We can't say that he's a liar because he's half our case. We got to go with what he says. And the problem with him is that he says that there wasn't the money and I was out of the will.

And my Uncle Carlos is going to come in and tell them, "I talked to Jose, and Jose told me that I want you to be the executor of my will, and I told the boys they are not in it." Yeah, he's coming in to testify to that. So I don't see how this money thing is going to hold up when I'm not even in the fucking will. And my Aunt Marta is going to come in and say that after my parents died she came to me and started stepping into all of these details of the estate.

I told her, "Listen, don't even talk to me about it because I'm not going to be in the will." She was shocked and then it turned out that they never did a new will and they just used one from 1980. So I don't know. To me that should cancel the spending image. Even the psychologist is going to come in and say that we came in and told him that this money—it wasn't the money because we weren't even in the will. So I mean, I think that holds up pretty good.

NORMA: Yeah, but then they have that whole computer thing—

LYLE: Yeah, but the computer thing is on our side, I would think. All they have is evidence that some relative, Carlos Menendez, says that there might be a new will on the computer. He couldn't find one but there was a category called "will." And that I flew out and erased it. And this friend is going to say that I flew out because I was concerned that there was a new will that disinherited me. Doesn't that support the fact that I obviously was concerned then? I mean, why would I fly out if I wasn't sure that I was out? I mean, so I don't think that that hurts me. It's just kind of like an overreaction.

NORMA: Let me ask you a question. If you had it to do over again, how would you have handled it?

LYLE: I don't know. I wish that I could just go back and have waited. Just waited another day or two and see what happened. I mean, I can't honestly say now that I felt that they were actually going to do something at the moment because now I know that they didn't have any weapons with them. Not that I knew for sure how it was going to go down anyway, but the fact—

NORMA: You don't think that you could have been over-reacting?

LYLE: Well, I obviously overreacted at that moment. No doubt about it. I fucked up. But whether something was going to happen that night—and I felt like it was pointing to that night. But

I don't know. Obviously, what the point of the moment—and I'm not going to go into court and say that it was.

July 27, 1993
July 28, 1993

NORMA: How did today go, love?

LYLE: Went terrific.

NORMA: It was terrific? OK, that's good. Who was there today? I know that guy was supposed to finish up today, wasn't he?

LYLE: He was destroyed on the stand.

NORMA: He was destroyed?

LYLE: Absolutely annihilated.

NORMA: By who? Leslie and Jill?

LYLE: Just Jill. I mean, she destroyed this guy. It was so embarrassing, I felt so bad for him. The guy had to admit to everything under the sun—conspiring, lying, and it was a joke. It was sad. It was fucking sad. And not only did—he also in the process took down with him, remember the guy that testified yesterday? He took the limo guy down with him because the limo guy said that he didn't go to a topless bar with the chief detective when he was out here. I don't know if you were there for that testimony? Straight out told the jury he didn't go—laughed about it and said, "Oh, I'd remember that if we went there." Everybody believed him. I even believed him.

He got on the stand today and said, "Yeah, I was with him. We went—I know what you're getting at—yeah, we went to a go-go bar.

She said, "A topless bar?"

He said, "Yeah."

It was unbelievable. The jury went like—that motherfucker was lying yesterday. He—we destroyed him on the stand and then Donovan [Goodreau] came in and he was in two minutes, he was made to be a liar. In two minutes because of the Bob Rand tape [Rand had interviewed Goodreau on tape]. We didn't even get into the main part of the Bob Rand tape that we wanted—the part that's all about molestation and all that. All we got into was just a few of the other things that Goodreau had said.

He said that I didn't have any money—and I always had five dollars—and I went to the airport one day and I couldn't get my car out, I had to borrow fifty dollars from my grandmother, right? On the tape, he saying all kinds of different things on the tape. We destroyed him on the tape. It turns out that the truth is the guy said that I lived a first-class lifestyle, everything I did was first-class. He said that I took him to lunch every day and paid. I took him to dinner and bought him margaritas on a regular basis. He said he borrowed $400 in cash from me.

NORMA: He said he borrowed it?

LYLE: And I don't have five dollars. But he borrowed $400 from me, right? He admitted because it was on tape that in fact Grandma didn't give me the fifty dollars. She owed me the fifty dollars and she was just paying me back. He said—he admitted that I told him that my father, he admitted that my father had told me that when I graduate from college he is gonna give me $2 million to start any business I wanted.

NORMA: He said that?

LYLE: Can you imagine that? They are trying to say that I killed him for money and this guy had just told them—their own witness—his father told him he'd give him $2 million to start any business he wanted.

NORMA: And he didn't say that, your father?

LYLE: He did say that.

NORMA: He did say that? Oh, and he was saying that he told him?

LYLE: He told him that that is what I told him. That my father told me that. So how can it be a money murder if the fucking guy is going to give me $2 million? It's a fucking joke. I mean their tape was just a shambles. Then Glenn Stevens got up there, I can't even tell you all the ways that Steve looked like a liar and we caught him in straight lies. I can't even tell you all the ways, but it would take an hour and a half because it was four hours of direct—of cross-examination. Destroyed. Completely destroyed.

NORMA: And I missed it.

LYLE: But he testified that he never went shopping with me.

He never—I never bought him anything before my parents died and every time I would try to give him something, either before or after, he always refused, he always said no. He wouldn't allow it. Right?

NORMA: Why?

LYLE: That's what he said. His testimony. They are trying to prove that I had no money before and tons of money after. We destroyed him. We brought out the fact that he went with me and bought a dog. He tried to weasel out of it and we brought the records in. Two hundred dollars when I bought a dog. Then she brought in that I bought with him a Movado watch, I lost it, came back to the store a week later and bought another one with him—that I bought for myself—a Movado watch. And then she brought out with him that—this is the one that kills me—that I had bought him a leather belt.

She said, "Isn't it true that he bought you a leather belt as a gift?"

And he said, "Yeah."

And it came out that I bought him a leather—he had looked in the store, this expensive store that I used to shop in—this is before my parents died when I'm supposed have no money and just never using. And he liked a belt but he couldn't afford it because it was $125 so I bought it and surprised him the next day and gave it to him as a gift.

NORMA: Did you?

LYLE: And he goes, "Oh, yeah, I forgot about that." You know what I mean? I mean, what kind of a piece of shit who says that he is your friend is going—how offensive is it for the jury that a guy is going to forget that somebody bought you a $125 belt?

NORMA: Yeah, how could you forget that until your memory is jogged. That is something you don't forget.

LYLE: You would think so—if you got any fucking scruples at all.

NORMA: Sure. That's why he shouldn't have forgotten what you said about your father. You know, wouldn't he deny when you told your father about—about the abuse.

LYLE: I never—that was never—with Donovan.

NORMA: Oh, that was Donovan. This is the other guy. Yeah. Yeah, but they both did it, huh?

LYLE: They destroyed each other. It was unbelievable what they did. They go into all this little act—he was so broken down that by the end—what happened was that he thought that we had the goods on him for everything that Jill was asking. He thought we could prove everything. Jill surprised the shit out of him. He mentioned the resume in his testimony. We had the resume. He lied on everything on the resume. He said he was valedictorian—he wasn't. He said he got the Yale Book Award, he never did. He said he was in charge of twenty employees in the restaurant, he had testified it was five. He said that he had sold $200,000 worth of ChemLawn, he never worked there. He said that—all this stuff. One after another.

The jurors looked at him like—unfucking believable. And then the guy says, we broke him down so bad he goes, "Well, you got to understand. I went to Princeton University and they teach us there to embellish and sell ourselves." He said that.

I was like—Jill looked at him and smiled. And kind of like shook her head and smiled and they were looking at him in shock. Like he was trained to embellish. It was so stupid—I couldn't even go on—but he was on—. At the end, she asked him—as usual I come out like the nicest guy in the world. People have come in and only said that he was the most generous nice guy. It came out that he was the one that pressured me out of—to kick Donovan out of the room and that I was reluctant and I was sad and all this stuff and I didn't want to do it. My Dad ordered me to. And he pressured me and all of this stuff because he was resentful. I mean, it was so bad.

And at the end he goes—Jill asked him, "Did you find Lyle to be a caring, trustworthy person?"

And he said, "Absolutely, to a fault." Because he was so broken down at that point that he was trying to be nice to me now. He was obviously a liar and so he was just like . . . that's a nice thing to say about somebody. That they are trustworthy to a fault. And so the jury was like—I don't get this. Everybody comes in and says that he was a nice guy. Man.

NORMA: Well, this is great. I wish I would have been there.

LYLE: Wait 'til the media. The media ran in—this is before Jill was even half through with him—the media ran in and said, "He's destroyed, perjury." And then she went on talking and totally destroyed him. He was so destroyed that when the DA came back on the redirect, the first thing he did was get on the stand and say, "Listen, I admit it, I want to just admit now before it comes out on the other side that I did steal from Lyle's restaurant."

NORMA: Did he?

LYLE: He admitted to stealing. That's wonderful. And then he tried to make a big deal about these watches. He said in the direct examination that I had basically forced him to wear the watch, that I told him, "Wear this so I don't lose it." And then it comes out that he fucking sells it. He kept it.

She goes, "Well, where is the watch now? 'Cause you were wearing it when you got arrested."

He goes, "I don't know."

She goes, "Well, didn't you sell it?"

It was like—they were expecting him to deny it.

"Yeah I did."

"And did you get $1,000?"

"I did."

"And what did you do with it?"

"I don't know. I spent it."

You know what I mean? That's like—you're a piece of shit. Like I was a good guy and he is a piece of shit. They are probably thinking to themselves, What is a guy like Lyle doing with a guy like this?

NORMA: Well, I'm glad it went this good for you. I just wish that I was there.

LYLE: Erik was so pleased that his jury wasn't there. He thought it was going to be terrible for me and he crushed the case. At least that part of it. We have other difficult things in our case but this money thing is slowly destroyed. I mean fucking destroyed. Because they just tried to make it look like I had no money in the spring and then it starts coming out. I bought people belts, I'm buying dogs, I'm buying watches, I'm loaning $400, I'm living first-class, I'm buying—I bought the guy a $300 plane ticket. All of this stuff when I'm a college kid in a dorm.

NORMA: Yeah, you're probably getting more shit than you expected.

LYLE: I'm fucking buying lunch every single day for them. I'm going out and buying margaritas. This and that and this is when I supposedly don't have a dime. You know they fucking say like— Jesus. The truth trickles out. Nice try, guys. I was amazed because I didn't expect them to admit to anything.

NORMA: Right. I mean I know you were expecting some flack but I thought you weren't expecting this kind of shit to come out.

LYLE: Glenn was so honest it was unbelievable. He never told a lie on the cross-examination. Fuck him. He lied his ass off for three years in all the reports of the Grand Jury. He lied his ass off when the DA was asking him questions on direct. We destroyed him so early on in the cross-examination—Jill did. He never lied again. Because he didn't want to be caught in the lie. All she did was just say, "Well, that wasn't true, was it? And that wasn't true, was it? And that wasn't true, was it?"

He refused to lie again. He said, "You're right, that's true. That's true." He said forget it, fuck these guys. You know what I mean. He just gave up. It was really sad. It was pathetic.

The fucking bailiff said "Man, your lawyer is phenomenal. Boy, that kid had a bad day, huh?"

I said, "He didn't have a bad day. He's a liar."

NORMA: Good for the bailiff anyway, looking for you.

LYLE: The fucking judge. The judge was looking at the guy right—

NORMA: I hope all your days go this good. Well, who's on tomorrow anyway? Oh, no there's no jury on tomorrow is there?

LYLE: Oziel is Friday. He's the worst. . . .

NORMA: Well, I'm going to get there tomorrow anyway. I'm going to sit on the left. Is the public going to go in tomorrow? There is public, huh? OK. So, I'm going to sit on the left-hand side. I can see you better over there. You can see me out of the corner of your eye, right? But when I sit on the relatives' and friends' side, I'm sitting directly behind you and I can't see you then. So, you can't see me either unless you turn right all the way around. So, I'm going to be on the left.

LYLE: OK.

July 29, 1993

NORMA: OK, Lyle. Who's next?

LYLE: We got that Oziel guy on Monday so we've got to do something about that guy. I need to somehow—I need to put some thought between now and Monday. When he gets on the stand Monday or Tuesday.

NORMA: This is a sort of preparation.

LYLE: I'm going to— How exactly we are going to cross-examine this guy? How exactly we are going to establish his motive? It looks to me like the stuff he is saying is really unbelievable and he says it in a way that is relatively convincing. Although the stuff he is actually talking about is not convincing at all. But the way he says it is convincing. He doesn't look like an honest guy and he looks a little shifty but he is a very smart guy. So he looks like he recollects everything perfectly almost as if he is seeing it in his mind. Which is just because he's a sort of a psychopath kind of a guy.

NORMA: So he is putting it over real well, huh?

LYLE: You know anybody that has had enough experience— really he's a psychologist. He knows to talk in the way that's convincing. They probably sit there for patient after patient and sound like they are very caring convincing people.

NORMA: Well, yeah. You have to be like an actor you know. It's just like when you are an attorney, you've got to be an actress or an actor.

LYLE: Yeah, so you do. I need to—my feeling is that I should not go in there like we originally intended and say that you know we just didn't tell him the truth and so we therefore said these things that he is saying we said instead. Because these things he is saying instead are just so far out of the character of anything I would say. Even make this stuff up is a sick person.

NORMA: Right.

LYLE: Talking about perfect murder and this and that and

all—stuff that's amazing. And all made up—never happened in our sessions. We had very casual sessions. Never really discussed anything. This guy has just made these tapes. I never did get to find out the motive 'cause I got arrested too soon, basically. But my feeling is we could already show that I paid him $3,000 for two sessions that happened the first two days after the memorial.

NORMA: What's he charge—$3,000?

LYLE: Well, he showed up after my parents died for two days and hung out at the hotel with my family. Six weeks later he charged me for it after my brother confessed. 'Cause he had me by the balls, what could I do? I gotta pay.

NORMA: Sure.

LYLE: But my feeling is, we could show that, right? My feeling is to stand that scene because I think we need to show that this guy and everything on this tape is just something he fabricated for a purpose.

NORMA: Right.

LYLE: This is my thinking and I have three days to figure out what's the best angle and if it's the right angle.

NORMA: To use other motives for why he did it, you mean?

LYLE: To go ahead and say something like—along the lines—I want to say that I knew that these tapes existed.

NORMA: Well, where were you? Didn't he tell you you were being taped?

LYLE: No.

NORMA: I thought you have to.

LYLE: This is not our voice on tape. This is his voice.

NORMA: Saying what you said. Oh yeah, right.

LYLE: This is straight bullshit.

NORMA: Yeah, but I'm saying before he—

LYLE: He doesn't have our voices on tape. He shouldn't do any of this shit. Anyway, and he destroyed his original notes when he made this tape supposedly what he said a week later—right. But, in any case, my thinking is that—to tell a story—talk about him coming and us having a meeting of some sort of which he basically says, "You know, I have this tape." Maybe play us the whole tape or a portion of it. And it is a blackmail meeting. You know what I'm saying?

NORMA: Yeah, right.

LYLE: 'Cause I'm going to have to make something up. To show this guy's motive. 'Cause sometimes people can lie too convincingly.

NORMA: Oh sure.

LYLE: Look at this guy Glenn Stevens yesterday.

NORMA: So you have got to be just as convincing.

LYLE: Oh yeah, which is no problem for me. I mean I can do that just as well as he can. I mean I'm a smart guy and he's a smart guy and we both know it. My credibility is less at issue really because I'm also a nice guy and everybody has said that so far even in their case. This guy is not, and we have many people who say that. So the difference is I need to establish some particular motive because I can't figure the guy out. Because before I could figure out where he was really going with this tape. And I don't know whether to say—I haven't figured out like that he made the tape for life insurance reasons like he was genuinely afraid for some reason. And he was paranoid. The guy thought I was going to kill him or something, right?

NORMA: Yeah. Did he use drugs?

LYLE: No. He gave them to millions of people but he didn't—

NORMA: He had to give them to others, didn't he?

LYLE: So, you know either say that he made the tapes for life insurance purposes saying basically I made this tape. And, I'm like, he and I know that that tape never happened that it's just a fabrication and it made me look like a killer and a dangerous person. And he'd say anything happens to me, this is going to the police.

NORMA: Yeah, right.

LYLE: And that was his lie. And he understood it and I understood it. And I said, "alright, fine." And then he asks me for money for the sessions for the two days and I paid him—$3,000. Boom, no problem. I knew he had me and I started giving him money and I knew that I was going to have to be seeing him forever. And paying him.

NORMA: Sure, if he would have asked you for $10,000 you would have had to pay.

LYLE: Yeah, and I don't know if I should even add in—you

know I've got a lot of people that should come forward for me—whatever I need. Maybe talk about there was a payment made—in cash or something like that. Or a meeting with a third party—because bringing somebody else into it saying yeah this happened and let him deny it and let someone come in and impeach him. You know what I mean?

NORMA: Yeah, I'm trying to think rapidly while you're talking.

LYLE: Just think about it for awhile because I don't have to decide today. I've got all weekend. I'm thinking of actually talking about a meeting that takes place shortly after these sessions in which he sits there with me maybe in a restaurant or we meet somewhere and I've got to be vague as to the time and I can't be vague as to the place. But as to the time—because I don't know if he can somehow verify if he was here or there you know.

NORMA: Right, because you don't know what kind of alibi he's got, right. You could pick a day you know you went to see him. Did he make a note of all your visits? He probably does, huh? Especially you guys, he probably does make a note of your visits.

LYLE: We have a pretty much a lot of information on that time period. From his girlfriend—from his previous testimony and all that stuff. And I think that I can get enough details to know pretty much where he was.

NORMA: Can you?

LYLE: I'm going to get them all from Mike tonight or tomorrow and that—maybe I can help piece together something from that. 'Cause I want to make sure it's as sound as possible.

NORMA: OK.

LYLE: What I may then do is have him say something like, "Yeah, Lyle said he had to go to this meeting with a psych at this restaurant. He came back and he was real frazzled and everything." Something like that might be good. That gives me a little more time to set that up because then I don't need to know by Monday. I don't need to know until I testify. So, I need to know basically what it's going to be so that when he comes on the stand just for the cross-examination they can say isn't it true you met with Lyle here and you said so and so and so and so—and then that's as far as we can take it. Because if we have anything that can prove that, we have to do that in our case.

NORMA: Does Leslie need to be in on this?

LYLE: I've got a visit. Oh no, definitely not.

NORMA: Oh, OK. I thought she'd seen each of your—I mean she knows what Jill is going to be saying, right?

LYLE: Yeah, this is going to be very difficult to add now.

NORMA: That's what I'm saying. If she's seen the stuff already that you are already going to say, you know.

LYLE: This is something that I'm going to have to just tell Michael. . . .

NORMA: That you just remembered it all?

LYLE: Well I mean he'll know that I did it but I've got to tell him this is my life—and once you see another way—you know what I mean? Once you see another way—for people to understand this guy, I got to do what I got to do.

NORMA: Yeah.

LYLE: And he understands. He'll—I'll just say you just ask those questions, that's all. Don't worry about a thing. He understands that. I think he understands that this guy is a problem. Because he is such a—

NORMA: So what time period is—

LYLE: I think people are going to wonder, Can anybody have made up all that stuff? He's got conversations and yeah I remember he nodded and I remember his face when—you know what I mean?

NORMA: Is this about the August period—August—September or what?

LYLE: What?

NORMA: This whole period that you are going to make this thing up. Where you are going to have to fit something in—what period of time is it going to be in?

LYLE: Halloween.

NORMA: Halloween time? Around there? OK.

LYLE: Exactly Halloween.

NORMA: Halloween day? But do you know where he was on Halloween?

LYLE: I have a friend in town at that moment—but he's in Greece so I would need to get that number out there. Like I said, I have a little time. And maybe he can help me out. He could say he dropped me off at the meeting or whatever—something of that sort.

NORMA: I know you didn't know many people around Beverly Hills at that particular time because you haven't been here long enough. To fall back on now I mean.

LYLE: Unfortunately that's true. I can also get verification from people in Jersey or anywhere in the country whom I told later this has happened or whatever. This could be a prior consistent statement. Like if they try to suggest that I'm lying, then I could bring in so and so to say that he told me that this happened or whatever. I can bring other people—it's unfortunate that I wasn't aware of this problem earlier 'cause there's a lot of people that can help me, but you know, I was going to use. . . .

NORMA: What about Jill though? Well, she'll have to go along with it, won't she?

LYLE: Oh yeah. They won't be happy but I don't give a fuck. It's my defense team. It's very honest but on the other hand you know if I say, Hey, I'm going to say this so you know. But they're not going to do anything about it. They don't have a control issue over me.

NORMA: Yeah, but who is actually going to say—okay he's going to be on the stand getting questioned back and forth, right? Michael's going to do it? OK, he's going to chip in with what you are telling him that you did.

LYLE: I don't know—I haven't talked to him yet.

NORMA: OK—you are going to try—OK—right. 'Cause he might want the waters not ruffled.

LYLE: I've got to think of something most believable.

NORMA: Right, yes.

LYLE: My feeling is . . .

NORMA: Something not too complicated.

LYLE: Yeah, it's clear on the tapes, right? That he's saying that I'm dangerous, that I might kill him—that he thought—he took the things I said as threats. I never said I'm going to kill you but he took these things as threats—you know "Good luck, Dr. Oziel" and stuff like that. And he actually—and there are lots of documented things. He went and bought shotguns, he upgraded the security system on his house, he moved his family to a hotel—it was clear that he was paranoid. It's unbelievable to just go ahead and conceive that this guy was paranoid with fear.

NORMA: Yeah, but Lyle, he was embellishing. This is on—the latest fashion word—embellish. He was embellishing his story.

LYLE: Even embellished. This guy is unbelievable. This is straight fabrications. I told Michael—he laughed and I said when he was testifying, Erik and I should be dressed in clown suits to make a statement. . . . The guy, I mean I can't even believe that my life is hanging in the balance of somebody like this. This was a guy that I didn't even want to spend five minutes with.

NORMA: Right. What a pity that your father picked this guy.

LYLE: I'm a very private, secretive person. I don't go around just telling anybody anything in my life. No confessions against me or nothing. And this fucking guy has the nerve to come and say that I've told him all things. And there's just no way in hell—there's no way in hell.

NORMA: Do you think he was—I think basically he was probably trying to push his business, you know. Bit of notoriety and fame. Don't you think?

LYLE: His business is through—the district attorney—

NORMA: It is now. But he didn't think so at the time, did he? So he's going to add things on.

LYLE: This is not his fault—see he never intended to go to the police.

NORMA: It's Judalon Smyth.

LYLE: The girlfriend turned him in.

NORMA: Right, Judalon Smyth.

LYLE: The girlfriend was lying—saying that she overheard this and that and the other and she didn't. So it was like a lie because she was so unstable—but to him and then this whole thing broke open and he realized that he had these tapes which he clearly was going to use for some other purpose and he figured, Fuck, I'd better stick with them.

NORMA: Yeah, I saw last week when he said, "I'm telling you Judalon, you'll get killed." He was just trying to frighten her off from going, wasn't he?

LYLE: Yeah, they know who you are.

NORMA: And he sounded like he didn't want to—

LYLE: We had no idea who she was. You know what I mean? I never heard of her until I got arrested. So how could she be in danger?

NORMA: Of course, he's not going to talk about his girlfriends—only to patients—so of course you wouldn't know her until afterward.

LYLE: The judge doesn't think it's relevant that he raped another girl.

NORMA: Oh really?

LYLE: He raped—it isn't relevant to his credibility. Give me a break.

NORMA: What a sleazeball.

LYLE: I don't think he's going to let it in that he raped another girl. The jury should know that. I mean, come on. . . .

NORMA: I know—there are a lot of things that they hide—it's not fair is it?

LYLE: If I rape somebody, you can be sure that I sure won't be coming in.

NORMA: That's like an injustice when somebody like him is going on the stand and the jury don't get to know his past—and they're going to judge him by how he's dressed and stuff. Yeah, and they're going to think he's a nice guy.

LYLE: Yeah.

NORMA: 'Cause he's doctor and it's all—yeah, it's wrong, a double standard.

LYLE: You know, my feeling is you fight fire with fire.

NORMA: I mean, they get to know all about your background. Why don't they tell about his background? That would make it fair then.

LYLE: That's how you find out about people—like resumes. They never would have known about this kid's resume unless it was allowed in and that really changed their mind on this kid—realized that he is a liar.

NORMA: So why are they letting him off? This guy?

LYLE: The judge—you know why—because the judge wants us to lose.

NORMA: Do you think so? Do you think he's still biased?

LYLE: Please, it's not even a consideration. He thinks we

should go to the gas chamber. Straight out. No doubt about it and hold on a second—so—I got a visit. But you think about it. Think about some scenario that you think makes sense.

NORMA: OK.

LYLE: Him coming to me actually scared saying that this is my life insurance and me telling him, "Hey I don't know why you are so concerned." You know what I mean? I would never do anything to you. You know what I mean? Or maybe blackmail—he wants money, you know. I can't figure out what—maybe a combination or something like that.

NORMA: Yeah, OK.

LYLE: And how the meeting would take place, and then this and that and the things that would be said because I'll have to recount all that. And Michael will have to ask him if that happened. My feeling is unless Michael comes up and says something like that, it's not going to put enough doubt in the jury's mind after they hear his direct. 'Cause his direct will just make me look like a fucking Jeffrey Dahmer.

NORMA: Oh, I don't know. I don't know about that. That's a really bad comparison, Lyle.

LYLE: I'll look worse than Jeffrey Dahmer. You haven't heard the direct. You haven't heard the things he's said. He says that you know it was a plan—there was no way to kill the father once—there was no way to kill the father without killing the mother 'cause there was just no easy way to just kill the father. So it was a plan—we thought about taking the mother out—maybe she didn't deserve to die but fuck it we figured it was a perfect plan and we'll just go with it. Stuff like that.

NORMA: Jesus.

LYLE: Him saying yeah, we're so . . . me saying yeah, I'm a sociopath, I have no feelings. Once I kill I just keep going. I can't stop myself. I'm one of those guys that I just want the perfect plan, I get so excited I can't stop. That's pretty close to Dahmer. Pretty close.

NORMA: That's pretty close to insanity. Yeah.

LYLE: I mean, you know—I mean give me a fucking break—this guy. Unfuckingbelievable. Like I'm ever going to tell anybody that, even if I felt that way. I'm just going to sit there and go hey,

I just thought I'd let you know—you know—give you enough stuff to put me in the gas chamber. You're already the most unstable person and I'm not happy—

NORMA: You're unstable and I'm insane. Yeah—which way are you going to make out.

LYLE: Unbelievable this guy. Luckily the things he says don't sound very believable. If he had just toned it down a little and made it look semi-real—it would be more believable. Because if you are going to lie you had better lie convincingly. But he just—

NORMA: Without the exaggeration.

LYLE: It's like a bad movie. And Erik's script. Erik is better than this. There would never be a movie because no one would believe that anybody actually said that. Unbelievable this guy—unbelievable.

NORMA: So you have got what—it's Friday tomorrow. What's going on tomorrow? Friday, Saturday, Sunday—three days you've got before he shows up again.

LYLE: What?

NORMA: Three days before he shows up again. Three days to work something out.

LYLE: Oh yeah.

NORMA: What's tomorrow?

LYLE: I'm going to try and think—finish it tonight or tomorrow.

NORMA: What is tomorrow anyway?

LYLE: Court hearings—to sort out issues.

NORMA: But there's jury in tomorrow isn't there?

LYLE: No.

NORMA: No jury tomorrow? I thought one of you were in for half a day. OK, they canceled that. OK then, so we've got Friday, Saturday, Sunday.

LYLE: They're taking me so I've gotta go. I'll call you when I get back.

NORMA: OK, I'm going to go out and get a bite to eat. Bye.

August 4, 1993

NORMA: Tell me about it.

LYLE: It's—there's not much to say. I mean, this guy is going to go ahead with this bullshit—stick to his plan and try to come out of this as good as possible and save his own ass which he's never going to have a chance of saving anyway. It's only a matter of time before he loses his license and criminal charges but—it's just unbelievable. In the *L.A. Times* they had me shaking my head, they said, in disbelief as Oziel said what he said. I liked that one. I don't know. I don't know if people are going to buy this or not.

NORMA: How do you feel?

LYLE: I don't like it. The guy rattled me the first day when he came in. I guess he shouldn't because I had the transcripts of exactly what he was going to say for years but it's not something I dwelled on. I don't know. It was a mistake not to be able to address him more clearly in the opening statement, I think. It was a big mistake.

NORMA: What do Michael and Jill think?

LYLE: It's hard to get Jill's feelings. She brushes them off all of the time. She doesn't like to deal with stuff like that. I don't know. She dwells on the defense side of the case so much and I felt that she was sort of unprepared for the DA's side of the case but—I was obviously wrong when she just dismantled Stevens so easily. And I thought for sure there was trouble with him. He turned out to be great for me. So—I don't know. I guess she's not worried because it's not her job. It's Michael and Leslie going in with Oziel even though Jill had obviously overseen the various steps of it.

Mike's feeling is he can discredit the guy. And that his statements on the face are not believable. It just doesn't seem to make sense the things that he's saying and the common sense of what was going on those few days with him don't seem to correlate with this tape in a commonsense way. They are going to all-out attack him. Let him go ahead and say everything he can say against me—bring in everything. Although we did manage to get a lot of the bad stuff excluded today. The judge excluded a lot of it.

NORMA: Like what?

LYLE: Just various statements here and there that were either his opinions or he wants his—or just speculation type stuff.

Or prejudicial because they seem to relate to these future crimes. He has a lot of stuff in there about perfect crimes which seems to give the jury impressions—we'll just continue to make them I guess. And that would be prejudicial so that's been taken out. But to me it doesn't amount to anything. What's the difference? What are you going to do? Cut out the stuff so much that what he's left with is relatively credible? But what they were trying to do is cut out stuff that they felt was semi-credible and just have the stuff left that was really like fantasy. As much as possible and they're going to attack him all-out so we're going to have a little humor— how much the judge is going to let us attack him as far as the raping his old girlfriend and things like that. What he feels is relevant in the law and all this stuff. It's going to be a battle. We want to bring it all in dirty—we think it's relevant. The judge is in a tough spot because it is relevant but it also is time consuming. So I don't know—Jill is just going to watch it play out and then she's going to deal with it.

NORMA: It was just hearings today or did he testify?

LYLE: It was hearings but he had to testify at the hearings. Verify this—who said this—who said that—was it only Erik speaking—was it Lyle speaking—were they adapting it? The guy is such a—he's fucking amazing. He's like he's saying things that never happened as if he's visualizing them in his mind going yeah, Erik was nodding to that—no actually Erik was not—or Lyle was adapting that or he didn't disagree. He's like—this guy is unbelievable. I shouldn't say too much because I'm very familiar with liars and I know myself that things can be—people can lie convincingly—I've seen them on the stand and the jury has too. Lie convincingly and then realize that they lied. And this guy is no different.

NORMA: So the difference between a hearing and testifying is that there is none.

LYLE: There's no jury with a hearing. The jury is not there with a hearing.

NORMA: So when does he testify?

LYLE: He testifies Tuesday.

NORMA: That's much later. Wasn't he supposed to testify Friday?

LYLE: Yeah, but there's just too many hearings involving him.

NORMA: What about the privileged tape?

LYLE: Well, I got on the stand today and Erik and Oziel and we all basically supported the fact that it was protected under the attorney-client privilege but the judge wanted to reserve ruling until he heard from the attorney himself as well, who was kind of hostile to us, but Mike said he had a conversation with him and thinks that the guy will come in and support us. He's not sure. We'll find out. We have to do it Monday.

NORMA: That will be the attorney for?

LYLE: It's an old attorney I had—who was my attorney at the time I was seeing this doctor, before I got arrested. So we are trying to protect the tape under attorney-client privilege because there are no exceptions to the privilege if it's attorney-client privilege—there's no way—no possible way. But doctor-patient privilege there are some exceptions.

NORMA: Does that override attorney-client privilege?

LYLE: No, it wouldn't—that's why we're trying to attack that. At the moment the tape is protected. It's a tape of my brother and my actual voice on it just talking about my feelings about what happened. Which would show that Oziel was lying about the different things that he said we said. But it's not good enough that I want it in. It's not that good because we weren't there to talk to him about my family history—I was there to give him the fucking story to keep him relaxed. So that he wouldn't freak out and go to the police with my brother's information.

NORMA: Your brother said something prior to you coming in to relax him?

LYLE: Yeah. The guy's way out. My brother goes in and confesses, right? The guy calls me out of the blue—on Halloween and says, "Your brother is in my office—he told me everything."

I said, "What's everything? I'm not coming in."

He says, "I think you should come in, your brother's here, he told me everything. I don't want to talk about it on the phone."

I said, "Well, what the fuck am I going to do? My brother is unstable. Alright, I'll go in."

So I show up and I come in, I sit down.

He says, "Well, your brother has told me everything."

"I don't want to hear what my brother told you, I don't want to get into details, I don't want to be involved in what he told you." I was concerned. My feeling is that this guy is going to the police tomorrow morning.

Then he did this thing. "Well, Lyle you look real unhappy about this, you look real angry." And I was. I don't understand why I should have any other reaction. And I was very upset that my brother would go to him before me which I thought was a betrayal of sorts. And also like I'm supposed to be closer to him—he goes to this whacko doctor who I didn't like in the first place.

So in any case, the meeting was very short because my brother, after seeing my reaction, immediately ran out of the room crying and so I ran after him and I told the doctor, "Listen let's schedule an appointment for tomorrow because my brother is kind of whacked out and I need to talk to him."

He says, "Fine," We schedule an appointment.

But this guy on tape has me saying that I came in and I sat down and I looked at my brother and Oziel and [when he said], "Your brother has told me everything that happened," I said, "Oh, great, now it's not a perfect murder." That's the kind of stuff that he says I said. Like I'm really going to sit down there and say that—and that's what he says right in the notes. Lyle sat down and said now it's not a perfect murder.

And then from there he went on to threaten me and from there he left. And then he has the next session which is like—I mean just the insanity of all these things that I said including calling myself a sociopath and saying that I just can't help but get turned on by perfect murders and perfect crimes and getting away with it—I couldn't stop myself.

NORMA: He called you a sociopath?

LYLE: He has, yeah. He said that I called myself that. It's really—it's a ridiculous story and it's all centered around this perfect crime stuff. How—the incentive of the perfect crime. He actually said on the stand that I said in so many words that I was going to kill—I wanted to kill my dad, that was the goal. But we had included my mother in the plan and we couldn't figure out—then we wanted to take my mother out of the plan but there was no way—I couldn't figure out a way to kill my dad without also killing my mother. I just couldn't figure out any physical way to do it so I just left her in. And that also taking her out would have altered the plan and the idea was to have it perfect so we left it otherwise it would have taken away the incentive which was to conduct a perfect murder. Like I sat down and I said this to this guy.

That's what this guy is saying—Erik was nodding and I'm like, If the jury wants to believe that, just give me the gas chamber now. And between flying out before I could go back and get furniture for my condo, I came out for the weekend and decided to do this for no apparent reason. It's really pretty extraordinary. Our feeling is, as long as we've gotta deal with a guy like this who is a loose cannon, it's better that he make statements that are outrageous than statements that are believable. He could really fuck me.

If I wanted to fuck somebody, I wouldn't be saying stuff like that, I'd be making them a lot more subtle. I'd just weave it into something that is obviously first-degree murder. He doesn't do that. He makes it something like you gotta do like Jeffrey Dahmer's cousin or something. It's outrageous that he sits there with a straight face and says all of this stuff.

The jury is going to be shocked. In a mouth straight open—like spinning. Because so far they have seen me as a very normal, nice kid who apparently got wrapped up in his parents' death somehow and they are waiting to find out why. And Jill has told them why and they essentially feel that that's an acceptable reason—they can't think of any other reason that could cause something like this. And this guy is going to tell them this and they sit there and go, Well that was a little too good to be true for the DA isn't it? I don't know. It's just not reasonable. I never did feel like this idea that people could just kill people for a perfect murder incentive unless it's like a serial killer or something like that. They—just my knowledge of murders here—I have yet to ever hear of a murder happen because he just thought he wanted to do a perfect crime. And there's nothing—what's perfect about this? What, fifteen shotgun blasts in the middle of Beverly Hills with no alibi is a perfect murder? Give me a fucking break. He's stupid.

That's the main witness to their case, their case rests on this guy. If they believe him, I lose obviously, because there is no compromise position between him and I. If they don't believe him—then they essentially, my case I still have to prove—get people to buy what I'm saying but it's not very difficult to believe what I'm saying. Pretty well substantiated. What he's saying has no substantiation at all. It's straight-out just—they told me this—that's my testimony. No substantiation. The original notes, he destroyed them.

NORMA: Of course.

LYLE: And this is what he's left with, these tapes. And Michael's theory is very simple. This guy went out and he got this information. He says this is a big deal, this is exciting, this is one of those guys, one of those tabloid type of guys, and he's got a history of crazy kind of stuff and he fucking put his wife in a hotel, he bought shotguns, he upgraded his security system. Puts his wife in a hotel on the weekends so he can go off and fuck the girlfriend in Arizona. Does he hang out and protect his wife? No, he uses it as an excuse to go see his girlfriend and scare her to death so that she thinks she is real important.

He fucks up and scares her too much. He realizes she is going to go to the police so he makes a tape to cover his ass to explain why he told her. And sure enough, she does finally crack and go to the police and sure enough these tapes are what he thought are going to help make him look fine about this whole thing.

NORMA: Why did he tell her?

LYLE: For no reason. Pillow talk. It's girlfriend talk.

NORMA: Right. And he made tapes to cover up that he told her?

LYLE: Yeah, 'cause you can't do that. It's illegal. He'd lose his license. You can't just tell somebody what happens in therapy sessions. You'd lose your license in a half-second.

NORMA: So the tapes are different from what he told her?

LYLE: Oh, yeah. She says he told her all different facts. But, what she has to say is worse.

NORMA: Well, I heard. Is this Judalon? Yeah, I heard.

LYLE: Yes. And she has said that she actually—instead of just saying that he told her—half of the time she says that she actually overheard, which makes no sense at all. Because if she overheard things that were worse, he would obviously be saying that, not his story. So she's not truthful either. She's a whacko. But there is no doubt that she was given all kinds of pertinent information. She knew about the gun as being in San Diego, so he told her facts. You know, with pillow talk. And he, in order to justify telling her, which you can do if you feel somebody is in direct danger, you can tell them things to try and help warn them. But we didn't even know who this lady was—how could she be in danger?

And his excuse that, well, these guys were such psychopaths—see, that's why he has to make me out to be a psychopath because these guys were such psychopaths that I felt that they could kill anybody associated with me and since my business has contact with her as she is in the tape duplication business and I sometimes give her my tapes, they could have seen a business card of hers sometime in the office and gone after her. That's his fucking theory. He actually said that in superior court, two years ago.

The judge looked at him like he was from another planet. Obviously they're not buying it. But nevertheless, because of the tapes, they ruled that it is admissible—that it's an exception because really these tapes are correct, this guy is afraid. They must have threatened him. And another theory, of course, when they ask him why he made the tapes, he says he made them for life insurance. If he died, he wanted these tapes to be out there to screw us. [unintelligible] is supposed to show that he may have altered them. I'm just going to watch the show, I guess. But it bothers me.

NORMA: I bet.

LYLE: I wish we had more on him.

NORMA: What is your feeling about the end of the trial? Your feeling?

LYLE: What do you mean? About what's going to happen? I don't know. I gotta go through Oziel first. Impossible to say at this moment. It's going way better than I ever expected. At this point, they have no case. They can prove that two people died.

The money motive is history, damage to their credibility. They've proven—they managed to independently prove to themselves that, in fact, my dad did abuse my brother and I sexually and that that was all a part of the family problems. Donovan and Glenn Stevens—so their case is a shambles. But they have this one guy—like an ace in the hole. If they can survive his testimony then there'll be a better chance to sway some of the jurors. If they don't survive his testimony they're in trouble.

NORMA: How much trouble?

LYLE: It depends. If anybody believes him then the jury will hang.

NORMA: And that would be what?

LYLE: There'd be a new trial then. Start over. But I don't want to start over. Jill has done too good a job destroying these guys. I don't know if she could do this job the second time around. We got a great jury so I'm confident.

NORMA: If it's not a hung jury, if it's a straight decision, something other than first-degree—

LYLE: It's gotta be manslaughter or I'm not coming home for awhile. If I get second-degree murder, I would be doing a whole lot more years. It shouldn't be second-degree murder. It should either be manslaughter or first-degree.

NORMA: Which would be?

LYLE: First-degree? It's like twenty-five to life. Second-degree is fifteen to life and I already have like four in—so that's going to be eleven years. But probably at least—but still it would not be a victory to me. Against me. We need to—

NORMA: And that would be?

LYLE: That would be manslaughter and I don't know how many years that is. From five years down to zero. 'Cause we have a lot of time in. Probably—I can't say what the judge is going to sentence us to. That's all speculation.

NORMA: You have a problem that you want to share? You said probably—do you want to share it?

LYLE: Probably what?

NORMA: That I can't say but probably and you stopped and—

LYLE: I imagine four years. A year and a half, two years, two and a half years, three years, I don't know exactly.

NORMA: If all goes—

LYLE: If it goes pretty well. They could send me home not guilty but I don't see that happening and I also don't see anything terrible happening. In between I can't say.

NORMA: I just need to know more immediate.

LYLE: I don't know—I can't say because the trial is just started. If we were to rest today, I'd go home, not guilty. But I imagine it's going to get worse from here because the coroner is going to come in and show a lot of pictures. They're not going to like that—probably—maybe I don't know. And the doctor is going to come in and say a lot of bullshit. It may go over terrible—he may look like a clown. It may go over great and he may look credible.

NORMA: The doctor.

LYLE. I don't know. And then I take the stand and if I do terrific, they may not—they may just say, you know what, there is no doubt that this kid is telling the truth. What a joke. I don't think I'll do too bad. I'll do at least okay. We just have to see. My case is much better than my brother's. I think that we are going to have the same results. At least I'd like to think we'd have the same results. It's a lot of real sensitive issues and it just sways day to day—every day is hard to predict.

NORMA: How are you doing?

LYLE: I'm okay. I'm not that comfortable with this guy. I want to somehow have more on him. I gotta talk to Michael.

August 5, 1993

LYLE: So far, it has been established to the DA's witnesses that I am like a white knight in a group of dark circle friends who tried to stab me in the back and were all found out to be liars. Exactly how I come across at the moment. I come across incredibly well. They all said I was extraordinarily generous, the jury was looking at me like I was just way too generous with the people—they didn't deserve it. The guy said that I was trustworthy and caring to a fault, absolutely. And I come across as very emotional. I was reluctant to kick this con artist out of my room. I was crying over it. I was sad. I was too involved with my girlfriends. I cared too much about their feelings. I gave them respect. My aunt thought they were bimbos and yelled at me, forced me to get rid of them, I refused. Even the bodyguard, I was respectful, I bought him things, I asked his advice. You know, I just come across as this really really nice kid.

And they look at me and I look all that they are saying. I look like a nice kid. And the DA has not been able to put on a single witness to say otherwise, nor would they dare in my presence. So that's the image they have of me so far and I'm sure they are sitting there thinking to themselves, How the fuck did this guy get involved with these parents? We're dying to find out. Then, the other thing that they have is that they see us, my attorneys, mainly Jill Lansing, as the absolute bastion of truth, honesty, and with the truth on her side and of honesty because of the way she chastised—literally chastised and made these witnesses be the liars that they are and held the marbles. They see her as a white knight which is what we wanted. . . .

LYLE: The judge is helping him every fucking step of the way.
NORMA: Helping who?
LYLE: The DAs. Their case is a shambles so far and he's pissed. He clearly wishes that he was prosecuting this case and clearly feels that they are incompetent. He's very upset. He wants me to go down so he can look good. And he's concerned. He sees me winning. And rightly so, he's concerned. He knows our defense very well and he's trying. He's very upset because they are not going to introduce the burglaries against me. He has tried to give them every hint in the world that he would allow them in. He says no, I've never even been questioned on it. They won't take it. They said no. He thinks that that's the perfect way to show that this is the perfect crime, that I fucked up a burglary and my dad really told me and so I killed him in a public manner. Something like along those lines. Because that's what Oziel said I said. And without the burglary, it has a lot less weight.

It's like all of a sudden I committed this perfect crime out of the blue a weekend that I just flied [sic] into California. It doesn't make sense really. Plus he's pissed. It's too late, though. They're not going to introduce it. It's unfortunate that mountain of evidence contrary to what we first thought, is against my brother. He has the benefits of being the younger brother and the kid but the weight of evidence against him unfortunately—I don't in any way think it is enough to convict him but it is clearly greater than it is against me.

NORMA: Greater against Erik?

LYLE: Oh, absolutely. Absolutely, the weight of the evidence is against him. The burglaries are painful and clearly tied into this perfect murder theory which is just so scandalous I can't even express to you how utterly ridiculous it is. And the big thing against me, the reason my case was so bad, was because of the money. And because they had Donovan and they had Glenn and they had this bodyguard and they have severely damaged their case. Jill Lansing has totally destroyed that end of their case. And in the process made me out to be a white knight.

And Donovan has literally gone as far as to substantiate that my father abused me and my brother in the ways that I told you a long time ago. [Donovan] said it on tape: "Lyle had this conversation with me." I told him I was abused by my uncle and then he started crying and he laid out what happened to him, on tape. And the DA didn't know that. [Donovan] got on the stand and said, "Oh, no, Lyle never told me anything" and suddenly this reporter comes forward and goes, I don't think so, here's the tape.

[Pam] freaked. And she's in big trouble. But whether that can even come in to support my brother is a question because it's my statement to him. The DA doesn't want to help him out. But that will all help me in the future but I want to get through this little obstacle which is a big obstacle—this fucking psychologist. So scandalous. . . .

But thank God the guy is obviously not too bright because the statements are kind of ridiculous. He literally said—he said on the stand today in front of like fifty people—which really pissed me off—that the plan was to kill my dad but the mother had to go too because there was no way that we could figure out to kill my dad without killing the mother too. We couldn't figure out how to do it because she would be around. And then we had some second thoughts maybe we shouldn't kill the mother but it was such a perfect plan, we thought if we altered it it wouldn't be perfect anymore and the incentive was to do it perfectly. Do you believe he actually said that I said that to him? I'm like, Jill, you tell me, you listen to that. Is that something that somebody would believe? I mean I'm not a half-wit. And she said, "No, it's not believable at all." Thank God he actually said that he said that. I mean like I couldn't kill my dad out in the fucking parking lot or something? I mean it is just ridiculous. I've got to be Jeffrey Dahmer to just throw my mother in just because I didn't feel like taking the time to kill him in the parking lot.

That's what I mean that the jurors are going to listen to this with their mouths open and go, "Wait a minute, how can this be?" And unless they are just won over by this guy. I mean it is one or the other, either you believe this guy and go ahead and send me to the gas chamber. I'm glad to go and I deserve to go. Anybody that's like that should go. Or this guy is probably completely lying because there is no in between. This guy's statements are either psychopath or he is lying, which is essentially where we wanted him to be. 'Cause I want to win this case, I don't want to be somewhere in between.

But just imagine that this guy is even involved in this case—he's a liar. So it sure was a very embarrassing day to have this fucking idiot on the stand saying these things with me in the room—strangling 'em. I was so tired, I started to fall asleep. Anyway, it was not a good day. But I did have a conversation with Mike who has calmed me down some and convinced me that we could really call this guy up and that the statements are not believable. And obviously they're going to know that Oziel is an untrustworthy asshole because all of his girlfriends are going to come in and say, he tried to strangle me, he tried to rape me, he did this, he did that. What are they going to say about this guy? A piece of shit.

The question is, Do they believe that I said these things to him? If they believe that then there's nothing I can do. Other than get on the stand and they'll look at me and go—there's no way this kid could say something like that. No way. Even if—not only could he not say something like that because he is a very private person who wouldn't say those things to anybody even if he felt them but there's no way this kid could ever feel that way to say these things that that could happen. I think it's fucking clear. They have a letter from my brother that showed that's bullshit. But, I don't know. The prick.

Anyway, everybody around the jail is telling me how great the case is going and everybody is calling in telling Jill how magnificent she's been. All this stuff. But it doesn't calm me down. I don't need to burden you with this bullshit.

NORMA: That's OK.

LYLE: Well, it's stressful, overwhelming stuff even for me and I'm in the midst of it. But I'm not letting this guy—this guy is a determined witty liar and I'm not just going to let him try and fuck me over and just sit here and take it. He's up against intellectual fire power, creative determined people and as well as the witnesses we have against him. I'm giving it a lot of thought. We're going to it, we're going to it. I will do what I have to do. This fucking guy is a—thank God that the DA's case fell apart before he took the stand so that they already have a very bad taste in their mouth about their case. That fucking guy—and they think Jill is like a pillar of truth and I come out to be an angel so far—thank God—because they need that cushion when they hear this fucking guy. . . .

I did call the lieutenant today from the jail—who loves me—and "Hey, what's happening Lyle, I hear it's going good." Yeah, yeah, right. Just keep watching TV. And I ask him what's up with the TV sets for me here and he said, "You mean, they didn't take care of that yet? That was supposed to be solved."

I said, "No you went on vacation and nothing happened."

He said, "I'll take care of it." Good. . . .

[The D.A.'s] case is supposed to rest on August 3rd, that's Tuesday I think it is. And Jill said that she would be surprised if they were done before the weekend. That we would probably start our case the following Monday is her guess at this point. 'Cause already we've had to take two days up on just hearing with this guy Oziel. . . .

NORMA: So, your five-month defense was a month and a half?

LYLE: Well, it was four or five months, we figured through November because our feeling was that their case was going to be longer. They said six weeks, it turned into two. That was something we couldn't control, they were saying six. We thought ours was going to be a lot longer, we were going to use a whole bunch of witnesses and then Jill and Leslie felt that because of their case falling apart, we don't need nearly as many witnesses to prove our case. And we want to use only the stronger ones. So that kind of shortened it up quite a bit and then also we had overestimated the case—that's what I didn't realize when I told you—on purpose to give the judge the impression that it was real long so that he doesn't rush us in any way 'cause otherwise he might have said, Well, you said that your case was going to be over in month and lately it's looking like it's going to be two. I'm not letting this guy in, I'm not letting that guy in, this guy's extraneous, we don't need this guy.

We want it to be the other way around where he's expecting four and he's kicking back, he's realizing our case is winding down, he's let us put on whomever we want. Plus he's made rulings that a lot of the experts that we felt were going to be able to come on, can't come in. Like he's not going to—it's clear he's not gonna let an expert testify for me that is not a physical doctor. We were going to have people like the former Miss America person, Paul Mones, people that aren't doctors. So that cut out days, days. All that stuff, so essentially it has been severely short. Actually I think it's going to be a month and a half at least—Jilly said. So it moves along fast. He doesn't allow you to say, OK, take a half day off. He goes, next witness, next witness, next witness. Everyday, nine to five. You go through a gang of witnesses in just a few days.

Although Pam is under this very mistaken impression that I'm a vulnerable witness, she says that she has extensive cross-examination to do on me and we'll have lots of fun. So she doesn't realize how big a mistake that is. She will, in like the first couple of hours. We'll see. Anyway, it will be a short case.

AUGUST 16–DECEMBER 15
1993

$\bullet$

The Defense

After the prosecution rested the defense began their version of the crime. The now familiar "abuse excuse" was used to explain the killings to which the brothers had confessed.

A lengthy list of school teachers, coaches, relatives, and friends of Kitty and Jose described events from the brothers' formative years. The defense also produced two photographs that Lyle said Jose had taken of his sons' genitals when the boys were young. Medical pundits from great distances have appeared, prompting an influx of self-proclaimed abuse victims to attend the trial. And the brothers testified dramatically in their own defense, detailing years of abuse.

The main thrust of the defense was to get the jurors' minds off the two dead parents and onto Dr. Oziel, by discrediting him in every way possible. To that end they produced Oziel's former girlfriend Judalon Smyth, who told the police about the brothers. Spectators were hard pressed to remember who was on trial as Judalon Smyth spewed forth an Ozielorama of sleaze in a little girl's voice. She also had memory problems regarding all she had previously recited regarding the defendants. She attributed the memory failures to brainwashing by Dr. Oziel.

Dr. Oziel withstood the onslought with amazing composure, despite the undisputed fact that his personal and professional life was in extreme disarray.

Rebuttal witnesses were called to refute earlier testimony and bring the trial to a close.

After five months of trial, closing arguments began for Lyle on December 8, and ended on December 10. On December 13, closing arguments began for Erik, and ended on December 15. Both juries listened to long and complicated jury instructions before retiring to deliberate.

September 10, 1993

NORMA: They are saying that you have two days' worth of defense and two days' worth of prosecutors but what's to say that you might go three days with the defense? Nobody knows yet.

LYLE: I'd like to get it over as soon as possible. They're killing me.

NORMA: So, did you like what you heard up 'til now?

LYLE: Yeah. I expected that it would be good. It was a difficult day and I think everybody felt great. Domínick Dunne came up to Michael in the—

NORMA: Which Michael?

LYLE: My Michael.

NORMA: Michael Burt.

LYLE: Before I testified about anything about my dad, just after my mother and the first break. You remember the break, right? He came up after the break and he said he was really sorry that he had no idea.

NORMA: He did? That was good.

LYLE: That was before the next segment. Unfortunately he had already written this very bad *Vanity Fair* article which I know he is regretting with everything that he has, but that's good. I felt that if we could turn around some people like that to some degree.

NORMA: Right, because he already had his opinion formed. This is the problem. People have their opinion before they've heard you.

LYLE: Yeah, they have their opinions but you can turn it around. It's very interesting. I was reluctant to testifying today because I know Jilly and—

NORMA: Well, aren't you glad now. Because I know that you'll feel better. Maybe tomorrow you'll feel better.

LYLE: I felt bad. You know I have my mixed emotions. But anyway, one of the television stations. I know they must be saying good things because I keep hearing good reports from people.

NORMA: Right, I know. One of the reporters just came on the Channel 7 news and she said that "I have just heard the most emotionally devastating testimony that I have ever heard in my twenty years of reporting." And that was a Channel 7 reporter. So that's pretty good.

LYLE: See, what happened was [Jill] wanted to ask me why I killed my parents, right off the bat, for the jurors. She didn't want to start with early childhood. She wanted to let the jurors know what the case was about. It made me very emotional just to talk about that. She wanted to do that in just one minute. And then she wanted—she didn't want to stay there because she didn't want to talk about what had happened in the last weeks. She wants to start from the beginning. So then she immediately jumped back to the beginning. Her feeling was and it was very dangerous to do it because in the first minute of my testimony I don't have any credibility at all. To ask me why I killed my parents in the first minute—I have to say what I said. It's very—if it doesn't come across very well, I'm in trouble.

It came across extremely well. I couldn't have come across better, I don't think, and it was just very—I was crying and I said that I was afraid. And I think even in the first minute people started to say, Well fuck, maybe he was—

NORMA: Oh right. I'm thinking that now. Well, you heard that lady didn't you? Every time you hear one person give their opinion.

LYLE: I don't know what jurors were crying.

NORMA: It was your jurors.

LYLE: Those are the ones he can see.

NORMA: Who? Terry [Moran]? Terry knows who—we recognize who your jurors are—and who are Erik's.

LYLE: Those are the ones he could see. So if he saw people crying it was probably my jurors so he could see best. Because Erik's jurors, they're back of them.

NORMA: The job of Terry Moran—it's his job to look around and make notes of all that's going on in the courtroom and so he knows who was crying and who was not.

LYLE: Too bad we don't have the jurors on film so I could see.

NORMA: We all know your jurors just by looking at a few of them and so Terry does too—even more so because that's his job. I like Terry because he gets everything pretty accurate.

LYLE: Abrahamson does not. Alan Abrahamson you can't trust. The writer for the *Times*. Because there have been times where I was crying where he said I was showing no emotion and times when I wasn't crying and he said I was crying. I can't trust this guy. But Terry Moran is real good. Alan Abrahamson writes good articles for me but he is just not real accurate. I think it would be hard not to cry.

NORMA: You found it hard not to cry?

LYLE: Well I obviously did. I'm saying the people watching. I know the reporters were dying.

NORMA: Did you find that the faces blurred out? Once you got into it?

LYLE: I didn't think about it. I'm back there thinking about the events. I'm picturing the events in my mind and I don't even think I'm in the present world when I'm doing that. I can't think of anything. I don't even know there is Jill. It's amazing that I hear the questions. I'm completely spaced out. The only thing I hear are the questions at all. I just concentrate on not moving around in my chair and not just like falling over or anything like that. Because I—it is very hot and sweating. I thought the blue was a good thing to go with. Blue colors.

NORMA: Yeah, you looked really handsome today. You looked like a handsome college boy. That's the best I've seen you in a long long time, I don't know why because you've been getting dressed up each day you've been in court. I don't see the front of you very much but you looked more handsome today and of course, you know when I see you at the front anyway, you've always got your jail blues on. And so this was a really good chance to see you frontward with your good clothes on.

LYLE: Blue is a good color for me. I've never worn it before on purpose.

NORMA: It was rather formative.

LYLE: We saved it for this. I felt that like a dark color is good and the blue was very effective. We wanted to get through it. I think once we took the pictures up they realized it was true. They didn't even have to hear me and then after they heard me, then obviously they realized it was true but the pictures were very important.

NORMA: One of the women who called in. She'll call you later on—you probably haven't heard yet. But she said that the picture did it for her. The sexual abuse part. And there was only one photograph, wasn't it?

LYLE: There were two.

NORMA: Well, one I could see that was a bit explicit.

LYLE: They were both. One of Erik and one of me.

NORMA: One of Erik? Oh, I didn't see that one then.

LYLE: It was totally explicit. It wasn't fuzzy, it wasn't out of focus. It wasn't like off-center. It was clear and it was clear that the person taking the picture was taking it for that purpose. It wasn't a mistake. It couldn't be—not twice in a row.

NORMA: I was surprised to see Erik in the courtroom today. Was this Weisberg's last-minute change of something?

LYLE: No, his jury was there.

NORMA: I thought one of the juries wasn't going to be there.

LYLE: It was a damn good thing that they were there.

NORMA: Yeah, I think it is a good idea because now—

LYLE: We'll see how well I do because there should be some discussion about limiting Erik's testimony. I don't even think—if I do well enough. If I keep doing well enough, I see no reason for Erik to even go on. Why even risk it? We're not going to be in any better position. They believe what happened. I mean I'm going to blow the cork about what happened the last weekend as well as Erik. Erik will just come in and say the same thing. Why let them have a chance of attacking Erik, who I don't feel is as good a witness.

NORMA: You're worried a little bit—he might—

LYLE: He's fine. They expect him to be fine now.

NORMA: But they expect him to be nervous too.

LYLE: The expectations now after me is that Erik has to be the same.

NORMA: Yesterday I played for Erik the part where they said, "Erik is so vulnerable, is so much the weaker guy compared to Lyle that I think the jury will treat him very tender and expect him to make mistakes when he gets on the stand."

LYLE: I sure hope so.

NORMA: I do too.

LYLE: I think they have a different view of me now. I don't see how they could think of me as very harsh.

NORMA: No, not at all. Especially if you keep it up the way you did today.

LYLE: I just don't have a harsh look or a harsh voice. I think that appearance and tone is very important. You come across as a soft person, it's kind of hard to make you out into anything else unless they have real proof that you are very harsh and they don't. There hasn't been one person that has come forward and said I'm mean or I'm nasty. Everyone who has come forward says I am the most polite person, I stand up when they get up to leave, I'm polite—so even the prosecution witnesses . . . I don't see anything different here. The most complicated issues are to come. In a sense, this was the easy stuff in a way.

NORMA: Because it was kind of real and you got emotional because you were remembering it all.

LYLE: I didn't have to think. What's there to think about? I'm just recalling things that I know—I've been there for years. I just had to just talk. I was surprised that Jill didn't go into more detail because I was prepared to just talk about it. I could talk about it for hours. I would not want to go through it but I could. She left it alone. I'm going to call her now and find out.

NORMA: Well, she might go into a little more of it tomorrow. The main thing you have to prepare yourself for is the prosecution, because like you said this is kind of the easy part even though it is kind of difficult.

LYLE: I don't worry about the prosecution. They never worry me too much. I mean, what are they going to say to me? What are they going to say that I can't answer?

NORMA: I think it is the idea of them changing from topic to topic real quick to make you slip. This is why it is a good idea for you to talk slowly with the defense like I said and that means that you are not thinking—it won't give people the impression—

LYLE: Whoa. I talk about as slow as anyone.

NORMA: Yeah, you did talk real slow today.

LYLE: I think before I answer every question.

September 13, 1993

LYLE: Hello.

NORMA: How are you doing?

LYLE: I'm fucking sick. . . .

NORMA: Were you sick with anticipation?

LYLE: Nerves and I'm sick. I've got the flu. So that makes me tired. I kind of looked a little drugged out and I was tired.

NORMA: Yeah, you did a little. This afternoon you did.

LYLE: And I was so nervous in the break because I was going to have to talk about some difficult things. I was hoping that people would see how I feel about it.

NORMA: I'm sure they did. It's kind of difficult to absorb. You don't want those words to hit your ears. It's the kind of thing you recoil from. When you were talking about your mother, I mean. And so I can imagine how difficult it was to actually say it. 'Cause it is the sort of thing you try to avoid—it's just awful.

LYLE: How did the last thing come over with the limo? 'Cause normally like I tell that story here—'cause I remember when it happened it was fucking brutal. But for some reason because the whole day was so exhausting. I was just spent—I was just totally spent. I just was not like mentally there when I was telling the story but I wanted to know how it came across.

NORMA: You kind of—because you were tired. It came across like that because you were a little tired. I can find that segment for you if you want to call back and I can find it for you and you can hear exactly how you sound yourself.

LYLE: I don't want to hear it. I want to hear the commentary. I don't—did it sound at least like—Do you think they'll believe what I said?

NORMA: Yeah. I do. I did.

LYLE: I feel like at this point I have a very, very high level of credibility. I mean, Friday gave me a lot of credibility.

NORMA: I think one of the things you did a little too much today was blinking.

LYLE: Oh yeah?

NORMA: Sometimes you really blinked in the wrong places like where you were thinking too much. I'm trying to think where you were blinking. You were sort of blinking unnecessarily. Let me think where you were doing that. Blinking too much. Ask Jill if she noticed that.

LYLE: Well, when I cry I blink a lot. That was the problem.

Today I was—Friday I cried very specific times when the pain hit me. But today it was kind of like on and off—on and off. I was feeling the pain all day and then I wouldn't cry for about a half-hour and then I would cry. And it was like hard to . . . At least the second half, my eyes were always watery so—

NORMA: OK, I'll tell you where you were blinking too much. Just before a question was going to be asked of you. You know where you were saying you were bent? Sometimes Jill leaves a long gap after you have said what you have said so that the words sink in. And then that leaves you sitting there and there are no words being spoken. And then that is when you blink a little bit and you kind of nod your head a little too . . . So just try to keep your head a little stiller as though you are really thinking—in deep thought. Because you look like you are preparing yourself pretty well for the next question.

It's really hard to explain but it looks artificial, that's why I'm telling you about it. Just don't blink as much as you do. That's when it happens, right—I think she just leaves you a little too long in between questions and that's why you're doing it. Because maybe you're just a little uncomfortable there.

LYLE: I think it is just because I'm nervous. They can tell. . .

NORMA: Yeah, so just stare at something so your eyes are not blinking. That's the only thing that I noticed that doesn't look credible. And it is nothing much—it's not the kind of thing that everyone would notice anyway because everyone is listening to your words, of course. But I'm just taking more notice than other people, I think.

LYLE: Right. I don't even think about it. It's not like I'm not being credible.

NORMA: It just doesn't look natural. It doesn't look natural blinking too many times and there is nothing getting said.

LYLE: Could be because it is really bright in the courtroom. Alright, I'll think about that.

NORMA: Ask Jill anyway. Just mention it.

LYLE: I wasn't sure if I wasn't going on a little too much when I was talking about my mother's tantrums and I was showing how they—she did with my brother's homework. I think that came across well, I don't know—

NORMA: That was fine. I didn't notice anything out of the ordinary—anything unusual.

LYLE: When I was setting the table.

NORMA: When I go over the tapes again tonight, I'll take an extra look at a couple of things.

LYLE: I'm worried about tomorrow.

NORMA: Why?

LYLE: Because I've got to talk about the actual thing.

NORMA: The actual—or the murder itself? That led up to it you mean. That's got to be difficult for you. I don't know whether Erik is better off or worse off now. What do you think? I think—because everyone is really riveted to what you're saying, you know.

LYLE: I think he is much better off. Because let's say Erik doesn't do well. I've carried a lot of people already.

NORMA: Yes, but I think people might get bored listening to Erik if they've heard it already from you. So with you, you've got all of the attention of the courtroom. So it's an advantage for you. I thought it was going to be worse for you but it isn't 'cause everyone is really listening to what you're saying.

LYLE: It's an advantage if you do it well. If you're not doing well, it's a disadvantage. If I just sit there going uh . . . uh . . .

NORMA: Well, I knew you could do it anyway because you always showed a lot of confidence before. I was amazed when you—no, you didn't even stutter or anything, in your very first scenes last Friday. I was absolutely amazed. I didn't think you could do it. That was the most surprising—that was the biggest surprise I've had in a long time. 'Cause I never thought you would carry it off the way you did.

LYLE: They said that it was some of the more amazing testimony that people had ever heard. I've heard—I don't know what it is—I've seen kids on the stand here and there who are abused and stuff like that. I don't know, maybe they just haven't been worked on enough to get the pain out. Because I don't know—it's not the same as—I mean that was really affecting everyone around me. Maybe some of it was also the fact that my brother was involved. Because there was a play going on between my brother and I think the jurors were affected by that.

NORMA: A lot of the tears—when you have been crying and been upset and stuff. I know it's hard for you to go back and stuff. You're going to have to cry like that when you are talking about that particular day. Not just like when something bad is happening to you because I don't want people thinking you are a whiner or something, crying just about your own problems. I want you to cry about your mom and dad as well because some people called up and commented that you didn't cry when the photographs were showing. I'm thinking to myself, Well that's because you didn't even want to look at them. 'Cause you had your head down, didn't you?

LYLE: I was sobbing through the whole thing.

NORMA: Oh, I couldn't see from where I was. . . .

LYLE: Yeah, I was sobbing in the holding tank. And I would come out and I wouldn't be sobbing. It was a very difficult day. I don't think that anybody in the actual courtroom could—it was not about how stirred up I was over the pictures. If you would have been in . . . well you were in the actual courtroom but you couldn't see my face. It was killing me. I was slumped over. I was fucking . . . It was bad. The jurors were kind of like—the jurors didn't seem to be affected at all. The fucking coroner was making jokes.

NORMA: You could barely see the photographs anyway. They weren't even blown up very much anyway. Compared to some of the criminal cases they show on Court TV. The photographs are humongous. It is just as well they didn't.

LYLE: They really did a bad job with that.

NORMA: It's just as well they didn't blow them up. I don't think the jurors got a good look at them anyway.

LYLE: I don't think they did. My jury was in the back too. I'm going to give Jill a call and—I think I'll call back in and see if there is anything. Okay?

NORMA: Alright then. Don't forget about that tomorrow then, when you are talking about your mom or your dad.

LYLE: Unfortunately I don't have a switch. If I had a switch, I'd be fine. But I don't. I just have to go with what I feel. That's why I was so nervous during the break today because I was like—I got to talk about this stuff with my mom. In my head, it comes, the pain inside you, but that is no guarantee that it's going to come up. When you get nervous you automatically start thinking about other things. You're not concentrating. You don't feel it. That's the sort of thing that is really surprising people is that I seem to be consistently showing that pain—it just seems to be there all the time. And hopefully that will continue to be tomorrow. I think it will because I'm tired, I'm worn down.

NORMA: It's funny how they only need to distract you and they can knock the whole feeling out of you. Like today when the judge interrupts and says—or somebody objects to your question. That's enough to knock you off the emotional feeling and then the tears didn't just come like they were just going to. Just some slight interruption, I know.

LYLE: Good, listen, I'll call you a little later.

NORMA: Don't forget to listen to your messages. Bye.

October 2, 1993, morning

[Editor's note: Prior to this date, the police had contacted all local gun stores requesting them not to give out information regarding 1989 gun sales.]

NORMA: Do you want me to talk, or do you want to talk?

LYLE: No, you talk.

NORMA: OK.

LYLE: I don't want him to know I'm on the phone.

NORMA: Alright.

LYLE: . . . And you can say you're with, uh, you're a reporter from the *Mind's Eye,* or whatever, and you . . .

NORMA: Mm-hmm . . .

LYLE: . . . you just want to get this information.

NORMA: OK. This 708—?

LYLE: You can say it's with regard to my case, I mean, I don't care. But don't ask unless he, he asks why.

NORMA: So I dial a "one" first?

LYLE: Yeah.

NORMA: OK, and then just ask him when was the last time they sold—

LYLE: . . . ask for Jim Peters, and just ask, uh, if he could please put you . . .

NORMA: Are you talking about handguns now?

LYLE: Handguns, yeah.

NORMA: Yeah.

LYLE: . . . if he could put you in touch with somebody who, uh, would know that information.

NORMA: OK, then. Alright, I'll . . . [ringing telephone] OK.

LYLE: Say, say you were referred by the manager in West L.A. [ringing telephone] The manager of the Sportmart in West L.A. referred you.

SPORTMART OPERATOR: Operator.

NORMA: Yeah, hello?

OPER: One moment.

NORMA: OK. [background noise/static] There are early callers today, calling in already.

LYLE: Yeah?

NORMA: Mm-hmm . . .

LYLE: I thought Erik did real well.

NORMA: Yeah.

OPER: Can I help you?

NORMA: Yeah, hi. Uh, this is Sportmart, isn't it?

OPER: Yes, it is . . .

NORMA: Oh, OK. Oh, alright. Do you sell, you sell sports guns, right?

OPER: Sports—?

NORMA: Guns?

OPER: Guns?

NORMA: Yeah.

OPER: I don't know, you'd have to talk to the store.

NORMA: Oh, OK, then. Do, do you have a number to put me through?

OPER: Which store did you want?

NORMA: Guns, and, uh, sports guns.

OPER: At what store?

NORMA: Oh . . . um, the West L.A. store?

OPER: Oh, wait a minute . . .

NORMA: Do you have a West—?

OPER: You're calling Chicago, did you know that?

NORMA: Oh, really?

OPER: Are you calling from California?

NORMA: Yes, right. OK, I'll find a, a nearer number to call, if you—do you have any numbers on hand?

OPER: 31—You can call the office there, if you want.

NORMA: OK, give me that one. [The operator gives her a number.] OK. Thank you very much. [Norma hangs up.]

LYLE: Hello?

NORMA: I wondered where the hell that number was.

LYLE: Norma, what the *hell* did you just do?

NORMA: [laughing]

LYLE: Norma?

NORMA: What?

LYLE: Did you listen to anything I said before you called?

NORMA: Yeah . . . I thought you wanted me to ask . . .

LYLE: I said call the fucking office, ask for Jim Peters, the guy who represents Sportmart, the regional manager, and tell him—

NORMA: Oh, *ask* for Jim Peters—

LYLE: —and tell him that you were referred by a store in West L.A., by the manager, to his number, and ask him if—when was the last time they sold handguns at Sportmart. What was the year and month, and when—

NORMA: Oh, I see. OK . . . OK, yeah.

LYLE: —they were actually selling handguns. What the *fuck* was that?!

NORMA: [laughing] I remember your asking me to do . . . yeah, I remember—

LYLE: Jesus Christ!

NORMA: Sure—I remember you saying Jim Peters . . .

LYLE: I would have had Marco do it . . . I would have had Marco do it, but I, I wanted to call someone with intelligence.

NORMA: I know, but I wanted to—I just wanted to find out if they—when was the last time they sold them.

LYLE: First of all, what the *fuck* is a sports gun? OK, what the fuck is a sports gun?!

NORMA: Uh . . .

LYLE: You know what?

NORMA: [giggles] A gun that you go out and shoot reindeer with.

LYLE: Norma, you are a, you are fucking retarded.

NORMA: A gun that you shoot reindeer with, right? That's a sports gun.

LYLE: What? It's Sport*mart*. It's a *handgun*. Oh, my God . . .

NORMA: Well . . .

LYLE: I guess it could've been worse—you coulda asked for a hand*mart*. Norma, you know, you are crazy. Now listen . . .

NORMA: [sighs, laughing] I was . . .

LYLE: Now listen. Just call—call the fucking number again.

NORMA: Again—the same one.

LYLE: And just say you were referred to them. And ask for Jim Peters. Don't ask for anybody else.

NORMA: Oh, OK.

LYLE: Ask for Jim Peters, and if he's not there, then ask to talk to somebody who can tell you when the last time they sold *handguns* in Los Angeles Sportmart stores—

NORMA: OK.

LYLE: —and what the month and year was, and no particular type, just handguns.

NORMA: OK.

LYLE: OK?

NORMA: Mm-hmm.

LYLE: Alright. Thank you.

NORMA: Alright. [laughing]

LYLE: You wish you would never . . .

NORMA: Yeah . . . Hello?

V.O.: [voicemail system] Thank you for calling Sportmart . . .

OPER: Operator.

LYLE: Yes. I'm calling for some information, uh, about, Sportmart. Uh . . .

OPER: One, one moment . . . [background noise/static] Hi. I'm sorry.

LYLE: Hello? Yes, I'm calling for some information about some stores in Los Angeles—some Sportmarts stores?

OPER: Okay. What did you need to know?

LYLE: I needed to know the last time, uh, Sportmart stores in Los Angeles carried handguns.

OPER: Just a moment. [background noise/static] One moment, sir. [noise/static] Hang on for someone to help you. One moment.

LYLE: I appreciate it. [noise/static]

OPER: One moment. [noise/static]

JIM P: Hello, this is Jim Peters. May I help you?

LYLE: Uh, yes. Mr. Peters.

JIM P: Yes.

LYLE: Uh, I am a reporter from the *Mind's Eye* magazine, and I was calling to find out when the last time Sportmart stores in Los Angeles carried handguns.

JIM P: Uh, may I ask you why you're asking?

LYLE: Uh, yes. There's a case in Los Angeles that it has to do with.

JIM P: And, are you do—writing an investigative piece on it, or—what are you doing?

LYLE: I'm writing a reportive piece on the—from the *Mind's Eye* article.

JIM P: Mm-hmm.

[Editor's note: The transcript ends here; most likely the tape ran out. The transcripts resume a little later; Lyle and Norma are still trying to find out about the handguns.]

October 2, 1993, afternoon

LYLE: Boy, oh boy. There is an employee that has been here seven years, maybe he would know. If Jim doesn't know what's going on—

NORMA: Right.

LYLE: Jeez, what's happening?

NORMA: So, am I back to Number One investigator again?

LYLE: You? No, you are still low, low on the totem pole. If you can come up with a reason why Jim won't talk to anybody. . . .

NORMA: We still didn't get the friggin' information anyway.

LYLE: Unbelievable.

NORMA: I know.

LYLE: Sorry I yelled at you.

NORMA: Anyway there's a Sportmart in Sepulveda— Sepulveda Boulevard.

LYLE: Don't call anymore stores.

NORMA: There are no more.

LYLE: Don't call anymore because we don't want to start . . .

NORMA: Oh, no—absolutely love.

LYLE: We don't want a panic—we should have called Friday immediately. Stupid fucking lawyers! OK, what do we say? What do we say? My feeling is that they sold them. They would just say no if they didn't. Don't you think? If they did sell them.

NORMA: Yeah. Won't this guy know? Because he's worked for Sportmart for seven years. See, I was wondering how long Sportmart has been in existence. So if he's been there seven years, that's pretty good. I thought it was a new store or something—you know—three or four years old.

LYLE: It's been there seven years? OK—great. So we'll call him after 5:00.

NORMA: OK, so I'll call now then. Do you want to do the talking?

LYLE: Is his name Jim?

NORMA: Yes, Jim. He's the part-time guy that works 5:00 'til 9:00.

LYLE: Alright. Yeah, is this Jim?

PAUL: No, it's not. It's Paul.

LYLE: OK, is Jim there?

PAUL: Yes he is. Hold on.

LYLE: OK.

JIM: Hello, can I help you?

LYLE: Is this Jim?

JIM: Yeah.

LYLE: OK, hey. I have a question for you. They told me that you've been working there a long time.

JIM: Yeah, I have.

LYLE: OK. I wanted to know something. Do you know when you guys stopped selling handguns? Do you know what year that was?

JIM: Oh, I don't know the exact year but . . .

LYLE: We're you selling them in 1989? Do you know that?

JIM: Yeah, started in '87—

LYLE: You started in '87?

JIM: Yeah, the beginning of '87. I think we got rid of them—

LYLE: Were you still selling them when you came off?

JIM: I was selling them when they came in '87. We were selling them. I sold a lot of them too. I think we started, like at the beginning of '89 we stopped carrying them. It might have been the beginning of '87—I can't be sure. But—

LYLE: The beginning of '87?

JIM: Yeah.

LYLE: I'm trying to—someone said they had purchased a gun from you in late '89 and I just wanted to know if that were about—

JIM: Who would this be that I am speaking to right now?

LYLE: Who are you speaking to right now?

JIM: Yeah.

LYLE: Paul Novelli.

JIM: OK.

LYLE: I called in the morning and they said that the person that would know would be yourself.

JIM: Yeah, yeah. I think it was in the beginning or middle of '89—can't be for certain though. I can probably—

LYLE: Is there anyway to check?

JIM: I can probably check and see if there was any of the old records—

LYLE: Do you think you can do that for me? I would really appreciate it.

JIM: Yeah, and what is this referring to so I can have an idea of what's going on?

LYLE: No, just a person that I am thinking of purchasing a gun from has said that he—you know—just trying to verify where he got it.

JIM: He doesn't have any—

LYLE: He didn't buy it from your store but—uh—he said he bought it in 1989—

JIM: But did he say he bought it from here?

LYLE: At Sportmart.

JIM: He didn't say which one?

LYLE: No he didn't say which one but I—I figured that you know if I could find someone who had been there long enough they would let me know—since they know the way to find out. I called the—like the local office or whatever for Sportmarts and they knew that it was a couple of years ago and it was—really . . .

JIM: Too far back. The majority of the time what they do— they have the reports because we send the majority of the paperwork back to the regional office and what—I think they hold on to it for like three years you know, from the—but I can see the log books maybe—it might have some in it. Do you know what this person's name is?

LYLE: I only know the first name is Jeffrey. I haven't gone that far with him because I wanted to verify this fact first. I'm a little uneasy about it.

JIM: OK—

LYLE: How long do you think it would take—should I call back?

JIM: Yeah, call back in about ten minutes at most.

LYLE: Sure, I'll do that. Fine, thank you.

JIM: Is it called '87? Or whatever?

LYLE: It was purchased in August of '89 and I—according to him—and I wanted to know if . . .

JIM: And what?

LYLE: I wanted to know if you still displayed handguns in August of '89 and sold them.

JIM: What model was this?

LYLE: I'm not sure—that you were selling any at that time and you had them in the display cases—then that would be good enough for me to go forward with it.

JIM: Alright, I'll see what I can find.

LYLE: I appreciate it. Bye.

NORMA: Alright. Well, we could call back anyway if you want. He said ten minutes right?

LYLE: Yeah, I'll give him a half-hour or twenty minutes.

NORMA: OK.

LYLE: Sure sounds like they do, huh?

NORMA: Sounds like they did.

LYLE: Sounds like it's going to be close. Ha ha.

NORMA: Can't be close can it?

LYLE: Huh?

NORMA: It can't be close, it has to be August of '89.

LYLE: Yeah, I know.

LYLE: The only thing he [Erik] has to take back essentially in a way is that the guy said—he didn't even say that the guy said that. He said that he thought that the pellet guns were on the right and the handguns were on the left. And he said he really wasn't sure about that. He said he thinks that that's what he remembers but he is not sure. Remember that he is recalling this conversation thinking that they do sell handguns. That's what he left the store thinking. That's what he thought when he was on the stand. So he's not even thinking about—well I'd better be accurate to say I wasn't positive they were handguns because he thinks that they were.

NORMA: Yeah, he'll have to say that once he realized that you have to wait fifteen days he kind of lost interest and didn't concentrate on much else he was saying—that the guy was saying.

LYLE: Yeah, he's always said that the main thing he walked from the store with was the two weeks. He also remembered the glass case and where everything was. If he thinks he remembers that they were pellet guns and real guns, well it's easy that they could have all been pellet guns and he just didn't know. It's very possible that the guy knew very well that there was a two-week waiting period because they had just sold him—they had just stopped selling them. They probably had just stopped selling them for that reason because it was a pain in the ass and everybody had to wait two weeks. The obvious place I think would be that Sportmart sold them.

NORMA: Yes, but is there a Sportmart in the area, in the Beverly Hills area, Santa Monica area?

LYLE: No, there's a Sportmart exactly where Erik says the store was—two blocks from the freeway on Santa Monica.

NORMA: A Sportmart shop? Really?

LYLE: Yeah. Yeah.

NORMA: That would be handy if he could verify '89.

LYLE: I remember the problem was that the Sportmart people are fucking not being helpful are they?

NORMA: The Sportmart? It's a big shop is it—like Big 5? Have you seen the size?

LYLE: What? Yes.

NORMA: So it could be confused with Big 5 even.

LYLE: They are like the same store. Yeah. In other words huge. Sportmart—I think that Sportmart would be the best. But—

NORMA: If we could, yeah, if they sold the gun at that time.

LYLE: But if they don't, I think that pellet gun thing—

NORMA: Good thing he was a little vague when he was giving that—when he was giving his answers. Just that conversation piece is a little bit—dodgy. Where he actually had a conversation—because you know how Lester reads it back word for word.

LYLE: Yeah, I know, but you know, I figure, I think that Lester has also given a false impression. But I think that Lester has given an impression that there were no guns there at all anymore. There was not even anything that could be taken for guns. And that's a lie. That's a—

NORMA: So you think there were still pellet guns there then?

LYLE: There still are now. They have pictures of it.

NORMA: Oh good. OK.

LYLE: They're going to bring the guns in—we bought a couple of them. And we're bringing them in to show the jury, hey, these look like guns. You can't fucking tell the difference unless you are an expert.

NORMA: Right, I do remember that Erik said that I think the real guns were on the left and I think the other pellet guns. So he didn't say that the guy said that these are real and these are pellet. He didn't say the guy said that. He's just saying that, isn't he? Himself.

LYLE: Right, in fact he said that he pointed to a gun and said, "I want that one" and the guy said, "It's a pellet gun."

NORMA: Yeah, right. So he assumed that the others on the other side were real.

LYLE: So, obviously it would be better if they just sold

handguns but I think that does enough to show that he's not lying. It doesn't prove that he's lying.

NORMA: It proves—the thing is—even if he got messed up over the gun—he can still—they still can't prove that he didn't go in—that you two didn't go in with the intention of getting handguns. They can't disprove that. That's the bottom line. Even if that conversation was a little bit of hearsay—it doesn't matter— the fact is they can't disprove that you weren't there and that's the thing that you've got to keep in your mind.

LYLE: Exactly. And you know what I think I'll do is on redirect is have Leslie read back his testimony to save Lester the trouble. Have Leslie read the testimony back and read the part where he says that he thought that they were on the left and that the guy—the only thing the guy says was that that's not a pellet—that that's not a real gun, it's a pellet gun. And read it back. And the description and the crossbows and everything. And then show the pictures and then bring in the gun and then let Lester do what he wants to do with that. I think that's the best way to go. And skip this whole . . .

NORMA: It's worth a try—it's worth a shot you know.

LYLE: Well, Lester is the one with the burden—he's going to have to fucking prove otherwise. Once you've got pictures and the guy said there was crossbows and there is crossbows in the pictures. And then there's—then they got the case that he describes exactly and they've got all these guns there and you know that's pretty much the way he said it.

NORMA: Do you think Jill will go for it?

LYLE: Jill? I think Leslie is making the call on this. We don't have any choice. If we could use the Sportmart, great. Otherwise, what other choice did we have?

October 12, 1993

LYLE: This has been a good day. So we will see. I've got another good one coming up later today.

NORMA: So who's in this afternoon anyway?

LYLE: Traci Baker is coming in next.

NORMA: She is? Traci? Now which one is . . . Where was she involved in the case?

LYLE: She's one of my ex-girlfriends.

NORMA: Yeah I know. But where was she involved? What kind of evidence is she going to give?

LYLE: She's going to talk about my mother poisoning the family—she'll be pretty good actually.

NORMA: Your mother was poisoning the family?

LYLE: Yeah.

NORMA: Or trying to I mean, cause obviously you are still here.

LYLE: My dad would leave—he wouldn't eat the food. So she was there one time—

NORMA: I didn't hear that before except when I heard it the other day.

LYLE: She'll testify to that. A couple of people have talked about that. That will be about it for her. That's where my mother assaulted her a little bit so that will come out a little.

NORMA: Was she the one that your mother objected to or something?

LYLE: No—she objected to all of them.

[*Editor's note:* Below is a transcript of a letter Lyle sent Traci Baker. The last page is missing.]

LAW OFFICES   Feb 5
Ms. Baker

Alright Traci this is the information we discussed on the phone about visiting Erik. Im going to get right to the point because after you read this and feel youve absorbed it, I want you to throw it away. Do that right away so you dont forget. Maybe you can take some notes in your own hand writing. OK well basically there are two incidents. They may seem strange and irrelavent to my case but I assure you they will be very helpful. Youll just have to trust me on it. Later on I can explain why but for now Ill just lay them out. I have given alot of thought to this and I really feel that you can do it however just let me know if youd rather not. Alright the first incident is as follows. You were at my Beverly Hills house about to eat dinner with me, my parents and my brother. Ed wasnt there. We will decide later around what date this incident occurred. It was a weekend however. (I hate writing in pen) You and I had spent the day together. Mrs. Menendez had cooked dinner and it was served in the dining room. Everyone was seated except Mrs. Menendez. She was still bringing this and that in from the kitchen . . . next to me with your back to the . . . seated at the head of the table to my left. Erik was seated accross from us. Behind Mr Menendez were the doors that open to the foyer. All the food was on the table. There was lots of it but you don't remember what the food was. Anyway all of a sudden Mr Menendez said in a stern voice to Mrs. Menendez who was standing behind you, "what did you do to the food?!" There was a long silence or at least it seemed long and then Mr Menendez shoved his plate forward, knocking over some stuff. He got up and said something like "go out and wait for me by the car boys, we're going out to eat." Then I got up immediately and said "come on Traci" and we both walked out into the foyer. Erik walked out too. You got your purse and jacket. We walked outside and stood in front of the big mercedes. Erik and I were discussing something, whispering. You were just kind of standing there confused and embarassed. Then Mr Menendez came storming out of the house. He seemed upset. Either Erik or I (you cant remember which) said to him "What's the matter Dad, you think she tried something?" As Mr Menendez was getting into the front seat he said, "I don't know, but I dont trust her today." We all got in the car, you and I in the back seats and we drove in silence listening to some radio station. We made a right coming out of our house but youre unsure the way we went after that. Anyway we ended up parking somewhere and eating at Hamburger Hamlet. It was a big one. We all ate dinner talking about various things. Mr Menendez was charming. He paid the bill. We drove back home. You and I stayed out front and kissed for a long time. You didnt feel you should ask about what had happened earlier. You then left in your car. It wasn't that late. You never saw Mrs Menendez. (It had just gotten dark when we left for Hamburger Hamlet.) You drove home still confused about what had happened in the dining room, although it seemed obvious Mr Menendez thought Mrs Menendez did something to the food. You were dying to ask me what it was all about but you just couldn't. OK, thats the first incident. You really dont need to know anymore detail than Ive provided here. It was a long time ago. It would be strange if you remember things too well. However you do remember the statements I mentioned above very well--who said what to whom. You dont remember the unimportant conversations like what was said at Hamburger Hamlet ect. The best answer to any question you dont know the answer to is, "I dont remember." Its obvious why you remember certain things and certain statements. It was scarey and confusing . . .

October 25, 1993

[Editor's note: This is three days before Dr. Oziel is due to testify for the second time.]

LYLE: I'm dying to talk to Jill and Michael but I can't reach anybody.

NORMA: Oh, right. They're out?

LYLE: Yeah, Can you imagine that, three fucking—a couple days before you are supposed to testify? It's the biggest case in the DA's office and they fucking try to revoke [Oziel's] license. Oh my God.

NORMA: Yeah, things are getting pretty murky.

LYLE: You would think that the DA's office would have enough pull to say, listen—fucking wait two weeks—a fucking murder trial, we need the guy's testimony.

NORMA: Well, yeah but he . . .

LYLE: I mean it's been four years, right? You would think if they hadn't done it in four years, they could wait two more weeks.

NORMA: Well, I think "Primetime," the other night when it

was on was really bad for him, like I told you. Remember the girls were all on saying how he was violent.

LYLE: All those girls were on a year and a half ago.

NORMA: Were they? On, this is the first time I had seen it.

LYLE: No, that was just a rehash. That wasn't even nearly as good as the original show.

NORMA: Well, I don't know what's going on then, or if they found out something else about him.

LYLE: Yeah, they must have investigated it thoroughly.

NORMA: Oh, course, because now that he is in the public eye, his background is really gone into with a fine-tooth comb.

LYLE: Part of it is that Jill and Leslie took his girlfriend that we have, Alex. And they went to the state authorities and they started the process to revoke his license and went before the committee. And nothing came of it. And that was like a year ago. It just takes awhile. I guess they decided, you just had to be—maybe it is a coincidence. It just seems to me that they must have said to themselves, You know what, we're going to revoke this guy's license. Let's try and do it before he gets on the stand, cause that's not fair.

NORMA: Do you think it will stop him though, Lyle, from going on the stand?

LYLE: Oh, no. They can't stop him. He'll testify but I hope, and I haven't asked Michael yet, that we can bring up the fact that they are revoking his license. I don't know that we can. The judge may say that's irrelevant.

NORMA: I'm sure that the jury is going to hear about it anyway. Because people—

LYLE: I imagine that it's relevant though. It's got to be. His credibility is relevant and if the state is investigating him for— wants to revoke his license.

NORMA: I bet Leslie is slapping her knees in glee.

LYLE: Oh my God. You know the prosecutor has got to be—I mean they got to be dying.

NORMA: Yes because on the 4:00 news it wasn't mentioned and neither was it mentioned on the 5:00 news. And Art Rascon got you two mixed up again. He said that Erik shouted, "Shoot,

shoot, shoot." Instead of—he did that once before as well, a couple of months ago.

LYLE: I think Cignarelli is such a liar although I don't know if Cignarelli is lying, my brother just told him—

NORMA: I know. It was a damning six words.

LYLE: You never know. But I heard on the news, they said that he said that Erik told him it was for the money. But he testified at the Grand Jury that he told him it was for the money. And that's not true.

NORMA: Isn't it?

LYLE: At the Grand Jury he testified that Erik never said that. They're getting it mixed up. The police put in the report that he said that and he actually called the police back and said I did not say that. And so as soon as he sticks to that story, it'll be okay.

NORMA: Well, you'll have to—are you talking to Erik tonight?

LYLE: I don't know—Beatrice isn't home, Harry isn't home. Listen, I need to call a coach of mine in New Jersey. I need to call a girl in Florida. Both are very important. So I need you to do that for me because my credit card is not working directly on the phone for some reason.

NORMA: Do you think it must be lack of payment, Lyle?

LYLE: My credit card was working. You know that little twenty-cents number, every once in awhile instead of ringing to the MCI operator, you just get a busy signal. I haven't figured out if the busy signal is because it is busy there or because this phone is—

NORMA: Might be too similar sounds.

LYLE: The general phone doesn't allow you to do that—it just cuts you off and my concern is that if I keep trying, they will shut the phone off.

NORMA: Yeah, well, if you try the same number through me then, will that verify whether it's the jail's phone or not? It will, won't it?

LYLE: Could be, why don't you try it?

NORMA: OK, I'll get my pen. You know, I got a pen the other day through the mail for nothing—one of those that you stick on the phone. The pen is there permanently so all I need now is paper.

October 26, 1993, evening

NORMA: It's 8:00 already.

LYLE: Oh, I got back late.

NORMA: You got back late? Oh did you? Did you have a discussion after everyone left? Or were you just waiting for the van a long time?

LYLE: Just waiting for the van.

NORMA: OK. So how are you feeling?

LYLE: Alright.

NORMA: Were you very happy with the tape being played—or was it okay with you?

LYLE: I don't know.

NORMA: You were very—

LYLE: I'd like to hear the Court TV reaction if there is a commentary.

NORMA: Do you mean you'd like to hear Terry Moran's commentary and stuff? Yeah, I thought it was little dicey where—somebody else pointed this out as well—where you say I wouldn't have killed my mother without Erik's consent. Somebody else emphasized that that sounded like—planned. You know what I mean? It didn't sound too good.

LYLE: I'm talking about a planned murder in the tape. No doubt about that. I'm talking about a planned murder but obvious—the question is—is what I'm saying with Oziel, are we coming up with the truth? If it's not the truth, then it doesn't really matter what is said. That's the point—the whole point to me is that—it's ridiculous for anyone to believe that I killed my mother because I loved her so much and she was suicidal, I wanted to do her a favor. That's ridiculous.

NORMA: You mean—but did you say that on the tape?

LYLE: That's the theory on the tape.

NORMA: Well, didn't you say it?

LYLE: I said it on the tape.

NORMA: Did you? Because I haven't heard the tape.

LYLE: That's what I said. That's what I testified in the trial before this—said Oziel suggested to me that the reason my parents were killed. This is the reason. And I said, "Because it was making Erik feel better," I said, "Yeah, that was the reason." And then he wanted a tape made. I couldn't say no because he would go to the police. So I figured, Alright—I got to make this fucking tape. So we spent a few hours working out what we were going to say and I went with the theory that she was killed because she was suicidal and you know, it's ridiculous but I figured who gives a fuck—it's just for Oziel. Now the tape is here and you know, that's not the prosecution's theory—that she was killed because I loved her. That's totally not the prosecution's theory so I don't know how the tape helps them actually, 'cause they're not—what are they going to do? Go up there and argue that I killed her because I loved her so much—that's ridiculous. So, I don't know what they are going to argue. I didn't like the tape. I was distraught with the whole thing.

NORMA: I didn't hear the tape but when they were playing part of her commentary back to—I heard her saying down on line nine on page such and such—where you said that—what I just said to you.

LYLE: He did a pretty good job, Conte.

NORMA: Who? Conte? Yeah, he did do a good job. Yeah, he was. He was sticking up for you good—it wasn't that he was sticking up for you good, he made sense in his explanations.

LYLE: I just may take the stand and try to explain it myself. I fucking know this case inside and out. I know and I know what happened with my parent's death. So this way, I feel not vulnerable on the stand. Like I can fill in every hole, every question I can answer. Because there is no reason why I shouldn't be able to answer a question. And everything to me makes a lot of sense and I think I can explain easily why the two—nobody should ever believe anything that's on this tape and why it shows that Oziel is lying.

To me it's like Conte couldn't do that well enough. He got the basics down and this and that but I can really show just line by line why this tape clearly doesn't make any sense. I mean under certain—oh that's possible—but as soon as you take a closer look, you know it can't be. And I can show that real clearly. And I speak well, I can do it and I know the case too well. But it's frustrating to be sitting there. I can't fucking say anything. I can't answer the questions for the guy. He gives these fucking answers that are not nearly as good as I can give. They're good—I mean they're okay—but they're not anywhere near as good as I can give. And it's frustrating, we just sit there. You can't get the information out of the guy, you can't pull it out of him.

NORMA: That was three years ago when you did the tape, wasn't it? Four years ago, was it? Three and a half years ago?

LYLE: I can give all the answers. I mean, Oziel knows. You noticed that Oziel is not going to contact the staff.

NORMA: It doesn't matter about friggin' Oziel now and it's got to be a persuasive story for the jury to hear him out. 'Cause he's manipulated you into saying these things. That's what's got to be emphasized.

LYLE: And it's not that he brainwashed me. It's that I was willing to give him what he wanted so he wouldn't go to the police. And I didn't give a fuck. And it worked. I gave him the tape and he never went to the police. It was this bitch that went to the police. It was Judalon that went to the police, not him.

NORMA: You were probably just going along with pleasing him at the time never dreaming that this would actually end up in a courtroom, you see. That's probably what you were doing. Pleasing him.

LYLE: That fucking Oziel never dreamed it would end up in a courtroom either. No way. And he didn't think it was going to end up in a courtroom when he testified earlier in the trial, lying his ass off. Oh, it was because of a perfect murder and all this bullshit. He didn't think this tape was coming out either.

NORMA: That's true.

LYLE: Because he would have said, "Oh man, none of these things are on this tape, so I'd better tone it down a little bit." He did it. He went way off the friggin' end because he figured, Well, who can say that it's not true? And so he went way out on the end and now this tape has come in and to me the tape shows that he was lying. Because there is nothing on there—any of those things that he said in court earlier are not on this tape. None of them. There's no hate—there's no perfect murder—there's no witness—there's no BBC [Billionaire Boys Club] movie. I mean where are all of these things? They just fucking disappear? Where are all these theories that we were hearing all like the last two months? They're gone. All of a sudden they are completely gone. So that should be the highlight of this tape. It shouldn't be focused on this crazy bizarre theory that I killed my mother because I loved her so much which everybody knows just cannot be.

NORMA: I think the prosecution was really disappointed in the tape. 'Cause they were expecting some really good heavy stuff in it.

LYLE: They're disappointed because now they realize that Oziel is a liar. Their star witness is lying. I did not go to him and say, "Oh, yeah, we watched this movie and we had to do the perfect murder so I killed them and I killed my mother because she was there and she was a witness." They actually testified to that under oath and then you listen to the tape and you realize that it's a lot of bullshit. And so now you're left with, well, fuck, now what are we going to do? Like reargue our theory now as this? They're not going to do that. They're going to like—I have no idea what they are going to argue. It should be very interesting.

NORMA: I heard Judalon Smyth saying to Terry—she was telling Terry how Oziel perjured himself every time he opened his mouth, he perjured himself.

LYLE: She reamed him today. I mean, it was clear that she was there on October 31st.

NORMA: I heard quite a bit of her testimony but I haven't heard this morning's yet. 'Cause I went out this morning but I left it on record so I can play some of it back tonight. But I believe listening to the tape was really difficult to hear. So you can't make out what you're saying on the tape. That's why everyone had to have transcripts. To try to follow it better, you know. So I don't suppose I'll be able to hear much either.

LYLE: Listen, do you have anything I can listen to?

NORMA: You can hear Terry. OK—

LYLE: Did they have any call ins?

NORMA: Yeah. How is Erik?

LYLE: He wasn't even in the courtroom.

NORMA: He came in this afternoon. He was outside, napping, I believe.

LYLE: He's dying.

NORMA: I know, they gave a real good quote above his face and he really looked bad. Did he tell you how it happened? He did? It probably was a physical altercation, wasn't it?

LYLE: No, no. He was having a water fight with Todd Bridges [television actor and fellow inmate] and he slipped and he fell on the table and—

NORMA: Oh, did he really? 'Cause no one seems to believe that story about him falling. They think somebody either punched him or threw him into a doorknob.

LYLE: If somebody punched Erik and he had to go through all of this, there would be a lawsuit so big, I mean, everybody in the world would know about it by now. What do you mean, covering up if someone beat up Erik? We would be telling the world.

NORMA: Yeah, well that's what I was saying. You never really find out what goes on in jail. Everybody covers up.

LYLE: —What you're doing with the Menendez brothers.

NORMA: OK, well, I'll talk to you tomorrow and I'll fill you in on the TV reactions.

October 26, 1993, later that evening

NORMA: So everybody is very happy with John Conte.

LYLE: He was awesome. He was great. I mean the best thing about him, you know all these people—the best thing that they can do is make themselves very well liked, and then people think they're smart people, that they—like they need to give the feeling that hey, he would know if I was lying, he would know.

NORMA: I think he gave that impression out already.

LYLE: Once he builds up that credibility just personally like liking him—

NORMA: Then they're just going to swallow everything else he says.

LYLE: Then the main thing is that he just says I believe. And then you walk away like—remember that Conte guy, he was a nice guy, he's smart—he believed. That's what you walk away with. You don't remember everything he says. He, Conte, does a great job of confusing the issues a lot of time. Like he, remember when we were just listening now and the prosecutor said what about the postcard and stuff—it's all documented. He goes, "Well, a lot of it is confusion and hard to understand." You believe him and it is. And you start—the problem for the prosecution.

NORMA: Because it is confusing. He's letting them know that it isn't all well planned out—otherwise you'd come out with stuff that followed in a nice, neat, organized pattern.

LYLE: The other thing he's letting them know is that this case is confusion so how can you reach a real decision? In order for the prosecution to win—it's just part of the defense strategy I think is that they have to prove something that's clear.

NORMA: Absolutely.

LYLE: They can't just say, "Oh yeah, everything is confusing so give them first-degree murder." That doesn't make any sense.

NORMA: 'Cause right now we got a jury that's going to go out there completely confused.

LYLE: They don't know what's going on. They don't know what the hell is going on. What, are they going to believe Oziel? They don't have any—there's no proof of anything. We barraged them with witnesses. Most—90 percent of the trial has been our part of the case. Almost the whole trial has been our side of the case. And we've taken two months and they've taken like four weeks. And that—

NORMA: I know. Well I've never heard of a trial that's gone back into history and family and—everything has been brought into this one, hasn't it? So they're really getting—like he said it's like all in the family.

LYLE: Well, we got all of the family members up there just about.

NORMA: The defense had made a hell of an effort. I'll say that.

LYLE: Really, Jill Lansing is responsible for the whole thing.

NORMA: Is she? More so than Leslie?

LYLE: Yes. That's why you see Jill doing all of the witnesses. She's the one who has talked to them and convinced them to testify. None of these people wanted to testify in the beginning.

NORMA: They didn't? They were probably too nervous.

LYLE: They were nervous or upset, they've grieving. And they're scared. And they meet Jill, they start liking her and they trust her and she convinces them. . . . And then they're gung ho. These people want me out, they would carry me out if they could.

NORMA: Now the—I noticed the deputy was talking to you—he looked like a nice deputy guy—real friendly.

LYLE: The good-looking one? Yeah, he's a good guy.

NORMA: The good-looking one. They were kind of both middle-aged. This afternoon?

LYLE: Oh, you mean this afternoon? Oh, OK. He liked—yeah. Erik said he was getting more mail than me and I said yeah, hate mail. So he came over and he said, "I hear you're getting most of the mail."

I said, "Yeah, well, I get all the girls over twelve—"

NORMA: Remember Dominick leaned over me and said, "That was a nice move Norma, wasn't it?"

I said, "Which?"

He said, "Those deputies there giving the boys their mail."

I said, "Yeah, it was a nice touch, you're right."

I don't think he'd seen that happen before. And he had a lot of good things to say about—Terry Moran had good things to say about Dominick. He was saying, he thought he was very fair, considering he only goes—he's looking at stuff from the outside in, he thought he was pretty accurate in his stuff. This was Terry.

LYLE: Dominick Dunne?

NORMA: Yeah, that Dominick.

LYLE: Actually I'll tell you this, you know what would be better. The problem with postcards is that I can't write anything personal because everybody can read them. You know those postcards that are like, they've got two creases in them and they have like a flap.

NORMA: Yeah.

LYLE: It's a postcard-type thing—it's not really a postcard but you write it and all you do is put one flap and the other flap over so it's kind of a sticker thing. It's open—it's not an envelope but it's closed. If you can find those and there's something that's nice like that and buy me a bunch of them.

NORMA: Listen, why don't I ask Terry to mention that you guys are getting a lot of nice letters from the court and you're getting quite a lot of letters which is going into the hundreds now, and you don't have a stamp machine, and from now on anybody who writes please, you know, give a self-addressed envelope.

LYLE: That's tacky.

NORMA: It's—the money. What about the stamps?

LYLE: No, no no. Let's not do that—that's embarrassing.

NORMA: Embarrassing—you're in friggin' jail.

LYLE: Ask on national TV for people to include stamps—that's ridiculous.

NORMA: Erik was adding up the money the other day and it would have come to $200 just for stamps. And then he got a bunch from Jeffrey and I sent him a bunch in today of stamps.

LYLE: Well, we won't need stamps if you can find these envelopes. These envelopes probably will require stamps—the ones I'm telling you about the ones that fold over. It will need stamps. Forget about the stamp part, just see if you can find that like the way it's designed. Don't worry about the stamps—I got a game—my grandmother gives me a fucking one hundred of them.

NORMA: She does? That's nice to know that you're going to get stamps fairly easily. I don't believe you 100 percent but still—

LYLE: Nobody does. So if you can find that—I can use like as many as you can buy. You know what I'm talking about like the way they fold over?

NORMA: Yeah.

LYLE: What I'm trying to do is cut down on time. I don't have time to like—

NORMA: You don't have time, pardon me laughing but carry on—

LYLE: I know and I have the weekend to—

NORMA: Yeah, I know. Well, what Erik was going to do was just type the same—he was going to write—

LYLE: I don't want to do that. I want to write it myself but I want it to be a quicker process. If you can't find anything that folds over well, then I'll just take basic postcards. Like one hundred—

NORMA: Well, you're not going to write anything personal. You don't even know anybody personal, do you? That's just writing.

LYLE: I write personal things.

NORMA: You don't even know these fucking people—how can you write personal?

LYLE: Because they tell me personal things and I just respond to what they tell me—I mean it's personal, I can't put it on a postcard. It's hard.

NORMA: Well if it's that personal you can write a little letter then and seal it but the others who are just like—

LYLE: Ninety percent of the people are telling me they were abused and these are personal things.

NORMA: But I mean you can't very well discuss it on a postcard even, can you?

LYLE: That's the problem—but if I have something that folds over that nobody else can see when I mail it, that's okay. You know what I mean by foldover.

NORMA: Yeah, it folds over. I understand English very well, you know.

LYLE: Good I'm glad you do. Alright, listen.

NORMA: I'll let you go.

LYLE: Am I going to see you tomorrow at all? Probably not. I'll call you at lunchtime.

NORMA: Are you asking me or are you telling me?

LYLE: I'm asking.

NORMA: Alright, well, I'll be here during the lunch break anyway for you to call and then if I do come over it'll be afterward as usual.

LYLE: OK, I'll call you at the lunch break.

NORMA: Is there anything you need me to bring in? How are you for dimes?

LYLE: I could use some dimes. What day's today? Wednesday?

NORMA: All day.

LYLE: I can use some dimes. I can use a pen with a clock on it but I won't mention it.

NORMA: OK, I'm still looking for you.

November 13, 1993

NORMA: You mean all of us or Jeffrey?

LYLE: I don't particularly like to hear it from anybody but

especially from a guy. You know what I mean? Like somebody that's supposed to be a friend of mine. I mean my attitude is I'm in jail, OK, so that means that I don't always eat what I want to eat. I don't always get enough sleep. I always have a headache a lot of times. I have stomachaches—and I'm in uncomfortable positions a lot—I get depressed occasionally. Those things happen all of the time. So stop asking about it now—that's what I told him. God sakes, I can understand it coming from my grandmother and I've got to put up with it because it's my grandmother, right?

NORMA: Oh yeah, well they're supposed to be fussy hens.

LYLE: Yeah exactly. But everybody else—

NORMA: I know Beatrice is always like a fussy hen. She goes oh, baby, how are you baby?

LYLE: I hear from Beatrice—she's sixty-seven years old. But fucking Jeff? Get the fuck out of here—I mean come on. I told him, this is fucking getting boring. I don't want to fucking call you anymore because I had a fucking day—I don't want a fucking—I can't stand it.

NORMA: Have you seen—have you talked to Erik?

LYLE: No.

NORMA: I was wondering how his kidney is coming along.

LYLE: I have no idea. No doubt he'll come in tomorrow for the appointment.

NORMA: You doubt it? Oh, he is. Oh, yeah it's Judalon Smyth again isn't it? I left you a message to see if you were warm enough.

LYLE: Why?

NORMA: I wondered if you still had those underclothes—thermals.

LYLE: Oh, yeah, I got those. No, I got plenty of them.

NORMA: That's what I wanted to know. Because it was fucking freezing when I called you. It was 4:00 in the morning.

LYLE: It's warm in here.

NORMA: Oh, really? 'Cause I was in the house and I was freezing, 'cause the fire had gone out and no more logs to burn.

LYLE: It was OK.

NORMA: As long as you're OK and warm. Did you get an extra blanket or anything?

LYLE: I mean, here we go. Did I not just spend ten minutes telling people that I don't want to hear, "Did you get an extra blanket?" You know what I mean?

NORMA: Alright. Give us my fucking words back.

LYLE: Are you fucking paying attention or what?

NORMA: Yeah, alright.

LYLE: I'm not finished yet because I'm sure I'll hear the same thing. Is it cold in there? Click. From now on if I ever hear that, I'm hanging up. . . .

NORMA: Well, do you need anything in the way of envelopes?

LYLE: No, I'm OK. I'm fine. You know I do need like—you're not even coming down—well, maybe you can come down. I need a thick black magic marker—the kind that . . .

NORMA: I've got a beauty here, Lyle. You've never seen a thicker marker this big in all your life. It's so thick, I don't even know if they're going to let you have it. It's like a quarter of an inch wide.

LYLE: I don't need it that big. A quarter of an inch? That's nothing. Yeah, I can take that.

NORMA: You can? OK, cause it's—the pen is so pretty fat— it's about an inch and a half 'round in diameter.

LYLE: That's fine. I don't need it that thick.

NORMA: Well, how far away are you from the guy that you're showing the message to? Give me an idea—distance.

LYLE: I just—you know what a regular fat black marker—it only comes in one size really.

NORMA: No, there's lots of sizes.

LYLE: Generally there's just one size. There's a regular size of magic marker and then there's the thick magic marker.

NORMA: OK, so you want that thick one.

LYLE: About the size of a highlighter.

NORMA: OK, so this is just a little thicker than that even so that's why I was telling you about it.

LYLE: I don't need it that thick.

NORMA: Alright, I'll get you the regular one—

LYLE: It's got to be waterproof though. It's got to be the kind that's kind of toxic—it's waterproof. You can't wash it off, it like stays on clothing forever.

NORMA: OK.

LYLE: And I actually could use it tomorrow—I need it tomorrow.

November 16, 1993

NORMA: So even though Judalon Smyth turned up turning you in, she's turning out to be pretty good for you in the end.

LYLE: Yeah. Well she's in love with Michael.

NORMA: Oh, she is? She's always in love with somebody. She needs a relationship, she said, didn't she, today?

LYLE: She's pretty, though.

NORMA: Yes, she is. She's attractive. She's got like a really young voice, hasn't she? When I heard her on the tape one time before, when she first came on. When they were playing what she was saying to Oziel, she sounds about twelve years old. Really young voice.

LYLE: I know she does.

NORMA: Can you—

LYLE: Well, I don't want to listen anymore. That's good enough. I guess Terry seemed to feel that it was good. It's not damaging that I say it was a mercy killing, because nobody is going to believe that. The dog thing is bad, but I mean, I thought Conte did real well with that.

NORMA: I don't think it's going to be something that's going to stick out in people's minds anyway, really.

LYLE: I think it will because they're going to have transcript in the jury room. They were listening carefully. There is no—the DA—'cause we would do nothing with it. But it's just that it's sort of there. You kind of feel like, fuck, maybe I should get up there and really bury this thing. Really just say that this is a joke, saying that you can't possibly put any weight on this, let me explain to you exactly how this was made.

NORMA: And emphasize the fact that you were doing it all.

LYLE: Exactly why I made it. This is what I was thinking when I made it. And this is why it comes out the way it does. Maybe just put it to rest, instead of all this mystery. And then they can evaluate my credibility—you know, I always come off. I think I come off very credible on the stand. So I assume I would again. There's nothing to get emotional about, I don't have that pressure. It's just explaining the tape.

NORMA: Right. And you did come over very credible. 'Cause even Dominick Dunne who never believed you from the very beginning was moved by your testimony and he's a real critic of yours, isn't he? And so, he believed you.

LYLE: And one-on-one with Bozanich, I went. Only last time I tore her up the first day, when I was fresh and we went over cross-examination. I mean everybody was saying that she just was destroyed. And I think I can really beat her on this one too because I don't think she has any clue what this tape means. And I think I can, I know it inside and out. So you would think if you put me in the ring with her, I would do well. And so I don't know. I want to go in there. I mean, there are some drawbacks to it, like you just, she'll ask me about the burglary thing and I'll have to talk about that. She might ask me about—

NORMA: I don't think the burglary thing has a lot of importance anymore, do you?

LYLE: I don't know. It came up today for the first time.

NORMA: What importance does it have though?

LYLE: I don't think it's relevant to anything. It's just a bad fact. I was pissed about the burglary coming out. Oh, yeah, what was I doing? I couldn't believe it either, I was just like—this is fucking amazing—$80,000. Give me a fucking break. These fucking people lied so bad on their insurance forms, it's not even funny. We took like some stuff and they put $80,000. Unfucking believable.

NORMA: I thought it was $100,000 your dad paid back.

LYLE: My dad paid $12,000 back. All he paid back is $12,000. We had a document, we had to check, $12,000 fucking is it.

NORMA: How's does that go?

LYLE: I want to bring that in but the problem is that I don't want to bring it in if it means that I've got to go through every fucking thing in his receipts.

NORMA: Right, it might be a subject best forgotten, you know.

LYLE: The other thing that's bullshit, the only reason that we got caught for that. We didn't even get caught. The only reason that my brother was sort of caught for it, is—I decided because I felt bad—that I wanted to give the stuff back. And I actually re-burglarized the house and put everything back. Right? And then I accidently put stuff from one house into another house's safe and when the lady got home . . .

NORMA: You mean you gave the wrong jewels back?

LYLE: And when the lady got home, she says, wait a minute, this isn't mine. And she connected it with her neighbor—since everybody was kind of friends. And that's how they realized that the burglaries were connected. Right? They couldn't figure out how the fuck one piece of jewelry would get into another piece of jewelrys' safe—it's because I felt bad and actually broke in and put it back. And I mean to me—like that should come out. Because what kind of real criminal goes in and re-burglarizes the house?

NORMA: Right, to put stuff back.

LYLE: To put stuff back. Only a kid that like wishes he didn't burglarize in the first place. But I just don't want to get into the details—'cause then she's going to go, "Did you wear a ski mask?" And I don't even want to answer those questions.

NORMA: How did you get mixed up with that anyway? Did you get—was there only the two houses?

LYLE: No, I wasn't involved in the first burglary. So I was really not involved in this. Right? It was my brother and his friend, Cignarelli. So I never saw the jewelry before in my life. So I didn't know what jewelry went back. I was just taking my brother's word for it and he really was confused and so I just did the best I could.

NORMA: You were just concerned for him?

LYLE: Yeah. How was I supposed to know that someone was going to get home and complain that they got too much jewelry? That's ridiculous. So I don't know. So anyway.

NORMA: Do you think that—well have you talked to Jill about going back on the stand?

LYLE: Yeah, she says we'll think about it this weekend. I mean, Conte did well. But I feel like fuck. If I were speaking for him, I would have tore her up. I mean, I would have destroyed this tape but, of course, I know it inside and out and so I shouldn't talk about it. But listen, I'm going to call Jill and tell her that Court TV said it was OK and talk to her about what they said.

NORMA: Alright. I'm surprised she doesn't have someone recording this for her and letting her hear it herself.

LYLE: She doesn't.

NORMA: She doesn't want to hear how she's doing?

LYLE: She doesn't want to hear it. She doesn't think their opinion is valuable. She doesn't look at Court TV to see how she's doing.

NORMA: Are you still getting mail?

LYLE: Yeah.

NORMA: Well, that will give you something to do over the weekend, anyway, love.

November 21, 1993, afternoon

NORMA: The thing that bothered me this afternoon is when they talked about the maid. Does he know where the maid is?

LYLE: They are going to bring the maid in to say that she didn't hear any arguments.

NORMA: Are they definitely bringing her in?

LYLE: Yeah, they are going to bring her in. But come on, who's going to believe the fucking maid? The maid has immigration problems, she's here on a visa.

NORMA: That's what I was wondering, if they found her. I thought she'd have gone back to Mexico.

LYLE: What is she going to say? Isn't she going to say anything that the police want her to say?

NORMA: Yeah, or she'll get shipped out. Oh sure, well you can say that. You just have to hope that she doesn't have a green card or something.

LYLE: Oh no, we already know about the maid.

NORMA: Does she have a green card?

LYLE: She's got immigration problems. Nobody fucking believes the maid anyway—give me a break.

NORMA: But when is she coming in?

LYLE: So far at the end of the trial.

NORMA: At the end of the trial. So she's not coming in tomorrow to topple him or something?

LYLE: No no. We know all the people they have.

NORMA: As long as he's prepared. Alright.

LYLE: He's prepared. We know already. Remember when he mentioned the pool guy—when we were playing tennis? Erik brought it up himself because he knows they are going to bring him in. So I told him, you might as well just let the jury know you know and it's not that you are getting caught but it's just that you know the guy is not telling truth.

NORMA: Yeah right.

LYLE: Because if we wanted to change the story we could say, "Oh yeah, we played tennis," and match with the pool guy, but we didn't. So my attorney said, "You know what, you didn't play tennis," fuck this pool guy. So I figure it's better to mention him. That definitely wiped out the validity of the pool guy. We could've made up all kinds of stuff . . . That fucking story is lame. I mean what I think is the most ludicrous thing is like remember that lady—I'll give you that—like the next day he was playing tennis on the courts?

NORMA: Take away the fear thing.

LYLE: So how could he be that afraid, right? First of all, how the fuck do they know that he was playing tennis the next day on the courts? Because my brother says so. They have no other way of knowing that, so I could just leave it out, right? If my brother was lying—

NORMA: Exercise and stuff like that is a way to get rid of your fear—like people lift weights and stuff to do the same thing—get rid of stress.

LYLE: Not even that. Maybe it was denial, is what it was. They never said it was denial. But it's like I don't think it's good logic to use somebody else's story against himself. Because like, wait a minute, if the guy is telling the truth then who cares how many times he played tennis? He's telling the truth. You can't use the fact that he said he played tennis on Friday and use that against them—you weren't afraid when he said he was afraid Sunday. And the only way you know that whole series of events is because he is telling you. I mean it would be different if they had somebody that came in and said, "I saw them playing tennis on Friday."

NORMA: Yeah.

LYLE: You know, then they could say, How afraid could you be? But if the kid is the one volunteering the information then you figure—you either believe his story or you can't use this fact against him.

November 21, 1993, evening

LYLE: Norma . . . I thought it was great.

NORMA: Great? Why? I thought he was a big fly in your ointment.

LYLE: No, no, no. As usual, you misinterpreted the whole thing. We destroyed the whole thing—the one limo driver they actually didn't do recross on because it was so embarrassing how much he was lying, so they sent him home.

NORMA: Which guy was that?

LYLE: The first guy.

NORMA: Oh, yeah, the limousine driver. I knew he wasn't much—

LYLE: He stopped remembering things as soon as Leslie was on.

NORMA: Yeah, but it wasn't him that I was bothered about. It was the second guy—the pool guy. Oh, the guy that came to do the repair.

LYLE: The pool guy that said he called the police department with information about the murder and they said, "We're not interested, don't call back."

NORMA: Yeah, he said so.

LYLE: Yeah, right. Do you believe that? Could that be possible? I mean, that's impossible.

NORMA: Well, I don't think—

LYLE: This is the guy that said that I had an argument with my mother and then they bring the second guy in and he says that he was told there was an argument with the father. And then he says that the conversation took place with the guy on Monday and then later he says that four days later, he was surprised, he found out about the murders when he went to the house, because there was a [yellow crime scene] tape on the house. And Mike asked him, "Well, how is it when you are surprised on Thursday, you found out there was a murder on Thursday, right? So how is it that you could have had a conversation on Monday about this guy's feelings about the murders and that he saw an argument there the day before?" Right, there's no answer.

NORMA: Not the day before—Saturday.

LYLE: How is it that if the boss found out about the murders on a Thursday, that the Monday before that he could have had a conversation with this guy about the murders?

NORMA: And he is supposed to have not had a conversation?

LYLE: No, we're saying that he is lying, there was no conversation. And there was no supposed call to the police by this guy—it's all bullshit.

NORMA: What about when he went to repair the [pool] pump though and he said that you and Erik were there?

LYLE: That's what the pool man says, right? But how do we know the pool man is telling the truth? He has no documentation. There is no documentation that the police department got a call.

NORMA: Well, you'd know if he was telling the truth if you were there, wouldn't you?

LYLE: Yeah, we weren't there. He's not telling the truth.

NORMA: So, you weren't there? Well, how do you know he wasn't there?

LYLE: Because he's saying that we were there.

NORMA: Right.

LYLE: So, not that I would remember him but I'd know if I was there that day.

NORMA: Oh, yeah, because you already testified that you both went out. Did you say you both went out of just Erik?

LYLE: Both of us. We went out. Look at the guy's testimony. He says that I had a coach with black hair, the only tennis coach I have is Mark Heffernan who has white blonde hair. He says that the patio table was right up against the fence of the tennis court. You can look at the picture in the crime scene and the patio table is about fifteen to twenty feet away from the tennis court—we're talking about a patio set with chairs. So you can't move it around easy. OK? So that's another lie.

Then he says that the argument was with the mother and when in fact the guy that comes after him says no, he said it was between the father and the son. So obviously he changed that around and made that up. And then he says that he called the police department to let them know about it and they said, "OK, we'll get back to you on it." And then when he's questioned further on it because we find out that there is no record in the police department that he called . . .

NORMA: I did say to myself, What the hell is he going over to do the pool for if he knows that there has been a murder there? Obviously your mother and father don't want the pool done on Wednesday. That was the only question mark I had.

LYLE: Question mark? What do you mean question mark, Norma? How can it be true? It means that he's lying. There's no question mark. . . . So [the DA] decided not to call the wife of this [pool] guy. She gave up on this guy—obviously why. You've got to pay attention when they're doing this. I hope the jurors do—the jurors were laughing at this guy. If the jurors are laughing, we're doing well. Then it's obvious. Because they never pay attention at all. They're like alternate jurors. You watch them all the time. They're like yawning and looking around. But it was fun because Leslie was going after this fucking guy.

NORMA: I'll have to watch it from the beginning because I've seen glances of it this afternoon and I sort of hear it bits and pieces here and there in between doing a few jobs and then I sat down. But some testimony had already been and gone—so I haven't watched it constantly. So I shall do that tonight though.

LYLE: Bits and pieces are not going to do it with this guy. Leslie just dismantled his fucking ass. . . . I mean, what's believable about this fucking guy except for that he is a trained rat?

NORMA: The jury is going to say, What is this guy lying for? That's what I'd say if I was on the jury.

LYLE: The guy's lying because he's a fucking pool man whose wife is obsessed by Court TV. Like he said, she watches every single day and tapes it. And is pushing him to be a witness so that she can be a witness. That's what Leslie said.

NORMA: Oh, you think so?

LYLE: Yeah. That's what Leslie said. "Does your wife watch Court TV every day?"

"Yeah, she watches it every day."

"And is your wife the one that went to the police and said, 'Hey, he's got this information?' "

"Yes."

You know what I mean? She went to the police so therefore you talked to the police—that she can now be a witness.

NORMA: So, you're thinking that they're looking for fifteen minutes of fame?

LYLE: Yeah, fuck yeah, they are man. They're fucking pool people in fucking Beverly Hills. They want to fucking be on TV. You know you can't look—I tell you there's a big mistake to try and figure out whether people are lying by looking at why they would lie. Because you can't believe the stupid fucking reasons people have for lying.

NORMA: Yeah, I can imagine the variations.

LYLE: I mean, I have seen so many people get up in this trial and lie and I cannot figure out why. You can't figure out why man. Some people you can figure out why—they want money, they want this and they want that. Oziel wants to save his reputation whatever it is. But a guy like this—I mean you don't know why. Why did the first guy lie?

NORMA: The limousine guy? I don't know.

LYLE: There's no reason. So you can't say it's perverse because you just can't. Why did he lie? You don't know. You don't fucking know why. So the only thing you know was that this guy was lying because you can't have that many mistakes. I mean, look at Erik and I—we're up there three fucking weeks and the only thing that could possibly be inconsistent—it looked like it at first is the Big 5. In three fucking weeks, everyday on the stand. This guy is up there for twenty-five minutes and you got ten fucking major discrepancies in a simple story. That's when you know people are lying. . . .

NORMA: No wonder Leslie was losing her marbles this afternoon. She was getting mad wasn't she?

LYLE: Oh yeah, because she can't stand it when some little punk motherfucker comes in and lies so he can be a big deal. He thinks he's going to outsmart her? No way would she let him get away with it. So really fucked that guy off.

NORMA: So, were you getting mad when you were sitting there?

LYLE: No, it was exciting. It pissed off me—when the guy—when he first pulled that first trip to the stand I was really upset because the guy sounded credible in the beginning, like all liars do. Until you get a chance to pick apart the story. And then once the second guy came on, forget it. It was so obvious, it was a joke. So then I started laughing. . . .

NORMA: Anyway, they're finished now. I don't know how the ending went? The ending of the pool guy.

LYLE: The ending was what did it. The ending was Mike asking the last question of this guy, "How can it be that you found out about the murders Thursday, if on the Monday before you had a conversation with this guy about the murders? There's no way. You're lying." And that was the end of the question. That was the last question—

NORMA: And then you sat down.

LYLE: And Pam did not get up and explain it. She said, "No questions" and the guy left. And that was the end of that. He fucking flaked out of the courtroom. That fucking rat. Piece of shit.

NORMA: So that looks like they're out on their asses now. Which one are you nervous about, what about Gill Small, is he going to be OK do you think?

LYLE: Who is Gill Small?

NORMA: Gill Small—the guy that knew your dad for fifteen years—that worked with him in LIVE.

LYLE: I don't care about business associates. What do they know about what's going on in the house? Do you think anyone is going to believe that this guy [Jose] is a nice guy at work?

NORMA: Well, I don't know. This is the guy that was on "The Maury Povich Show" with Henry and he said—

LYLE: Oh great. That ends his credibility right there, what's he doing on "The Maury Povich Show"? Hold on. Hello? You know I was going to listen to the Terry Moran wrap-up to see what his opinion was. Did he give you a wrap-up?

NORMA: Yeah, yes he did. Do you want to hear that? What about Jamie, is she going to be a threat?

LYLE: That'll be a good day too.

NORMA: Are you bothered about her?

LYLE: I wish she wasn't testifying—bitch. I can't believe that she's testifying. All I ever did was buy her presents like I did with all of my girlfriends.

NORMA: Did she go to the library? You asked her, or you didn't ask her?

LYLE: This is fucking bullshit. OK, explain this to me. There's another time when you know people are lying. She didn't know that I was even involved. She thought the Mafia did it all the way up to October until she was told for the first time by me, right? Now, how is it that she thinks that the Mafia did it in October, if in June supposedly I'm asking her to look up cases where kids get off for killing their parents because they claim child abuse? Isn't that kind of a hint that maybe I'm involved there? Wouldn't you start asking questions like, Wait a minute, what's that got to do with the Mafia? You fucking lying bitch.

These fucking people, they don't think when they lie. They just think, Oh, I can say this. He can't prove otherwise—even there, he wasn't at the library. I just wonder how she is going to answer that question. I can't handle with people lying—you can figure it out. There are times when the guy lies—there's just nobody there—he sounds credible and there's nothing you can do about it.

NORMA: Especially you. You're just sitting there and you can't say nothing.

LYLE: I can't say anything. I just . . . Oh, it's lock-down. I'll try and get back out.

November 23, 1993

[Editor's note: Lyle is discussing the testimony of his former girlfriend Jamie Pisarcik.]

LYLE: That fucking call went down in flames. Oh my god, you've never seen anyone lying so bad and get in trouble for it in your whole life. It wasn't as bad as Glenn Stevens but it will be by the end of tomorrow.

NORMA: What's she going to say tomorrow?

LYLE: She's not saying anything.

NORMA: Oh, you don't know what they're going to ask her yet, do you?

LYLE: No, I know she's trying to keep her lines straight, but it's getting hard, it's getting very hard. Why is she doing so many lies that don't even matter?

NORMA: I don't even know anyway because I don't know which is the lies or which is the truth, some of the time so I have to rely on you to tell me or—

LYLE: Not really when we got work records and documentation and plane trips and phone calls and that has nothing to do with me. I didn't make those calls, or go to work or take those flights. She did.

NORMA: I know, but do you think the jury is going to consider that as important anyway—the fact that she is using you. To me personally, I don't see it's important anyway if she is using your phone card.

LYLE: You don't think that the fact that she made up a story that my mom gave her permission when in fact she had been using it all summer, is relevant?

NORMA: Saying your mother gave permission?

LYLE: You don't think that saying that she had a conversation at the time when she actually was at work is relevant?

NORMA: Who was at work? Your mother?

LYLE: She was at work.

NORMA: Oh, she's at work.

LYLE: She was at work, every day.

NORMA: Yeah, that's true. That's why Jill went through it all, isn't it?

LYLE: Look at that—she keeps pushing it back a month and

we—fuck. Bitch. Is there anything . . . we wanted to know what Terry Moran said if you have anything taped on him.

NORMA: Yeah, he had a spin. Let me go in there and I'll put on for you. OK, hold on. I'm rewinding a little bit—What did you think about the maid?

LYLE: The maid was a joke.

NORMA: A joke—I knew you would say something negative.

LYLE: Even in a normal family, do you think that people occasionally argue? Just occasionally. Maybe just once?

NORMA: Yeah.

LYLE: So, this maid goes in there and says, "I lived there nine months and nobody ever got mad at anybody else, nothing strange ever happened, nobody ever raised their voice." OK, my mom is a documented alcoholic, right. She said my mom never took a drink. The kids never talked back to their parents. It was a perfect family. OK thank you, you can go now.

NORMA: Yeah, she did say that.

LYLE: Man. I don't believe that. Unbelievable.

NORMA: That's in your friggin' defense cause—

LYLE: When people come in and they just blatantly lie like that, you got to be fucking upset about it. It's one thing if they have people that actually are like credible to come in and—but to just come in there and go, "Oh, no there was never . . . nobody raised their voice in nine months." Come on.

NORMA: Personally I don't give a shit between who is telling lies and who is not because I'm not on the jury anyway. I mean I'm not swallowing everything that gets said, even—I don't even swallow everything you tell me because I know what you've got to do to get your freedom or even—or save your life. I don't believe everything.

LYLE: We would have struck you from the jury a long time ago so you don't have to worry about it. Got anything?

NORMA: Yeah, I have a report of Jamie Pisarcik's testimony. I'll read it to you. [reading] "Jamie Pisarcik is really what the prosecution hopes to be the knock-out punch against the entire defense. She is to attack the brothers' elaborate story of what happened in the week leading up to their parents' killing. She says that in 1989, she heard Erik Menendez talk about Lyle Menendez's hairpiece. And the reason is that Erik Menendez and Lyle Menendez have testified that their fear of their parents, their sharing of the incest secret in the family, their threatening to bring it out, culminating in their parents' death began with Erik's discovery in August of 1989 that his brother wore a hairpiece. So Jamie Pisarcik's testimony may destroy the defendants' case. It is possible that the last witness in this case on rebuttal would be Lyle Menendez in order to address this testimony and some of the other rebuttal testimony that's coming up. His lawyer, Jill Lansing, certainly delivered a lot for him this afternoon in her cross-examination of Jamie Pisarcik, in a very low-key way to show that Jamie Pisarcik may not have been able to be in the same state at the time she says that Erik Menendez told her about his brother's hairpiece." [end of reading]

LYLE: OK.

NORMA: So, anyway, I thought she was pretty, Jamie, when she testified.

LYLE: I didn't think so. She looked pretty bad.

NORMA: Why? Everyone looks better on television, have you noticed?

LYLE: She looked better when I was there for sure. I think her hair was longer. People never look good when they're lying.

NORMA: No, but she looked good considering that she doesn't wear makeup.

LYLE: She does wear makeup.

NORMA: She does? Oh, she has got none around her eyes, I didn't notice anything. And her cheeks were kind of—

LYLE: There's a difference between wearing makeup and knowing how to wear makeup.

NORMA: I suppose. She looked good anyway considering she had makeup then. So anyway, she's on again tomorrow, is she?

LYLE: Yeah, unfortunately for her. Yeah.

NORMA: Fortunately for you? I love the way you put that.

LYLE: We're going to have fun with her tomorrow. Tomorrow is going to be great.

NORMA: Who else is on with her? Afterward?

LYLE: After her it's going to Brian and he's going to be a motherfucker.

NORMA: He's going to be a pain in the ass. I heard about him already.

LYLE: No doubt about that. OK, but listen I got to call Jill and I'm going to call a few people and try to get ready for tomorrow. I just wanted to hear what Terry Moran had to say.

NORMA: Why don't you give your grandmother a call? How long is it since you called her? Four days, five days. Maybe ten.

LYLE: Not that long. I'll tell her though that you told me I should call her.

NORMA: No, she did call me this afternoon though, to see if I heard from Lyle. Bye.

LYLE: I'll give you a call tomorrow.

November 25, 1993
Thanksgiving Day

NORMA: Have they served you turkey in the jail?

LYLE: They did. On Thanksgiving they do.

NORMA: So what did you have, turkey, potatoes, and gravy? Did you have a dessert?

LYLE: Yeah, pumpkin pie.

NORMA: I wonder if Erik has any? 'Cause he has a problem eating anything, doesn't he?

LYLE: He'll get that. I'm sure he ate well today.

NORMA: Well, who's coming in on Monday? I wasn't listening to the argument on Friday to see what was going to be allowed in and stuff.

LYLE: I think my Uncle Brian is coming in.

NORMA: Is Brian coming back on? Is the judge going to let those comments in where you were in the limousine? You don't know yet.

LYLE: It sounds like he is.

NORMA: It does? 'Cause it was kind of negative stuff that you don't need.

LYLE: Yeah, but as usual I'm sure we'll make him look like a liar like the rest of them. Everything looks negative until the person gets up there—but you take them apart and they look like idiots. Everybody thought my ex-girlfriend would be bad for me too and look at that.

NORMA: Right, she got blown up, didn't she? That was even worse the next day. Remember when you said to me we'll have a lot of fun with her—

LYLE: It was worse the next day. I told you that the day was going to be fun. These people get up there like they think that all they got to do is tell their lies and they just get to leave. Wrong.

NORMA: There should be some sort of a threat to people, even though they take the oath, there is nothing to stop them going up there and still lying. But I think once people get found out, they should be—I don't know—sent to jail for so many days or something. And that would really stop them from coming up.

LYLE: Yes. She should get perjury charges.

NORMA: Yeah, they never do though.

LYLE: I'm going to have them filed against her.

NORMA: Oh, are you?

LYLE: Yeah, I'm going to try. We caught her in enough lies that were proven on paper with her own words.

NORMA: Yeah, I know because the dates did seem way off, the dates wiped all of her testimony out.

LYLE: Even if you take away that part of the testimony, it's the other things that she talked about that were lies. Because in her own handwriting, we showed her the letters and she just lied.

NORMA: And then it was pretty good how Jill trapped her into that wedding thing where she said that really weren't wedding plans and she wasn't really engaged. And two stones fell out of her ring. I don't think so, it's very rare one stone falls out of a diamond ring and she said a few of the stones fell out.

LYLE: Right and she said that she tried to return it to me twice. Like I wouldn't take it back. And I've been trying to get that ring back for three years.

NORMA: Really? I thought it was kind of—this is just my own little personal thought. You know how you broke up and then I know your father had said she was a gold digger, right? And then you got arrested and then you wanted her to be your girlfriend again for the time being. And then she really couldn't wait to get back into it because I think she could see her becoming your wife after all and living in the house and you're going to get the money. 'Cause you hadn't confessed to her then you see. So I thought, Oh, oh, she's getting back in with Lyle again so that she can live in the house and they can continue there once he gets released and she'll get all that money that's coming to him.

LYLE: Then she found out what happened—got a new boy-friend.

NORMA: Soon as you confessed to her, that was it, wasn't it? She saw all that money disappearing.

LYLE: Bitch. She got what she had coming. Embarrassment.

NORMA: You know the secretary? Is she going to say anything that is ominous? Is she already?

LYLE: She's like the rest of them. She'll just say whatever the police need her to say. So she is going to tell a bunch of lies and then we're going to go up there and try and show that she's a liar. Probably we'll do that pretty easily. They think my Uncle Brian was a liar already and some of the things that Brian said were totally ridiculous and he was proven to be a liar. It'll get worse for him. And then we'll make her out to be a liar too. They all went down in flames. So far they haven't had one person that's been credible on rebuttal. Who have they had? Nobody. The limo driver went down in total flames. The security guard went down in flames. The pool man was a joke.

NORMA: It's funny because every time they bring in anybody that's going be the absolute dynamite witness, I always go, Oh, my God and I get all this anxious feeling. And then after they've been on I go, Well what the fuck was that supposed to be? 'Cause there's never anything really concrete. Either verbally or on paper. They don't have proof of anything. This whole fucking trial is built around words.

LYLE: They don't even have a theory that—they can't even support a theory. What are their theories? It can't be for money. That's already been destroyed because they can't even prove that I was in the will. So that's ridiculous. Once you don't have money, then you've only got hatred.

NORMA: And even this thing about Erik going back on the plane trip when that girl said yesterday that he was in a hurry. She still couldn't say exactly what he was in a hurry over. Do you know what I mean? Because he didn't actually say to her I've got to get back to the computer for something.

LYLE: The point of that was that the limo driver—that he took Erik on the ride—he said he took Erik to the computer store on the way to the airport. Right? And he said before he went to the computer store, he went to the U.S. Open with that lady, her husband, me, my girlfriend, and Erik. Right? So then we show him that I'm on a plane to California at 6:00 A.M., so I sure as hell wasn't at the U.S. Open. Right? what was a lie. And then the lady gets up there and says she went to the night matches. So she couldn't have been at the U.S. Open before Erik left for the airport. And the husband wasn't even there. He left for a seminar. The fucking limo guy is totally lying. He just made up the whole fucking story.

The driver of the limo came in and testified. He hasn't come in yet but he's coming in later. And he says that we were in a hurry to get to the airport. No way would we stop at some computer store. They were in a hurry to get to the airport. He was—my brother was in such a hurry that he left clothes behind at the hotel. So you think he had time to browse around at a computer store before they got to the airport? No way. So the guy's a total lie.

NORMA: Is there anyway you can get back up the stand and have Jill ask you those appropriate questions?

LYLE: Well, I can get back up there but I don't know if I need to. I mean what do I really need to address? Originally we needed to address the tape but I don't think that's an issue anymore after Smyth and after the experts. That tape is just—doesn't prove anything. What else do I need to get up there and say? If I get on the stand, they're going to bring out all of the burglaries against me and they're going to make me talk about that bullshit for a fucking hour. Right? And I don't want to have to talk about burglaries. And then—

NORMA: Well they are not that important really. I don't know why the burglaries bother you.

LYLE: They're not even relevant. But they don't bother me. It's just, Why do I want to get up there and talk about them?

NORMA: You won't get the attitude if you talk about them as you would on some of the other things that you want to dispute.

LYLE: I can talk about it well. I can explain why I was sorry and all this other bullshit but the point is that I don't want to leave the jury with a discussion about burglary. But that would be no problem. The main thing is that if I get up there and I'm very emotional and I do well like I did last time, I'll leave the jury with that. That would be nice.

NORMA: What bothers you the most about what's been said about the rebuttals? What's been said? Does anything stick out in your mind?

LYLE: Nothing. Not yet.

NORMA: What do you mean, "Not yet"? There's only two people to come on isn't there?

LYLE: Yeah, but we'll have to see what they have to say.

NORMA: One is Brian and who's the other? Oh, that's right, the secretary. Yeah, you want to see what she's going to say.

LYLE: Because these people make things up as they go along so you don't know what they're going to say exactly.

NORMA: When the prosecution brings them in doesn't the defense get to know what they're going to say?

LYLE: We get to know but then they start coming up with— Jamie came up with a DBC book a half-hour before she went on the stand. What the fuck is that? A half-hour before you come to the stand, you come up with new information. This is ridiculous. You never know what they are going to say. We're going to get up there and we're going to try and show that—I mean this is my dad's secretary, right? She won't even talk too much to attorneys and she's going around hugging. The secretary is going to come on and say that I was an asshole.

NORMA: The way you are at work doesn't mean that's the way you are at home. At home you're different as to what you are at work, when you're out with other people of course you're different.

LYLE: She's going to try to make me out to be cold and all this stuff but nobody is going to believe that because I mean, she's my dad's secretary for all these years. Chances are they had an affair.

NORMA: Did you have much to do with her, Lyle?

LYLE: I never spoke to her.

NORMA: Oh, well, how can she say you're cold then?

LYLE: I had nothing to do with her, you know what I mean?

NORMA: So, she can't say that you came in every day and stopped talking with her or anything or you were unresponsive every time she spoke to you. She can't say that?

LYLE: She comes up with these statements three years after she was first interviewed. After she had gotten a chance to watch the trial and see what she needs to say and figure out what she wants to do. And then she says, "Oh, yeah, I remember this." Come on. That is incredible. We would never put a witness up there that suddenly had memories. I don't know how many people they are going to put up there in a row that are obvious liars. My Uncle Brian—this guy is vicious. We're going to destroy him hopefully.

NORMA: Yeah. I heard Weisberg saying, you know we could be going through to January with this case.

LYLE: No, we're not going to go to January. Well, we could especially if the jury can't make a decision. Erik's jury probably will go into January. My jury could come up with a decision before Christmas.

NORMA: Do you think so? I thought they'd both go out together and then come back when they're ready, separately.

LYLE: Well, my jury is going to have an extra week. They're going to be out while Erik's jury is still arguing. They're going to have a little bit of time. But this part of the rebuttal is going well. It pisses me off that they can just put so many liars up with a straight face.

NORMA: I know, especially when you've got to sit there and you can't jump up and say, "Hey you, you friggin' liar."

LYLE: After they put up a couple of liars, the case should be dismissed. They should say, "Listen this is bullshit." They can't just put people up here and lie and hope that the defense can't prove they're wrong.

NORMA: That's what I'm saying, there should be some sort of a threat against them instead of just putting their hand up and swearing on the oath. They should know that if they do get up there and lie, then they're going to go to jail for a week or whatever it is, you know.

LYLE: They could go to jail for a long time if they're risking somebody's life.

NORMA: Absolutely, that's what I'm saying. That's what I mean. Make them think twice then.

LYLE: The pool man did a talk show. Did you know that? He fucking did a radio talk show.

NORMA: Huh? He's going to have a radio talk show?

LYLE: He did a radio talk show.

NORMA: The usual thing, isn't it?

LYLE: First he goes up there and they go "Why are you here?"

"Oh, I just have to do my civic duty."

Is that your civic duty to do a talk show? Please. But listen, I got to go.

JANUARY 1994

The Verdicts

The jury deliberations extended over a long period of time, in part due to the Christmas and New Year holidays. On January 13, exactly a month after they went out, Erik's jury came back without reaching a verdict; after twenty days of deliberations, a mistrial was declared.

On January 17, while Lyle's jury was still deliberating, the Northridge earthquake affected the lives of most jurors and court personnel, and damaged the courthouse itself. When Lyle's verdict came in, it was announced in a trailer courtroom that is stationed permanently behind the main building. Once again there was a turn-away crowd. Six months after the trial began, Lyle's jury returned to say that they could not reach a verdict, so another mistrial was declared.

Los Angeles District Attorney Gil Garcetti announced to a huge gathering of the press that there would be a retrial and the death penalty would be sought.

Lyle had been laboring under the mistaken notion that he could not be tried again when the death penalty was possible. Mr. Garcetti's announcement must have dispelled that delusion.

Lyle's defense team declared the hung jury a victory, but Erik's did not. In the open-air post-trial press conferences outside the courthouse, before hundreds of reporters and spectators, neither team made any mention of Paul Mones. Though he was standing right beside them, he was ignored and shunted aside as if he had played no part in the years before the trial or during the trial itself. It is interesting to observe that Paul Mones is the only person about whom Lyle Menendez never speaks ill.

January 7, 1994

NORMA: So are you still getting letters or what?
LYLE: Oh, yeah, Jesus . . .

NORMA: Oh, yeah . . . couple of tons?

LYLE: There's no way to stop these letters from coming. New people every time, so it just keeps getting worse.

NORMA: Oh, really?

LYLE: But it's terrific, you know, I mean, I'm glad—

NORMA: Of course it is, because it's nice to know you've got all those supporters.

LYLE: I mean, I don't have time to read them all, almost, I mean I try, I'm going to get to every one, but it like takes forever.

NORMA: Yeah. So you're writing them, are you—?

LYLE: It's wonderful, it's just wonderful, though, it's really wonderful.

NORMA: Yeah. So you're answering some of them—still?

LYLE: Yeah, I answer all of them.

NORMA: OK. It'll keep you busy for awhile, I know, answering them.

LYLE: Forever.

NORMA: Can I read some—?

LYLE: When I'm an old man . . .

NORMA: [laughing] Well, everybody's different aren't they in the world then? Are they saying different things? I would imagine they are.

LYLE: Yes, they are. They're very different.

NORMA: OK, that's good.

LYLE: Yeah.

NORMA: Give you something to do. I stuck a little Dell word-finder book in there, too.

LYLE: OK, good.

NORMA: Because I wanted to give it a flat envelope, but I didn't just want to put this little reflective mirror in a big envelope, you know?

LYLE: OK, good.

NORMA: So I thought, Well, I'll ship one of these little magazines in . . .

LYLE: I'll look out for it.

NORMA: Yeah, it's kind of a simple thing, but I thought, Never mind, I'll just stick it in there, so something with the mirror, you know.

LYLE: Well, good. Thanks, Honey.

NORMA: You're welcome. So . . .

LYLE: I'm gonna go . . .

NORMA: Alright, then.

LYLE: And I'm feeling pretty good, so don't worry about me.

NORMA: Alright then.

LYLE: And then tom—Monday—we have a long day, but I'll, I'll talk to you tomorrow, so . . .

NORMA: OK, yeah let me know if you have plans for the weekend—gosh, doesn't that sound nice? Out of your cell, I mean, to phone, you know what I mean . . .

LYLE: Right. Yeah.

NORMA: You know what I mean [laughing].

LYLE: Yeah.

NORMA: Never mind that. We might be saying that for real one day, soon.

LYLE: I think so, you know?

NORMA: Yeah.

LYLE: I think it's gonna be surprising how well the—it's gonna be hung, but I think . . .

NORMA: You think so?

LYLE: I think it's gonna be hung in our favor. I think it's gonna be something like ten to two, you know what I mean?

NORMA: Really?

LYLE: In my favor.

NORMA: Yeah.

LYLE: And I think it's gonna be like six to six, on Erik, with like two people for acquittal, and so on . . . I think you're gonna be surprised. I mean, I know a lot of people have said, "Oh, no, it's gonna be murder," or "It's gonna be conviction," but these are people that really don't know. They have not watched the trial.

NORMA: Right.

LYLE: They didn't realize how well we did in this trial.

NORMA: Right. And I heard that the longer they're taking like this, the better it looks for you guys.

LYLE: Oh, yeah. Going, going into the room, I think we had most of the votes already, and this is just wearing down the people who are against us.

NORMA: Mm-hmm.

LYLE: You can't, you can't wear down people that are for us.

NORMA: Oh, right, absolutely not.

LYLE: No way. Once you're for us, you're for us. I think if you're for the issues, you don't get worn down. But if you're against us, it's just a question of how long you're willing to just sit in the room—because if you're against something, you tend not to be very passionate about it, you know?

NORMA: Right.

LYLE: You know what I mean? You're just kinda like, "Yeah, I think they planned it," or "Yeah, I think they did it for this reason," but, you know, it's certainly not something that you feel like you really care a lot about.

NORMA: Yeah, I think that's a good psychological evaluation. So you've been analyzing a little, huh?

LYLE: Well . . .

NORMA: Or analyzing a lot.

LYLE: I'd say analyze a lot, yeah [laughing].

NORMA: So they're definitely having a problem with some of the jurors, aren't they?

LYLE: Yeah, well . . .

NORMA: —not agreeing with the other jurors, you know.

LYLE: Well, I think on my jury, they've got this lady that's married to a district attorney, they got her right?

NORMA: Yeah.

LYLE: 'Cause she's gonna vote the way her husband is, so that has no credibility, that vote, but it's gonna be against me. And then they got . . . there's a guy in there who's kinda really an eccentric, kinda hippie-type?

NORMA: Yeah?

LYLE: And he's a real nasty guy. I think he's going to vote against me.

NORMA: Do you?

LYLE: Everybody, everybody on the jury hates him—you can just tell. And, he'll vote against. And I don't think more, I don't think anybody else will. That's my feeling, you know. I could be wrong, we'll see.

NORMA: Well, there was a guy in the mock trial they were

holding on Court TV. They were holding a mock—not a mock trial, a mock jury—

LYLE: Yeah.

NORMA: Debate.

LYLE: Yeah.

NORMA: Well, what the judge was, was for your acquittal, the guy who's an ex-judge?

LYLE: Well, he's a guy that knows, because he's done all the abuse cases.

NORMA: Right, yes, he said he's dealt with them, too, and he wanted for your acquittal, yeah.

LYLE: Yeah.

NORMA: So that looked promising, you know.

LYLE: Yeah. So I think—

NORMA: Do you think—?

LYLE: I think their case was a joke. And so, you know, we destroyed their case. They had no case. Basically, it just came down to whether they believed our case, because there was no opposing case—

NORMA: Right.

LYLE: —of any worth. It was just a bunch of liars, and fools, and bad, bad jobs.

NORMA: Mm-hmm.

LYLE: So, you know, our case was put on very, very well . . .

NORMA: Right, I know.

LYLE: I think with a lot of emotion, and a lot of integrity, and so, I, you know, I think that we swayed almost everybody, but, it's, it's hard, you know, it's hard to sway twelve people. It's hard to get twelve people who agree on anything.

NORMA: Of course, yes.

LYLE: It's hard. I'm pissed off about it because, you know, I want them to come to a decision for me, and I have a feeling that, you know, there's always gonna be one or two people that just don't wanna do it.

NORMA: Right. Now, if it does come back hung, like you think it will, is that gonna be a retrial?

LYLE: Well, if it comes back like I think it will, then, you know, I don't know if Garcetti will retry the case. There'll be a lot of pressure for him not to, because, I mean, if it comes—let's say it comes backs ten to two, or nine to three, or something—

NORMA: Yeah.

LYLE: —in our favor. Well that's a strong signal that he cannot win the case.

NORMA: Well, have some cases been . . . have you heard of people who've just been, you know, let go, because of a hung jury?

LYLE: Oh, oh yeah, absolutely, yeah.

NORMA: I mean, is that what you're thinking, if you get a hung jury, you might just be let go?

LYLE: No, what I'm thinking is, if it's a hung jury—

NORMA: Yeah?

LYLE: —he's gonna give me a deal for manslaughter.

NORMA: Oh, I see . . . OK. Because I wanted to know what your options were, if they came up, if a hung jury came up.

LYLE: Well, if that occurs, I'm gonna have a bail hearing.

NORMA: Oh, really? Wow!

LYLE: Oh, I should get out.

NORMA: That's interesting.

LYLE: And if I get out, I get out; if I don't, I don't. But I have a good chance, and the bail hearing alone is gonna scare the hell out of 'em.

NORMA: Yeah, it's not like you're a serial killer or something, you know?

LYLE: Oh, yeah.

NORMA: There's no reason why you shouldn't be let out.

LYLE: There's no reason why I should not be out.

NORMA: Right, because you're not like a danger to society now.

LYLE: No, no . . . Are you kidding me? I have a priest—that priest could take me in. I probably could produce, you know, 10,000 letters from people that say they would let me stay in their homes.

NORMA: Oh, really?

LYLE: You know, so . . .

NORMA: Well, that's good.

LYLE: I mean, I've gotten 5,000 letters already, right? And between my brother and I, we have about 7,500 letters?

NORMA: You have? Are they—

LYLE: Every single one of those people would take us in their home.

NORMA: Do you think so?

LYLE: No, no. I don't think so—

NORMA: Well, that—[laughing]—you *know* so.

LYLE: Yeah. They love us.

NORMA: Well, that's nice. That's nice and promising, anyway. You get a big choice.

LYLE: Yeah. Unfortunately, like, they're from all over the country, so, I don't think . . . put me under house arrest with my grandmother in Calabasas.

NORMA: Yeah, that'd be nice.

LYLE: I'm not going anywhere. Where am I gonna go, that they're not gonna know who I am?

NORMA: And then you can finally play me that, that game of tennis. [laughing] Well, you can.

LYLE: I'm not allowed to associate with known felons, and with all the, all the horrible things you've done in your life, you know, I can't be a part of that . . .

NORMA: [laughing] Oh, listen to you . . . stop. Anyway, yeah, things could just twist, just like that, couldn't they?

LYLE: Huh?

NORMA: Things could just twist like that, you know?

LYLE: They *could,* they could . . .

NORMA: You never know the moment here.

LYLE: If he decides to retry me?

NORMA: Mm-hmm.

LYLE: Alright. If he decides to retry me, I'll tell you this—I'm not taking any more deals.

NORMA: Oh, really?

LYLE: No way—forget it. You know what I mean?

NORMA: Yeah.

LYLE: I'm not taking any. I mean, if he tries me again, he's gonna lose. I'll tell you right now, I'm gonna beat his ass *worse* than I did the first time, because the se— The first trial had a few mistakes in it, and there won't be any mistakes in the second trial.

NORMA: Right. Of course, then you can fill in all the things you didn't do in the first place. Can't they—

LYLE: You know, like all that Big 5 stuff.

NORMA: And then you can add on what you didn't say.

LYLE: You can only do that once.

NORMA: Right.

LYLE: So, he's got all those people that lied in his—in the first trial—that he's not gonna even use in the second.

NORMA: Uh-huh . . .

LYLE: So he's gonna be down to like, one or two witnesses against me that have any credibility at all. You know, basically the tape is all they can use against me.

NORMA: Right.

LYLE: And so he'll do that, and we'll go again, and . . .

NORMA: Do you feel that the tape's your worst portion right now, of the trial?

LYLE: It's the only reason that I'm not home already.

NORMA: Yeah . . .

LYLE: That's the only reason.

NORMA: Yeah.

LYLE: It's bullshit, because this tape is, you know, totally Oziel . . .

NORMA: Yeah.

LYLE: It's like an Oziel thing, you know what I mean? I mean, there were never—it's got Oziel all over it, but still, it's enough that it could make some—one or two people say, "Hey, that's enough."

NORMA: Right.

LYLE: So . . .

NORMA: Well, you know, like I said, there was a lot of people in this, in this mock jury, that wanted you to be acquitted, even though they knew about that tape.

LYLE: Oh, yeah . . .

NORMA: So, why shouldn't your own jury be thinking the same thing?

LYLE: Yeah.

NORMA: You know.

LYLE: Well, that mock jury is a joke, because the mock—but none of those people—

NORMA: Well, of course it is, but it still—

LYLE: None of those people watched the trial.

NORMA: Well, not all of them, no, that's true. But they didn't—

LYLE: But they haven't watched every moment.

NORMA: I know, yeah.

LYLE: You have to deal, you have to be—watch every moment before you can honestly say, "Well, I have this opinion," because—

NORMA: Right.

LYLE: Because, you, you can't have an opinion if you missed a day.

NORMA: Yeah.

LYLE: Because it could be an important day.

NORMA: Of course, yeah, sure. And that, you know, that's why, they picked sort of not older people, and they were all like—there were youngish and there were middle-aged, so obviously some of them were working.

LYLE: Yeah.

NORMA: So how could they see it, you know—the whole trial.

LYLE: Yeah.

NORMA: So it would have been hard really, to get a mock jury, debating, who had seen it all.

LYLE: Even if they watched it, if they watched it on Court TV, it still doesn't matter, because they've seen things that the jury hasn't.

NORMA: Yeah.

LYLE: They've seen tons of things the jury hasn't.

NORMA: Well, yeah, that's true.

LYLE: You know, so that's not representative of a real opinion of, of trying the case.

NORMA: Yeah . . . yeah, because I even forgot about that, you know, where they're seeing something—well, your jury's seeing some things, but the other jury's not—

LYLE: What's amazing is that a few people who have watched

Court TV have seen every single thing, even the things that are bad, that aren't admissable—they've seen, right?

NORMA: Mm-hmm?

LYLE: And they still are for us. So, it's a—

NORMA: So that's good, yeah. So it *is* looking pretty good right now. There's a lot of support . . . yeah.

LYLE: And I think it's gonna be very shocking. I think every, you know, I think there's a, a whole group of people out there, probably yourself included—

NORMA: Yeah . . .

LYLE: —that, that think that it's gonna be bad, and there, there's no way you can win, and this case is not "winnable," and it's gonna be at least a one-murder conviction, and Erik's gonna go down or something . . . and I think you guys are totally off—completely. And I think it's gonna be very shocking for people to hear that this case is not gonna be won by the district attorney's office, ever. And I, I don't even think it's gonna be close. It's not like they almost won—they had to try it again—I think it's gonna be like they just were a thread away from losing, and they just barely made it so that they didn't lose.

NORMA: Right.

LYLE: And at the next trial, they *may* lose.

NORMA: Well, now if they *did*, would you still have Jill and Leslie?

LYLE: If they tried it again?

NORMA: Yeah.

LYLE: Oh, yeah, definitely.

NORMA: OK, 'cause, wouldn't they want to be paid again?

LYLE: They'd have . . . well, the state would have to pay them.

NORMA: Oh, I see . . . oh, OK.

LYLE: That's another reason they're not gonna retry this case—they might not.

NORMA: Oh.

LYLE: They're gonna have to shell out a few million dollars.

NORMA: Oh, dear.

LYLE: At least I know, I'm not gonna pay for it.

NORMA: Right.

LYLE: You know . . .

NORMA: Yeah, 'cause they are expensive, aren't they now?

LYLE: Oh, yeah! And I could raise the money to pay for them, right?

NORMA: Yeah.

LYLE: Easily, but I'm not going to. Let the state pay for it. Let the prosecution's office use their money to pay for it. If they, if they want to prosecute our case again, you know, if they want to prosecute it again like we're some kind of a serial killer?

NORMA: Yeah?

LYLE: You know, which is a total joke [interference from another conversation] . . . then *spend* the money.

NORMA: Mm-hmm, right.

LYLE: And embarrass yourself a second time.

NORMA: Yeah.

LYLE: And then after you lose the second trial?

NORMA: Yeah?

LYLE: When you don't have a verdict from the second trial, either—I might not win it, but, after you don't win it either—

NORMA: Can you imagine that?

LYLE: Then, then don't come to me and say, "Oh, we'll give you manslaughter." No, no, forget about it. Forget about it. I'm not taking it. Dismiss the case. Or, or, go for a third trial, and spend another couple million. You know what I mean?

NORMA: Yeah.

LYLE: Why should I take a deal then, you know? Every time I come here, I say, "I'm willing to talk."

NORMA: Yeah, but don't, but manslaughter's only—

LYLE: I mean, "Fuck you."

NORMA: Well, how many—manslaughter's only a couple of years, though, isn't it?

LYLE: Yeah . . .

NORMA: About four years . . .

LYLE: No, not that much.

NORMA: And then you do half, which'd be two . . .

LYLE: Yeah, they'd give me two.

NORMA: Why wouldn't you want to take that?

LYLE: No, I would.

NORMA: You would?

LYLE: I would take that.

NORMA: Oh, I thought you just said "I wouldn't take it," and you'd go for a third trial.

LYLE: I wouldn't—I wouldn't take it if we—if they forced me to go to a second trial—I would *not* take the four years.

NORMA: Oh.

LYLE: I would tell them, "Listen, I don't want a felony conviction." You know, 'cause what am I gonna—they get to try the case twice to see if they can convict me. Only after they, they realize there's no way?

NORMA: Yeah . . .

LYLE: *Then* they want me to take a deal?

NORMA: Yeah . . .

LYLE: Well, why should I take a deal? Forget about it. I'll go again. You know what I mean?

NORMA: Yeah . . .

LYLE: They're not gonna try the case three times.

NORMA: No . . .

LYLE: So, so they got a choice to make. They either go the second time, and they better win, or they don't—or they give me a deal now.

NORMA: What happened to that friggin' law where you can't be retried for the same crime twice?

LYLE: Well, you can be retried as many times as long as—you can't be retried if you get found "not guilty."

NORMA: OK, if you're found "not guilty," that's what the clause says.

LYLE: Right. And I'm not gonna get found "not guilty."

NORMA: OK, yeah . . .

LYLE: You know . . .

NORMA: Right . . .

LYLE: Because see, there might be a few jurors that think we should be acquitted, but not twelve, or not, not even—probably not even, like eight. Probably just a couple.

NORMA: Yeah, but there is some. I think this is what's causing this long debate, because some of the others are trying to, trying to persuade the others to see their point of view, and vice versa.

LYLE: Yeah. Well, I think the debate is between the minority of the people that are against us—that's my feeling.

NORMA: Do you think so?

LYLE: I think so. I think that we won the trial, too. I think we're—you know, in my opinion, if you have the majority of people, then you won. You may not have gotten "not guilty" . . .

NORMA: Mm-hmm . . .

LYLE: . . . but you didn't get convicted, and you got the majority of the people, and you won the trial. You swayed more people.

NORMA: Yeah . . .

LYLE: And unfortunately, the law is, it's not a question of swaying more people, it's gotta be unanimous. But, uh, still, I mean, essentially, the way I would look at is, I won. Like, like, if it was like nine against me, and three for me?

NORMA: Mm-hmm?

LYLE: Then I would consider that I had lost the trial.

NORMA: Right.

LYLE: You know, and it wouldn't be that I was convicted, but essentially they did better than we did, they convinced more people, so they won . . .

NORMA: Yeah . . .

LYLE: They won the trial.

NORMA: Right . . .

LYLE: I think, I think that they . . .

NORMA: And then again, it's not only the prosecutors that are doing the convincing. Sometimes it might be the other jurors convincing the others, mightn't it?

LYLE: Yeah, that's true, too.

NORMA: Yeah . . .

LYLE: That's true too. But I think generally they go into the jury room pretty much set on what they want. I don't think it's people convincing a lot of people.

NORMA: You don't think so?

LYLE: No. You know, once you sit through the trial, you don't think you have a pretty strong opinion by then?

NORMA: Yeah, I do, I think so, yeah.

LYLE: I agree.

NORMA: So, the problem is, coming to what, to what degree.

LYLE: Well, it's not gonna get—I don't think they're gonna reach a decision on that.

NORMA: Yeah, it looked like both the juries are having the same problem, because they're both asking for things, aren't they?

LYLE: Yeah, well people are trying to convince people of things.

NORMA: Right.

LYLE: You know what I mean? Like right now, there's a big debate in my jury room?

NORMA: Yeah . . .

LYLE: About whether some fuckin' juror thinks that I was thinking about fingerprints when I purchased the shotgun shells. You know what I mean?

NORMA: Yeah.

LYLE: They think that I testified to that. And I didn't testify to that—obviously.

NORMA: No.

LYLE: Because that would mean planning. So, he's arguing that I actually testified to planning, you know, which is ridiculous, obviously, right?

NORMA: Which juror's that? They didn't tell you which one it was?

LYLE: Yeah, I know which one it is.

LYLE: Oh, God . . .

LYLE: And so he thinks that, so they asked for a read-back two times already on that fingerprint thing?

NORMA: Uh-huh?

LYLE: And they asked for a read-back, and when you read it back, it was confusing, you know what I mean?

NORMA: Was it?

LYLE: I can see, when I, when I read it back, why he would think that, because—

NORMA: Oh . . .

LYLE: —I was kinda talking about like different things at different times, and it looked like it was all—it was all, you know, it was confusing. So they've asked for another one . . .

NORMA: On Monday?

LYLE: Now they've asked for my entire testimony of that whole day, Sunday.

NORMA: Oh, shit.

LYLE: And everything that was ever said about Sunday, from me and Erik, which is gonna be like a whole day in read-back.

January 11, 1994

NORMA: Hello. Yeah, like I was waiting today and you didn't call.

LYLE: They wouldn't let us use the phone. No because Erik's jury was hung and—

NORMA: Your voice is coming in better now.

LYLE: The judge wouldn't let us hear the vote.

NORMA: Oh, really? In case you spread the news or something? Oh I see. Yeah, I had Terry already for you to play tonight. Did you hear him already?

LYLE: I heard he said something about Garcetti.

NORMA: Oh yeah, he said a bit of everything. But anyway what do you think about it? Do you think that is OK for Erik?

LYLE: Yeah, I told you he would never get convicted of murder.

NORMA: Do you think it's going to be a hung jury?

LYLE: Yeah. It's already a hung jury.

NORMA: Well, Gil Garcetti said he was upset about that. He said he would rather go for a new trial. He was saying that tonight on the news. Well anyway, we'll have to see won't we? When they go out again or come in again.

January 14, 1994

NORMA: I think [Erik's] sick because he's got to go through it again. Well, Lyle I don't think it will last as long, do you?

LYLE: No.

NORMA: Especially as I don't think that Leslie is going to bring in all those people again. That costs money.

LYLE: She doesn't care how much money she spends, she'll bring them in.

NORMA: They'll bring a jury in right? Show them videos.

LYLE: They can't. They are not allowed to do that. I don't think you can do that.

NORMA: I wonder if the exact same thing happens. I wonder who else has been in a trial before, twice.

LYLE: There is no laws about whether you can use a video because there is no other trial on TV. But she wouldn't be able to do that. She can bring the people back in.

NORMA: Well, anyway one thing about it, she could demolish all of the negative ones. She can get rid of them.

LYLE: Yeah, right. We'll clean up the bad ones. We did all right. I told you he wasn't going to get convicted of murder.

NORMA: But you know what you said all along—it's going to be a hung jury.

LYLE: Yeah.

NORMA: But didn't you think it was going to be for you too?

LYLE: I think it will be—I'm hoping that they will give me a verdict. But I don't think they are going to.

NORMA: Garcetti said if they come in with manslaughter for you—did you hear it? It's very likely that it will screw up for Erik, for getting a murder charge for Erik. So that'll be good, 'cause then they will have to consider manslaughter for Erik then too.

LYLE: Is that what he said?

NORMA: Garcetti said if they come back with manslaughter for you they will probably have to go with manslaughter for Erik.

LYLE: Oh, I thought he said that even if they come back with manslaughter for me, he was going to try Erik for murder.

NORMA: No, I didn't hear that at all. He definitely said it would screw up what they wanted to do for Erik. They wanted to bring murder charges—he didn't say screw up—he said something else instead of screw up but that's what he meant. Yeah, and he said we'd probably have to go with manslaughter too. Because you will most likely both be charged with the same degree whatever it is.

LYLE: Really, I'm just hoping they come back with manslaughter. God I hope.

NORMA: Yeah, sure. So do I.

LYLE: Fucking people that are involved though.

NORMA: So if you do talk to Erik you can tell him that. Yeah, because I wouldn't have you repeat that to him if it was a mishearing—I definitely heard him say that yesterday.

LYLE: They put a gag order on Garcetti so you won't be hearing him say any more.

NORMA: I'm trying to think. What I'll do is I'll rewind to where Garcetti is on and give you the exact wording and leave it on your message machine.

LYLE: Fine. Good. Thanks. He won't be saying anything more.

NORMA: I don't remember what else he said. But I'll try to catch all what he said and leave it on your machine tonight.

LYLE: He won't say anything new because he's got a gag order on him so he can't say anything new.

NORMA: A gag order on Garcetti? Really?

LYLE: Yeah, he's talking too much.

NORMA: He did say that before he got gagged.

LYLE: Yeah, I heard he did. Hopefully I can get a fucking manslaughter. But I don't know—these two women—I have this one woman and this one guy—I don't know. The one woman is married to a DA. The hippie guy, I think we can win him over.

NORMA: Which one is the hippie? The one who had a beard and shaved it off?

LYLE: Yeah. I think we can win him—

NORMA: He seems jolly doesn't he?

LYLE: He's an idiot. But we're working—he seems real kind of quirky.

NORMA: I've seen the jurors walking in and out but I really didn't analyze any of them. I just look and see if they look pleasant or if they are smiling or whatever. But most of the time they are in a good mood.

LYLE: They were in a very good mood Friday.

NORMA: Were they? I didn't see them Friday. I wasn't at the courthouse, I watched it all on television.

LYLE: It's been really gloomy lately but Friday they were in a good mood.

NORMA: OK.

LYLE: So they should come back Tuesday or Wednesday.

NORMA: Tuesday because Monday is a holiday.

LYLE: If they come back hung then we'll see—I'm fucked.

NORMA: So first you want manslaughter right? And then secondly you'd like a hung jury so you'd go back again with Erik?

LYLE: No, secondly I would want them to acquit me on first and then hang on second.

NORMA: OK—of course—silly me. [laughing]

LYLE: Manslaughter would be the best. If not manslaughter then at least acquit me of first-degree murder and then hang between second and manslaughter. And then if not that, then it's just—then I know it's going to hang. They are not going to convict me of murder because I got too many people

NORMA: No, everyone agrees with that.

LYLE: But I think they—I got a chance if they are not—I think if they can only agree if it wasn't planned and maybe they just can't agree on whether it's second-degree or manslaughter and then it will hang there but they can't try me on first-degree anymore.

NORMA: Right.

LYLE: That's what Erik was hoping for and it didn't happen.

NORMA: I thought he was pissed. He looked real dejected on the screen. He didn't look very happy. He was just hanging his head there.

LYLE: Yeah, he was really upset about it.

NORMA: It's a fucking shame that he's got to wait all over again. It gets me. It's horrible when you have to hang right there in the middle and not know. Not knowing is worse than getting a miserable verdict. It depends how miserable it is, of course. But not knowing is fucking—

LYLE: It doesn't look like murder.

NORMA: Nobody thinks so that I've heard.

LYLE: A lot of people thought so originally.

NORMA: Yeah, at the beginning of the trial they did. Some of them were still thinking so originally. But just lately now, well there is so much being talked about the manslaughter and the involuntary manslaughter and the things they've been asking for have been leading to that. So it looks like it's coming down and down.

LYLE: Yeah, but it only takes one person.

NORMA: To fuck everything up. It could have been just one to fuck Erik up, couldn't it? We'll never know—

LYLE: I think it was about five.

NORMA: Oh was it? Maybe we'll find out later on in the week or something, after the trial. They'll probably tell everything then.

LYLE: My case goes more deeper than Erik's did. But I got a better jury. We'll see, a lot of things are going to happen between now and the next trial so we'll see.

NORMA: I think for Erik it will be less time—shorter trial because of the people that she'll dismiss, that she won't want back on again.

LYLE: Definitely a shorter trial. I don't think he's worried about the length of the trial. He's upset that he may have to testify again.

NORMA: Right. Well the thing that I was upset about early on was when Garcetti said he had new evidence. So I thought, Now what has he got? So we won't find that out until later on.

LYLE: That's a bunch of bullshit. It always is. Look at all of the evidence they had in the first trial. They had me on tape. I don't think new evidence will have anything to do with the outcome. What has he got? Another person who says that Erik—

NORMA: Could be more heresay—exactly.

LYLE: I don't believe these people.

NORMA: It's all wind—everything's wind up to now.

LYLE: The only reason he is screaming about new evidence is to save himself the embarrassment of having had his ass kicked in the first trial. He's trying to tell everyone we're the ones who are right—we are still right. We were right even though well over half the jury feels that he was wrong.

NORMA: Well already last week he was saying that he was definitely bringing murder charges against Erik Menendez. And now yesterday he's come down from that even now. Well if they come down to manslaughter for Lyle, it's going to screw—what the hell did he say? I've got to find out the words that he uses—but he meant that it's going to screw things up for Erik and they would have to go with manslaughter for him.

LYLE: That's great.

NORMA: He said they wouldn't be able to bring murder charges. It would alter the whole course of the trial.

LYLE: They could bring them but the problem is it wouldn't stand.

NORMA: Yeah, he thinks that they would lose if they did that 'cause obviously any jury is going to say, How can we give Erik worse than Lyle? We'll have to go less or the same.

LYLE: Plus I'll take the stand and say that I just got manslaughter.

NORMA: Of course, because you'll be a witness won't you?

LYLE: Yeah, I'll say that I got manslaughter and they would be like, Well what are we doing here? The one brother that had planned it and the one brother that didn't.

NORMA: You will already have been dealt with so it won't matter what you say after that.

LYLE: Right. I could take the whole rap. He could say he was at the movies.

NORMA: Well [laughing] I was going to say now that is stretching it. That's taking an elastic band—that one is.

LYLE: It's just the agony—he has to go through it all again. I think maybe we can avoid it.

NORMA: [Leslie] did throw a hint about last night—a hint about getting a fund-raiser going. And she is already fielding calls. Offers of money. So I think she will do alright there. What she can do Lyle—she can already afford to do it. But she's saying if I can get some money coming in all the better. I'll use less of my own money.

LYLE: The state is going to have to pay her. The county is going to have to pay her. At $100 an hour. Absolutely, they can't avoid that. More than that.

NORMA: What if they do send money in then? Because she's fielding calls already.

LYLE: Technically she can't use that money but I can use it to pay other things.

NORMA: Well that would be nice.

LYLE: I'll use it to pay Mike and investigators and things like that.

NORMA: She'll take her cut before she tells you how much she got.

LYLE: I know that. I wouldn't doubt it. No, she'll be—well we'll see.

NORMA: It depends how much comes in I suppose.

LYLE: I'll definitely talk to you tomorrow and hear what Garcetti had to say.

NORMA: OK, love. I hope you get through to Erik and kind of cheer him up.

HOW THE JURORS SPLIT

Two juries considering evidence separately against Erik and Lyle Menendez failed to reach a consensus on any of the charges in the 1989 slayings of their parents, Jose and Kitty Menendez. Mistrials were declared in both cases. Here's how the juries split on the charges.

ERIK MENENDEZ: (6-man, 6-woman jury)		LYLE MENENDEZ (7-woman, 5-man jury)	
Murder of Jose Menendez		*Murder of Jose Menendez*	
1st degree murder	5	1st degree murder	3
2nd degree murder	1	2nd degree murder	3
Voluntary manslaughter	6	Voluntary manslaughter	6
Involuntary manslaughter	0	Involuntary manslaughter	0
Murder of Kitty Menendez		*Murder of Kitty Menendez*	
1st degree murder	5	1st degree murder	3
2nd degree murder	3	2nd degree murder	3
Voluntary manslaughter	4	Voluntary manslaughter	5
Involuntary manslaughter	0	Involuntary manslaughter	1
Conspiracy		*Conspiracy*	
1st degree	5	1st degree	3
2nd degree	1	2nd degree	3
Not guilty	6	Not guilty	6

July 1994

[Editor's note: Six months after the verdict, Lyle and Norma discuss the retrial—and another famous inmate.]

NORMA: Hey, what about O. J. Simpson? There's been a lot of lookin' at the TV?

LYLE: Yeah, they've been preparing for his arrival where Erik is, but I, uh, I don't know if he's gonna get arrested or not, but I assume he will.

NORMA: Yeah, well, there's no other suspects except him, is there? And I think that's why Weitzman gave it up, because I think he must have confessed to Weitzman, you know. I guess Weitzman said to him, "Did you do it?" I mean, once the attorney knows you did it, I don't think you can represent him, because you're supposed to—the attorney's supposed to believe him, if he says he didn't do it, isn't he?

LYLE: The attorney can represent you, even if you say you did it.

NORMA: You think so?

LYLE: Just because he did it, doesn't mean it's murder, personally. I don't think that he—the first stage of the case is proving that he did it, the second stage is proving that it was murder, and that's something else.

NORMA: Yeah.

LYLE: Because it's something, I mean, it doesn't seem like it's a planned murder to me.

NORMA: No, I think he just went berserk, you know?

LYLE: That's what I think . . .

NORMA: Yeah, he just lost it. Because look at all the clues he left around, you know. And the trail of blood up his driveway that they're showing on TV? So it just doesn't look too good for him at all. It's a shame for the kids, you know.

LYLE: Oh, yeah . . .

NORMA: I mean those kids were saying, "My father's O. J. Simpson, blah blah . . ." you know, "We're all proud of him." And now look at him—what's he done to them? It is a shame.

LYLE: I don't know, did he get arrested? I don't know, we'll see. . . . I think he fired Weitzman, I don't think that Weitzman will say it on his own, but . . .

NORMA: Yeah.

LYLE: He, he'll have Bob Shapiro right now, and he'll get rid of Shapiro, too.

NORMA: He knows what he's doing, this Shapiro guy. Did you see him on television?

LYLE: I had him as an attorney. He was Erik's attorney for about four weeks.

NORMA: Oh, he was? Oh, when you first got arrested? Maybe that's why his face looks familiar. I've seen him on TV before.

LYLE: Yeah, he represented us for awhile, and then he represented Brando after us.

NORMA: Oh, really?

LYLE: So that's probably where you've seen him, with pictures of Brando, but . . .

NORMA: Yeah.

LYLE: But he's not very good.

NORMA: Who?

LYLE: Bob Shapiro.

NORMA: He's not?

LYLE: I don't think so. He's pretty bad.

NORMA: Oh, I thought he looked pretty confident, that he knew what he was doing.

LYLE: That doesn't mean that he's good though.

NORMA: Oh . . .

LYLE: You know, it just means that he's confident. [laughing]

NORMA: Do you think—Isn't that odd why Weitzman gave up though? Why do you think he did that?

LYLE: Because O. J. told him he didn't want him.

NORMA: He did?

LYLE: You think Weitzman would give up this case . . .

NORMA: I was gonna say, 'cause that's a lot of money to throw away, isn't it? There's been a lot of publicity.

LYLE: No attorneys give up cases; it never happens. If they get fired—

NORMA: Oh, bloody hell.

LYLE: —then they go to the public and say, "Oh, I decided I didn't want to do it," and things like that, you know. And Bob'll be told the same thing, is my guess. He'll either end up with like, Johnny Cochran, or with Leslie.

NORMA: Oh . . .

LYLE: Somebody like that. He needs somebody good, not Bob Shapiro. It's gonna be a hell of a case.

NORMA: So you think if he gets arrested, he'll go up where Erik is?

LYLE: Oh, yeah, they're already prepared for him.

NORMA: Really? Well, what about down by you? Why wouldn't he go on your cell?

LYLE: Erik is up where famous people go.

NORMA: Oh, I see . . .

LYLE: I'm in a decent place, but not where, you know, I should be.

NORMA: Oh . . .

LYLE: Only one of us could be up there—they didn't want to put us together.

NORMA: Yeah. Right. You have to be separate.

LYLE: So, that's why I'm here, but it's not too bad.

NORMA: What's this shit in the paper, anyway, that I read about you last night, separating from Erik, because of, uh, Leslie Abramson?

LYLE: Yeah . . . the paper is totally out of balance. It's total bullshit.

NORMA: Well, I know that's what she wanted to do in the first place, though, Lyle. She always wanted to turn Erik against you in the very first place, you know.

LYLE: Well, I'm not so sure that that's true, but, in any case, it's totally ridiculous, it could never happen. I wouldn't even know if my brother wanted to turn against me, what he could say that would make any difference.

NORMA: Well, no, in the paper, he's supposed to be going to say that he was frightened of you.

LYLE: That's not—that's the DA's bullshit analogy . . .

NORMA: Yeah, because Craig Cignarelli said that "Erik wasn't frightened of Lyle; Erik was his own man—he did what he pleased."

LYLE: Well . . .

NORMA: That's what Craig Cignarelli said.

LYLE: Well, you can't believe anything Craig Cignarelli says, so that doesn't really mean anything.

NORMA: Yeah, but, it's gotta be one way or the other. Either he was afraid of you, or he wasn't afraid of you.

LYLE: Yeah, but there's no reason to be afraid of me—I don't even have a temper.

NORMA: No, I know.

LYLE: I mean, I don't know what my brother would be afraid of *me* for, because I was the only person in his life who tried to help at all. It's totally ridiculous. I mean, Leslie does do stupid things to try to get a semblance of some kind, you know?

NORMA: And yet, well, also, she's trying to get a separate trial, right?

LYLE: She's trying to get a separate trial—no, but she doesn't really want a separate trial, no.

NORMA: Well, I thought she wanted to blame you for most of the stuff.

LYLE: No, no, no, that's ridiculous. That's not true—she does not—she doesn't want to blame me. If she wanted to do that, she could have done it in the last trial—obviously didn't. Obviously can't . . .

NORMA: Still, it's still a sticky situation. I mean, I would still be a little worried.

LYLE: No, I'm not worried. I don't have to worry about it. I mean Leslie Abramson is not a relative of mine.

NORMA: Well, have you talked to Erik since? Did you talk to Erik within the last week?

LYLE: No, I haven't spoken to him.

NORMA: So, well, how do you know which way he's, he's thinking, then?

LYLE: We're brothers. And I know what happened, and I know, I know who he is, and that could not happen in a million years. I mean, that's just—my brother and I are very, very close, I think he loves me, and, uh, he would never do that. Some people are bad people, and they just do that to other people. Erik would not.

NORMA: Let's hope it's just wind.

LYLE: Oh, it is. She's already said on TV, Leslie was furious— she called the editor and tried to get him kicked out of the paper, and so on. It was totally unethical, what he did.

NORMA: Yeah.

LYLE: Trying to make a story out of something that was pure nothing. But you know, if a person's out of control . . .

NORMA: Yeah, well, in the paper anyway it said that the prosecutor said, "There's no way we're going to be separating these guys in the trial. They both did what they did together, they both decided together, and they both committed the acts together, so why should we separate them? They're both equally to blame." That was the attitude of the prosecutors, you know.

LYLE: Well, the reality is, they just don't want to spend another million dollars, you know?

NORMA: Right.

LYLE: But prosecutors can never tell the truth about what their real motives are. They, they go with their little excuse. But, they just don't want to spend the money, obviously.

NORMA: Yeah.

LYLE: So now I'll wait. And my guess is that we'll be tried together, which is fine with me.

NORMA: Is it improved at all down there? Nothing?

LYLE: No, nothing, really . . .

NORMA: Just your reading.

LYLE: There's a little bit nicer guys around me, but . . .

NORMA: Huh?

LYLE: I mean, there's kind of nice guys around me at the moment.

NORMA: You sound awful far away again.

J. Lyle Menendez

January, 1995 A.Δ.   BK # 1887106
P.O. Box 86164
Terminal Annex
Los Angeles, CA
90086-0164

Hello. *I hope you've enjoyed the holidays and are looking forward to the new year. I wish that I was writing this letter under better circumstances. I would like to thank you for your love and support. It has been really helpfull. it has lifted our spirits and is a constant reminder to Erik and me that we are not alone. Being insulated here in the jail is both scary and lonely. Letters from those that care makes a difference.*

*As you probably know, my retrial is around the corner. It's hard to imagine going through the process of another trial and the painful experience of testifying all over again. I don't believe I could have done it the first time without my attorney, Jill Lansing. Her skill, compassion and common sense were the soul of the trial and gave me the courage to continue. The mistrial last January was a tremendous disappointment to everyone involved. Ms. Lansing had given so many years of her life to it and she needed to spend some time with her husband and 6 year old daughter. She took a leave to be with them. For the last year, however, she has continued to work hard assisting the public defenders assigned to me. She did this without any compensation. The trial is set to begin in just a few months and the public defenders here have said they can **not possibly be ready**-- only Ms. Lansing can be prepared to present this case in time. In order to have her present at the re-trial, however—acting as my attorney of record, I must now hire her privately. She can not afford to defend me for free. If she could—she certainly would do so. She is willing to work for the same minimal fees that the public defender receives.*

I need your help! I have never needed it more so than I do at this time. I believe that if those that have supported me through correspondence, each donate a small amount of money --that I will have enough to hire her and possibly enough to hire Michael Burt-- the attorney that worked so brilliantly along side Ms . Lansing in the first trial. Every time I'm in court-- his absence is felt.

If you're willing and able to contribute financially, there are two ways that would be most helpful. The first would be to give what you can afford to give all at once. The second way would be to pledge that you would send a certain amount each month. Since the attorneys would be relying on their bills being paid each month—it would be very important that you send the amount you pledged by the 15'th of each month. Please only pledge what you truly feel you can send without hardship. The attorneys will need to be paid through sentencing in this case. I will certainly notify you of her representation ending . If you are able to send a lump sum now and a monthly pledge thereafter it would be especially helpful, as Ms. Lansing can not commit to represent me until I can be assured that the amount needed to represent me is available. The same would be true for Mr. Burt.

Time is running out. If she is going to substitute in, she will have to do so this month or next month at the very latest. I would not send you this letter if it was not a last resort. I hope that 1995 brings some resolution for Erik and me. Thanks again for your love and support—we appreciate it tremendously. Take Care and God Bless...

J. Lyle Menendez

Hi! thanks for taking time to read the enclosed letter. I appreciate the prayers and support.

Take good care

Love

Lyle

Lyle Menendez Legal Defense Fund

Pledge Card Certificate

I, _____, do pledge to send $ _____, by the 15'th
of each month for the Legal Defense Fund for Lyle Menendez.   My first
donation for January 1995 is enclosed in the amount of $_____.

<u>Please forward to</u>:   **Lyle Menendez Legal Defense Fund**
P.O. Box 5115
Beverly Hills, California 90209

This pledge card is necessary for record   keeping   purposes.   These pledge cards are not legally binding—Should you decide to discontinue your pledged amount   or wish
to increase it- - Please notify us at your earliest convenience.   Personal Checks or Money Orders   should   be   made   payable to: *Lyle Menendez Legal Defense Fund*
and forwarded to the above address. To verify the validity of this letter and Defense Fund—you may call Ms. Jill Lansing's office at 310.470.4317. Any funds received will be used to
cover attorney fees and expenses not funded by the court. All names will remain confidential. Thank you for your consideration and support.

4

LIFE AFTER LYLE

It had started with a letter, expanded to regular jail visits, then escalated into an all-consuming "job," catering to Lyle's purchases, errands, and phone calls.

Originally I had been happy to assure Mama Menendez that I would visit Lyle while she went back to New Jersey, because he had no visitors. Mama was expected to be gone only a short time, but the days and weeks rolled on before she returned. Meanwhile, I continued to visit two, three, and four times a week. I didn't complain because I felt it was important to get Lyle out of his cell as often as possible. Somehow, what began as a favor had become an obligation. Of course, no one could have anticipated when Lyle was arrested in the spring of 1990, that he would not come to trial until the summer of 1993.

After the trial commenced, monitoring and taping Court TV, newscasts, and commentaries, then playing all that back for Lyle on the phone at night, was full-time work. In addition to Lyle's errands, I was buying, cutting, and filing the daily newspaper articles and magazine stories, operating the telephone network, and waiting for his daily calls. Zero time was left for anything else. On days I was attending the trial, waiting in line, and delivering Lyle's requested items (an exceedingly time-consuming project) the regular daily jobs were delayed, so I had to rush home and play catch-up and be there for his after-court call.

Shortly before the trial I had ceased publication of my magazine. Ever-increasing costs of paper and printing made it too costly to continue. Now helping Lyle became my primary concern.

It is true that no one forced me into this situation. I had offered to assist Lyle when he was in need of friendship and help, and he had made the most of it. Given this opportunity, he maximized it, manipulating and molding me into his righthand on the outside.

I knew all along I was being used and controlled by a master manipulator, but once you are drawn into a vortex, there is no way to extricate yourself, no way to come up for air. You are trapped.

I never wanted to let anyone down who was counting on me. Lyle told me how much he depended on my efforts, how much he appreciated what I did for him. Of course he criticized, berated, and ridiculed me as well. Was I foolish? Maybe. Would I do it again? Never! Did I bask in his sporadic gratitude? I think so. Doesn't everyone like praise?

I was never surprised at his criticism or lengthy harangues, even when the supposed offense had not taken place. I knew no one could or would ever achieve the degree of perfection Lyle demands. Was this trait inherited from his father Jose, who demanded so much from his family and his employees?

Lyle knew I didn't believe in his innocence. Early on, although he hadn't admitted the killings, he knew I thought he did it. Long after he had confessed, he suddenly came up with the abuse story. We had talked about every subject you could imagine for a couple of years, and there was no mention of molestation. He knew I wasn't buying it. As he expanded on the theme after reading Paul Mones' book and visiting with him, it was obvious he was practicing on me, but to no avail. We just went on to other subjects.

After the trial was over, Lyle's daily phone calls dwindled. I heard from him now and then. Others with whom he had corresponded or spoken reported the same thing. He seemed to be dropping his circle of friends and supporters. I still heard from him, but now that there were no Menendez Court TV shows to tape, no news commentaries to follow, no newspaper articles to cut, no chores were required of me. The brothers' notoriety had downscaled to the occasional unflattering justice system cartoon or a comedy monologue mention.

One day, after I hadn't heard from Lyle for longer than usual, I was worried and left a message on his machine. He didn't return my call. A day later I called again, left another message, but I didn't hear from him.

Abruptly, with no hint, no warning, no notice, Lyle Menendez dropped from my life. As they say in the business world, I was free to pursue other interests.

Weeks went by and I was in Menendez withdrawal, remembering so much of what had transpired over the years before the trial, then the trial and all the emotion and excitement attendant to it.

Everyone else I had met was going on with life. Court-watching was no longer just the purview of retired people with plenty of time. All America had a new consuming interest: O. J. Simpson, the "Trial of the Century." I was left behind staring at the detritus of my Menendez years, knee-deep in pictures, clippings, books, videotapes, letters, cards, court transcripts, notepads, and unpaid phone bills. Included in this treasure trove of Menendez memorabilia is the pair of shoes Lyle was wearing when he was arrested.

I only remember crying three times relative to this case. The first time was when I met Maria Menendez and my heart soared with admiration for her courage and strength and broke with sorrow for her loss and what was to come.

The second time was on the way home after my first jail visit, when the enormity of the tragedy, the lost lives, and the devastated future of the family overwhelmed me.

The third and last time was when I read along at home a transcript of the Oziel tape as it was played in court. It was not clear to me why for years the attorneys had fought all the way to the Supreme Court to try to keep the taped confessions out. During that time, Lyle and Erik languished in the Los Angeles County Jail, hoping in vain to win that legal battle.

Hearing Lyle's and Erik's own voices, which I knew so well, confessing to the killings destroyed any wee speck of hope I might have held that perhaps there had been some explanation. I realized this was as close to the truth as anyone would ever hear from them.

This had been their opportunity to get it down on tape exactly like they wanted it. They knew they were being taped. Lyle told me he pushed the button that started the tape recorder. Where was one word about abuse? Where was there even a hint of incest, or a word about molestation? Where was there any reason to kill? Where was the *fear?*

I cried for hours. There was no way Lyle could defend the indefensible, refute the irrefutable, or remain believable with his contrived testimony of lies and alibis.

Menendez Update

◆

Maria Menendez, now in her eightieth year, lives in the North Hollywood area. She no longer speaks to her daughter Marta, whom she disowned for her damaging testimony at the trial. She has expressed plans to relocate to a place near whatever penitentiary will house the brothers if they are convicted at the retrial and sent to the same location.

The Calabasas house has been sold to the only bidder just two weeks before the house was to be sold at auction. The Menendez family had purchased the property for $1.4 million and put in around $500,000 in remodeling and improvement costs. The selling price was in the $1.4 million range. The proceeds were slated for repayment of a $700,000 mortgage, commissions, and taxes, leaving the estate coffers on empty.

Dr. L. Jerome Oziel and his family relocated to another state. Judalon Smyth continues to pursue lawsuits against Dr. Oziel.

Lyle's friend, Harry, remains loyal and attends some of the Van Nuys hearings. Throughout the trial he has always been the best-dressed spectator, usually clad in a dark suit, with dress shirt and tie. Sometimes he is alone, but usually he is accompanied by different women. Sometimes a gum-chewing blonde with exceedingly long hair or a dark-haired woman with a dour countenance is with him.

Only one or two of the original groupies ever attends anymore, but if any do, it is as though a dress and color code has mysteriously been imposed. Gone is the Frederick's of Hollywood mode. Smart black outfits, stockings, and stylish shoes have replaced the micro-mini tight skirts and low-cut, one-size-too-small tops.

Gone, too, are the herds of reporters, the video trucks blocking the street, the camera operators, and other media. Presumably their ranks will increase as the trial gets underway.

Because the cameras are gone, the spotlight hogs, those who show up primarily to get themselves on TV behind the news reporters, are of course, not present.

The cast of participants has also changed. Gone are Jill Lansing and Michael Burt. Lyle is now ably represented by Terri Towery and Charlie Gessler of the Public Defenders office, at the taxpayers' expense. Lyle has claimed he is indigent and, after expert testimony, the judge ruled that he is.

Erik is still represented by Leslie Abramson, this time at the taxpayers' expense. Abramson is seen regularly on various TV shows acting as a legal commentator on the O. J. Simpson case.

Gone are the prosecutors, Pamela Bozanich, and Lester Kuriyama, currently prosecuting in other branches of the court system.

Deputy District Attorney David Conn now heads the prosecution team, assisted by Deputy District Attorney Carole Najera.

Detective Les Zoeller of the Beverly Hills Police Department is still on the case.

The Menendez Brothers will be retried together before one jury.

Judge Stanley Weisberg will preside at the retrial, as he did in the first trial, in Department N of the Van Nuys Courthouse.

The retrial is scheduled for the summer of 1995, two years since the first trial began.

Lyle and Erik remain in custody in the Los Angeles County Jail.

Reflections on the Con Artist as a Young Man
by Pierce O'Donnell

---◆---

By now the story of the brutal Menendez killings has been told so many times that there is a natural tendency to forget the horror of the crime. That is not only a cruel disservice to the memory of the victims (and precisely what the defendants tried to do at trial), but it is also an impediment to any understanding of what dark forces prompted one of the most infamous cases of parent-killing in the annals of jurisprudence. The Menendez case is a harrowing journey into the heart of darkness, but the trial offered only shadowy clues about how the mastermind Lyle, a bright, attractive, athletic young man, could become a vicious killer.

The Private Diary of Lyle Menendez has afforded a rare opportunity to delve into the demented mind of an admitted killer who, in my opinion, fabricated a "self-defense," claiming his parents drove his brother and him to murder. From the mundane to matters of life and death, we have had revealed the twisted psyche of a self-professed sociopath. It is in his almost matter-of-fact description of the murders of his parents that we get one of the most insightful—and disturbing—insights into Lyle's mind.

Based on the boys' own admissions under oath, it would appear to be an open-and-shut case of first-degree parricide. Guilt was even more apparent in light of their initial lies to the police and cover-up; falsely suggesting that the executions could have been the work of the Mob or someone doublecrossed by Jose in a business deal; the spending spree immediately after the murders; attempts (including bribery) to get friends to lie about their parents' abusive conduct; a taped confession to their psychiatrist; the motive of greed because they would inherit a $14 million estate; and their utter lack of remorse. As for his feelings about slaughtering his parents, Lyle testified that his only pain was like "you miss having these people around. I miss not having my dog around. If I can make such a gross analogy."

People v. *Lyle and Erik Menendez* was never about guilt or innocence. The defendants admitted that they killed their parents in cold blood, showing neither mercy nor remorse. What the trial was about, however, was two things: first, the sons' refusal to accept personal responsibility for their own acts—instead blaming their parents for a seemingly endless catalogue of abuse that supposedly transformed the defendants into killers—and, second, the state's attempt to prove that the defendants killed out of hatred and greed and were lying sociopaths who invented the sensational allegations of sexual, psychological, and physical abuse.

With the benefit of hindsight, we can now see how an apparent slam-dunk murder prosecution was derailed by carefully rehearsed testimony, brilliant defense advocacy, underfunded prosecutors caught by surprise, a well-meaning but indecisive trial judge, and a group of jurors manipulated to accept an outlandish defense. The resulting mistrial was a miscarriage of justice.

In *People* v. *Lyle and Erik Menendez,* the victims were not only Jose and Kitty Menendez: a fundamental tenet of our society—accepting responsibility for our acts—was also blown away. If *The Private Diary of Lyle Menendez* makes anything clear, it is that a willful, intelligent, and cunning defendant, represented by clever lawyers and unchecked by a strong trial judge, can subvert the legal system, turning on its head the notion of personal responsibility and blaming the victims for the perpetrators' deliberate acts.

Unfortunately, the Menendez prosecution is not unique. Increasingly, criminal defendants who are caught red-handed are refusing to accept blame for their anti-social behavior. This abdication of responsibility transcends racial and class lines. The urban ghetto youth who wantonly kills an ethnic grocer is portrayed as the victim of his impoverished upbringing which has taught, if not programmed, him to kill. Likewise, the Brothers Menendez who premeditated their parents' murder are helpless "battered children" and their parents, not they, really pulled the trigger.

We must distinguish between legitimate cases where chronic abuse of the defendant by the victim justifies a plea of self-defense and the use of self-defense as an excuse to blame the victims, such as in the Menendez case. The failure to make this distinction can lead to serious antisocial consequences. The concepts of deterrence and punishment become meaningless. The resulting loss of public confidence in the rationality and fairness of the criminal justice system will lead eventually to cynicism and, if the disaffection is wide and deep enough, to some form of vigilantism.

In the retrials of Lyle and Erik Menendez, far more is at stake than whether the defendants can reprise their dramatic first trial performance and con some or all of the jurors into buying their sob story. Literally, the role of law as a civilizing influence is being put to the test. Society is being given a second chance to secure a conviction in a prosecution where all the credible evidence shows that Erik and Lyle Menendez, ice water coursing their veins, were sane actors who logically planned, reflected upon, and then "rationally" carried out their parents' execution-style murders—not as spur-of-the-moment reactions to a clear and present danger of harm from their parents but solely for financial gain and revenge.

Before proceeding any further, let me briefly disclose my qualifi-cations for rendering such a harsh judgment about the brothers and their first trial. Early in my career, I defended men and women accused of a cornucopia of crimes: murder, aircraft hijack-ing, terrorism, robbery, killing a witness, tax and securities fraud, perjury, and bribery. From time to time, I raised almost every conceivable defense: alibi, self-defense, mistaken identity, politi-cal motivation, insanity, diminished capacity, intoxication, and SOD ("some other dude"). I know a sociopath when I see one because I represented my share of defendants with antisocial personality disorders.

Shortly after the Menendez murders in 1989, the Board of Directors of LIVE Entertainment, Inc., the public company headed by Jose Menendez at the time of his death, appointed me as an independent special counsel to investigate the murders and to determine whether they had any connection with the corporation's business activities. My team of lawyers, accoun-tants, and private investigators conducted a thorough investigation of the company, its employees, financial affairs, customers, vendors, and competitors, and the Menendez family itself. We shared our findings with the Beverly Hills Police Department. My 200-page report to the Board of Directors, submitted a week before the sons' arrests, concluded that the company was clean but that the Brothers Menendez were dirty.

I have no doubt whatsoever that Lyle and Erik fabricated large portions of their testimony about the nature and extent of abuse that they suffered at the hands of their parents. Nor do I doubt for a moment that they engaged in hard-hearted character assassination—perhaps a more heinous crime than the murders themselves. In performances worthy of Oscars, they lied, schemed, and faked emotional trauma to save their lives.

To be fair, the evidence demonstrated that the Menendez family was dysfunctional. Jose Menendez was a controlling, demanding, and difficult father. Tough as nails, he drove his sons to excel in tennis, tolerated their criminal and antisocial behavior, drummed into them a patrician notion that they were better than everyone else, and was not in tune emotionally with his sons' feelings and needs. Jose saw his sons as the extension of his own life, and his dreams must be their dreams.

Jose was not a good husband either. He had often treated his wife with contempt. He had recently ended a long-term affair that devastated Kitty, but in their last year he tried to be a supportive, loving husband. For her part, Kitty was devoted to her sons, but was concerned about their growing antisocial behavior. She was in poor mental health, perhaps suicidal.

The crime was overwhelmingly precipitated by the sons' desire to kill their father. The mother's murder was almost incidental, an afterthought. At one point, Lyle even rationalized that the killing was merciful because his already suicidal mother would have eventually killed herself once Jose was gone.

The pivotal factual dispute at trial was the motive for the murders. The prosecution claimed that the greedy sons killed out of hatred and for financial gain (to inherit their parents' estate, which they thought was worth $14 million) and that they killed

Kitty to silence her as a witness to Jose's murder. The evidence was strong, if not compelling, that the brothers finally struck when they believed that their parents were about to cut them out of the family will.

The defense, on the other hand, claimed that "the boys," after a lifetime of brutality, reasonably feared that their parents were about to murder them. The immediate trigger, they claimed, was Lyle's confrontation with his father after he learned from Erik only a few days earlier that Jose had been sexually molesting Erik for the past 12 years and Lyle's threat to go public if his father did not stop immediately. When Jose told Lyle to mind his own business, the defendant felt they were left with no choice other than to kill their parents.

There was no evidence to support these pivotal defense assertions other than the self-serving testimony of the brothers themselves. Credible independent evidence of sexual abuse was never offered, and testimony about supposed psychological abuse was either spotty or subject to an innocent interpretation. Finally, the brothers never gave a plausible explanation of why they did not leave home or go to the authorities or relatives—instead they spent their time planning the murder of their parents, purchasing shotguns in San Diego using a stolen driver's license, going on a fishing trip with their parents the day before, and then lying in wait to exterminate their mother and father as they dozed in the family room.

In the final analysis, it should make no legal or moral difference whether Jose and Kitty Menendez would ever have been featured on the cover of *Parents* magazine. Regardless of which view of the evidence was closer to the truth, supposed parental abuse should have been irrelevant. As prosecutor Pamela Bozanich suggested, the testimony about sexual abuse and the numerous opinions of defense psychiatric experts were just so much "psychobabble." At no time were these defendants—to the manor born, well-educated and sophisticated—reasonably fearful that their parents were about to murder them.

Two other facts support the prosecution's claim that the alleged abuse was a ruse. First, before they changed their defense strategy and while they were still denying any complicity in the murders, the Menendez brothers never told their psychiatrist or anyone else that they were physically threatened by either of their parents or that they killed them in self-defense.

Second, during our investigation for the LIVE Board of Directors, we conducted hundreds of interviews, including sessions with close family and friends. At no time did any of the interviewees give the slightest hint of the dark secrets of the Menendez family that would form the core of the defense. While Jose was depicted as a demanding and driven father, no one suggested that he was a pervert or that his wife knowingly tolerated long-term sexual abuse of her boys. Strange, isn't it, that not one person, one intimate, lifted the curtain ever so slightly, for just a tantalizing glimpse of the supposedly sordid world of the Menendez family.

One of the most significant things to understand about the outcome of the first trial is the evolution of the defense employed by Lyle and Erik.

The crimes themselves provided plenty of foundation for an insanity defense. What normal son would assassinate his parents without any immediate provocation or threat of harm? Skillful defense lawyers could easily paint a picture of abnormal behavior, a sudden paroxysm of filial anger, a near-hypnotic blood bath, and almost anything else to negate premeditation.

But an insanity defense, even if successful, can lead to a conviction for manslaughter and/or a long period of imprisonment and/or psychiatric commitment and no assurance of prompt release from confinement. No, the Menendez brothers needed a more potent defense, one that offered some prospect of freedom if they could sell it. Legally, that promise of walking could come from either an outright acquittal or a succession of hung juries and eventual dismissal of the charges by the judge "in the interest of justice."

That defense did not immediately spring to mind, however. Professing their innocence to family, friends, and the public, the brothers spent over three years in jail waiting for the California courts to decide the admissibility of their psychiatrist's damning notes and tapes of their therapy sessions. At no time during this long hiatus was there any hint of "self-defense" or that this defense would be predicated on the extraordinary allegation that Jose and Kitty Menendez, over many years, had verbally, psychologically, and sexually abused their children and that the murders were the inevitable culmination of the sons' justifiable inability to tolerate any more abuse at the hands of their monster parents. Based on longstanding California caselaw, most lawyers and judges would rule out self-defense when, as it appeared here, there was no imminent danger to the sons from the parents and they did not have a reasonable fear of jeopardy of serious bodily injury or death from the conduct of their parents.

Once the California Supreme Court held that the defendants' therapist, Dr. Jerome Oziel, could testify about two of their highly-incriminating sessions, the defense was forced to shift gears. Denial of guilt was no longer a feasible strategy, and an insanity plea was unpalatable.

The defense concocted an imaginative theory with roots in the "battered wife" syndrome cases. This special variant of self-defense involves women who have murdered their abusive husbands after being beaten but while the perpetrators slept or were otherwise passive at the time of their death. In some instances, the wives have successfully claimed that, while there was no immediate provocation, years of abuse and fear for their lives triggered the murder. The Menendez brothers argued that they honestly feared that they were immediately in harm's way and that the jury must be allowed to hear testimony about how they had been raised by their parents over the entire course of their lives.

The prosecutors vehemently objected that this defense was not legally tenable. Judge Stanley M. Weisberg may have agreed with the prosecution, but despite his strong reservations, he concluded that he had to follow an appellate decision, *People* v. *Aris* (1989). That case held that it was error not to allow testimony about a severely battered wife's state of mind at the time she killed her sleeping husband. Accordingly, the trial judge allowed the defense to introduce flimsy, marginal, and outright unsubstantiated allegations about the parents. In effect, the victims were put on trial, thereby diverting attention and blame from the murderers.

Unfortunately, as demonstrated by the two deadlocked juries, lay jurors do not neatly compartmentalize evidence like lawyers and judges. Stripped of legalisms, the jury was allowed to hear months of testimony about the minutest flaws of Jose and Kitty and totally uncorroborated testimony from the defendants about their supposedly nightmarish childhood and adolescence. The entire center of gravity of the case shifted. The jurors were now given a choice: convict the defendants or exonerate them of first degree murder because of the alleged sins of the father and mother.

If the prosecution miscalculated, it was in not perceiving the cumulative effect on the jury of months of testimony about alleged sexual and mental cruelty, and the like. The prosecution mounted a weak and ineffective rebuttal that largely ignored the main thrust of the defense: the defendants' mental state due to the supposed abuse. In my opinion that was a fatal mistake.

In retrospect, we can see that the jurors were almost brain-washed. After the sexual abuse and psychological torture claims were repeated so many times, and defense experts were allowed to testify (incredibly!) that they believed the allegations were true and that the long-term abuse excused the crimes. The unsubstantiated charges took on a life of their own, gradually becoming fact and then the basis for juror sympathy.

It was a brilliant strategy, flawlessly executed. As effective as the defense lawyers were, the major credit must go to Lyle Menendez. There is no doubt in my mind that he was the Grand Architect of the Defense who pulled the strings and wrote the script. Any doubt about this was resolved by his candid statements in his conversations.

As we can now see, the subversion of justice began once the trial judge let in the parent-bashing evidence. His first instincts to bar the testimony were right, and he should do so in the retrial, in my opinion.

*   *   *

As I read this book, I was reminded of the villains in the true crime works of Truman Capote (*In Cold Blood*) and Norman Mailer (*The Executioner's Song*) whose nonfictional accounts of brutal, senseless murders of innocents became not only best sellers but classic works of American literature. Lyle Menendez and Capote's and Mailer's characters have several things in common.

*In words that aptly characterize the Menendez murders, Capote describes the shotgun slaying of the four members of the Clutter family by Richard Hickock and Perry Smith in the course of a $40 robbery as "virtually an impersonal act; the victims might as well have been killed by lightning."

*Lyle Menendez could be Richard Hickock—an intelligent con man and ruthless sociopath who cooly planned "the perfect murder" of four strangers in a small Kansas town and got a rush thinking about the exploding shot gun shells and "plenty of hair on them-those walls."

*Lyle could also be Hickock's sidekick, Perry Smith—a dreamer, "stuck on himself," who was contemptuous of the rights of others and " 'a natural killer,'—absolutely sane, but conscienceless, and capable of dealing, with or without motive, the coldest-blooded deathblows."

The parallels between Lyle Menendez and Gary Gilmore are not as exact, however. While Lyle and Gary each killed in cold blood, Gilmore at least had some remorse. And, to his credit, he did not protest his innocence or blame his acts on his miserable childhood.

One of the most intriguing qualities of Lyle Menendez is that he makes no bones about who he is. He knows that he is a sociopath, a young man without a conscience or compassion whose moral compass pointed him in the direction of cheating, lying, and killing. According to his psychiatrist, Dr. Ozeil, Lyle admitted:

> "We're sociopaths. We just get turned on by planning the murder. Once we plan it, nothing gets in the way. Once we start, nothing will stop us. Furthermore, we don't think much about what we're doing before we do it. Once

we get going, we just go ahead and commit and make it happen. And we can't change the plan because it's already formed perfectly."

Lyle certainly fits the classic definition of sociopathy or psychopathy—synonymous lay terms for the clinical diagnosis of "Antisocial Personality Disorder." According to the official Diagnostic and Statistical Manual of Mental Disorders ("DSM-IV"), published by the American Psychiatric Association, this illness involves "a pervasive pattern of disregard for, and violation of, the rights of others that begins in childhood or early adolescence and continues into adulthood." Deceit and manipulation, as well as theft and serious violations of rules, are central features. "They may repeatedly lie [or] con others . . . and also tend to be consistently and extremely irresponsible," including with money. Sociopaths also "may blame the victims for . . . deserving their fate." In addition, they "frequently lack empathy . . . and they have an inflated and arrogant self-appraisal . . . and may be excessively opinionated, self-assured, or cocky. They may display a glib, superficial charm. . . ."

Lyle's arrogance, superiority complex and twisted view of the world are graphically revealed in his own words. One witness, a pool service man at the Menendez home, is "a trained rat," "a fucking joke," "a piece of shit," and a liar who is only testifying because his "wife is obsessed with Court TV" and its daily coverage of the trial and she "is pushing him to be a witness so that she can be a witness. . . . They're fucking pool people in fucking Beverly Hills. They want to be on fucking TV."

Everyone testifying for the government is lying. The cops "lie their fucking asses off," and his psychiatrist is "the worst witness . . . a lying shit." "I have seen so many people get up in this trial and lie and I cannot figure out why," Lyle complains. But Lyle seems unconcerned about this putative conspiracy of liars arrayed against him because "I've got better lawyers" who are "kicking butt," he brags. His lawyers are the Equalizers, particularly Leslie Abramson, his brother's lawyer.

Not only are the witnesses liars and dunces and the prosecutors inept, but "the judge is biased totally . . . for the DA."

Typical of his thinking, Lyle, even though he admits that the judge has been "pretty fair," premises his allegation of judicial bias on his belief that Judge Weisberg

> "was a prosecutor five years ago in the only other case in Beverly Hills where a kid killed his father. And he lost. And the kid went home on self-defense. He actually lost the case because the father was wealthy and he argued that it was for the money and he lost. And he's out to get us. Plus he fucked up the McMartin case and he fucked up the officer case—the [Rodney] King case. He was the judge that let them go."

Lyle is egotistical and opinionated. I particularly enjoyed Lyle's account of O.J. Simpson joining the famous Menendez brothers in the Los Angeles County Jail in 1994 while Lyle and Erik were awaiting their retrial. Noting that *People* v. *Simpson* is "gonna be a hell of a case," Lyle cavalierly dismisses Simpson's then lead counsel, Robert Shapiro (O.J. "needs somebody good"), and predicts that Los Angeles' newest celebrity criminal defendant will eventually hire Johnny Cochran or Leslie Abramson. In his next breath, Lyle complains that Simpson will be housed with Erik in the wing "where famous people go . . . where, you know, I should be."

In discussing writing a book about his case, "Trial Lyle," as he calls himself, brags that "just about any writer would want to work on it" and a publisher would eagerly buy it because "my name is on it."

The trial is just another Big Game. While Lyle admits to being scared because he faces the death penalty, he nonetheless finds sport in the destruction of hostile witnesses. At one point, when Leslie Abramson does an effective cross-examination, Lyle confesses that he finds it "exciting."

If nothing else, Lyle is brash and cocky. When asked if he is nervous about the anticipated testimony of an executive from his father's company, Lyle mocks the witness. "I don't care about business associates. What do they know about what's going on in the house?"

When it is suggested that Leslie Abramson might turn Erik against him at the retrial, Lyle is not worried.

> "We're brothers. And I know what happened, and I know who he is, and that could not happen in a million years. I mean, that's just—my brother and I are very, very close. I think he loves me, and, he would never do that."

One of the few times he seems concerned is when his former girlfriend, Jamie Pisarcik, is mentioned as a prospective prosecution witness. She never believed Lyle's claims about his father molesting the brothers. Pisarcik testified that while awaiting trial, Lyle sent her to a law library to find cases about child molestation where "children had gotten off after killing their parents." Lyle also tried to bribe her into testifying that Jose tried to molest her. About his former girlfriend turned witness for the prosecution, Lyle notes:

> "I wish she wasn't testifying—bitch. I can't believe that she's testifying. All I ever did was buy her presents like I did with all my girlfriends. . . . This [testimony] is fucking bullshit. You fucking lying bitch."

Lyle's confidence that he will beat the rap oozes from almost every page. He knows that he is charismatic and will be a credible witness. "Everyone who meets me, loves me," he boasts. In his own words, he discusses "the theory" for his defense and arranging for the testimony of witnesses. The admitted author of the original "alibi concoction" immediately after the murders, Lyle undoubtedly choreographed the parental abuse defense. It is impossible to read this diary and not conclude that Lyle, with his gift for telling stories, is a pathological—and convincing—liar.

Lyle is fixated with the idea of perfection. He always considered himself smarter and better than his peers. From earliest childhood, his father indoctrinated him about his superiority compared to the lower classes—like pool men in Beverly Hills. In the excellent book *Blood Brothers: The Inside Story of the Menendez Murders,* Ron Soble and John Johnson note that "Lyle was a great experiment, a child raised so carefully and attentively that he would literally be a kind of ubermensch, man raised to a higher power." Lyle could be a character straight out of Tom Wolfe's *The Bonfire of the Vanities*—a younger Sherman McCoy, a Master of the Universe.

Lyle's father had drilled into him the sayings of Og Mandino from *The Greatest Salesman in the World*:

> "I was not delivered into this world into defeat, nor does failure course in my veins. I am not a sheep waiting to be prodded by my shepherd. I am a lion and I refuse to talk, to walk, to sleep with the sheep."

Ironically, Lyle Menendez may face defeat in the retrial. Some of the admissions made in this diary are damning and will likely be used against him by the prosecution. For this young con artist, a conviction secured by his own words would be poetic justice. Imagine, just for a moment, Lyle being hoisted on his own petard by the correspondence and taped conversations with Norma Novelli, the woman who befriended him in his darkest hours and whom he then manipulated and discarded like he had so many women before. Or, worse yet, imagine Erik copping a plea to save his life and testifying against Lyle.

"That could never happen in a million years," said Lyle. He is not worried. Perhaps he should be.

This is the stuff of great drama.

Will Lyle Menendez, already drained of funds and no longer able to afford high-priced legal talent, end up disgraced and friendless like Sherman McCoy?

Will Lyle Menendez, like Dimitri Karamozov in Fyodor Dostoevsky's *The Brothers Karamozov*, be convicted of the violent murder of a despised father?

Will Lyle Menendez, like Richard Hickock, Perry Smith, and Gary Gilmore, face the executioner for his cold-blooded murders?

If there is any justice, he will.